CANOE CAMPING

Also by G. Heberton Evans III

Lacrosse Fundamentals (with Robert E. Anderson)

Canoeing Wilderness Waters

CANOE CAMPING

G. Heberton Evans III

Drawings by Elinor Virdin Evans

SOUTH BRUNSWICK AND NEW YORK: A. S. BARNES AND COMPANY
LONDON: THOMAS YOSELOFF LTD

©1977 by A.S. Barnes and Co., Inc.

A. S. Barnes and Co., Inc.
Cranbury, New Jersey 08512

Thomas Yoseloff Ltd
Magdalen House
136–148 Tooley Street
London SE1 2TT, England

Library of Congress Catalog Card Number:75-20590

ISBN 0-498-01825-3

PRINTED IN THE UNITED STATES OF AMERICA

To
Section A
in appreciation of our summers
on Ontario and Quebec wilderness waters

CONTENTS

ACKNOWLEDGMENTS

Keewaydin Camp has been sending out organized canoe trips from the base camp on Lake Temagami, Ontario, for three-quarters of a century, and while none of the present staff made that first trip into Devil's Island, few organizations can boast of equal experience and knowledge. Howard and Jane Chivers have recently passed on the reins of ownership and direction of the camp to Fred and Marg Reimers, but generously allowed me to call on the camp's resources in producing not only this volume but *Canoeing Wilderness Waters* as well.

Except as noted, the photographic illustrations in the volume are the work of the author, but some situations are better explained by drawings, all of which are again produced by my mother.

My canoeing and camping education owes a great deal to having been fortunate enough to travel with some of the finest Canadian guides from Mattawa, Ontario—men like Eddie Bernard, Leo Belanger, Clid LeFabrve, Jack McIssac, and especially Nishe Belanger. But there have also been many veteran staffmen whose suggestions have contributed greatly—Rod Cox, Bill Russell, and Roy Waters to mention only a few.

Section A no longer enjoys the association with native guides under whom I learned. Canoe-trip guiding is a part-time occupation and not financially rewarding enough these days to interest younger men, so we have had to develop our own experts on camping and canoeing by bringing them up through the camp organization. For their assistance and comradeship on trips in the last ten years, I am indebted to Mike Fish, Tom Lathrop, Tom McDuffie, George Revington, Matt Ridgway, and particularly Dan Carpenter, Jr., who has now made six long trips with me—and my poorly disciplined Springer Spaniels.

CANOE CAMPING

1

A DAY OF TRAVEL

An orange red glow reflects from the fleecy clouds over the western hills; gentle waves lap against the smooth rock shore; the canoe rests on its gunwale for the night; the dying embers of the evening fire remain in the kitchen area where all is secure; the tent waits behind, sheltered by the forest. Inside, a warm sleeping bag beckons, for tomorrow's travel should begin early before the winds rise.

New canoe country lies ahead. New waters to travel. New sights to see. There are miles to cover on lakes, streams, and rivers, and portage trails for sure, but this is a pleasure trip. Probably two-thirds of the average day involves camping features that have little to do with the canoe except that it is the vehicle by which the travelers arrive at their campsite.

There are many samenesses about any camping, but canoe camping also has its idiosyncrasies. Camp is rarely far from water large enough to float the canoe. A canoe can transport a considerable amount of cargo in addition to the crew, which affects the equipment and supplies available. The route of the canoe is dictated by nature's highway—other campers travel on man-made routes, or perhaps can strike out on their own. Speed measured in miles per hour is comparatively slow; civilization and supplies may not be far distant in miles, but at a considerable distance in time. And weather can particularly influence both travel and camping. And the canoesman must always be prepared for the possibility of an upset and consequent threat of a soaking.

Handling the canoe with skill and confidence is an acquired art; one gained through experience. *Canoeing Wilderness Waters* (A.S. Barnes, 1975) was designed to assist. How to select the canoe, handle it in all kinds of water, find the portages, get it across the trails, and care for the canoe are items included in this volume. Methods of handling the cargo, packing, and portaging are discussed. Where to go and how to travel in various weather conditions are also covered.

But the camping aspects of canoeing are yet to be considered. The modern canoeist goes into the bush not just to get from one place to another as did the voyageur of old. He wants to enjoy an experience different from that met in the everyday work-a-day life. Canoeing is demanding in terms of effort and just physical work. But a dawn to dusk routine with head bowed low, pushing on the paddle hour after hour, and crossing portages, eyes riveted on the ground, getting loads across at a dog-trot only to collapse in exhaustion at the evening fire to catch a few moments of sleep before taking the trail again as soon as possible in the morning, may have been the pattern followed by the Montreal voyageur—but few modern canoeists enter the wilderness just to bend the paddle and cover miles. If so, little is gained from the experience other than the ability to brag to those on the outside of the distance traveled.

But if that is the kind of experience the canoe party wants, so be it. The voyageur actually enjoyed himself in spite of the long, hard, physically demanding days spent on the water and portage. Each Montreal canoe intentionally had at least one man able to lead the crew in songs, which were always a part of their paddling day. And while there was competition among men as to how rapidly they could cover the ground and how much they could carry, there was also a comradeship. A *pork eater* of the Montreal canoe had to undergo an initiation before becoming an *homme du nord* or *hivernant* in the North canoe after he got past the Grand Portage at the western end of Lake Superior and became a member of the wintering group coming down from Athabasca or some such distant inland post. There were the hourly pipes as they rested on their paddles during the long day, and always the jovial relaxation over their evening pipes when camp was pitched and they gathered around the roaring fire while their pot of rubbaboo boiled away just before time to roll up in their blankets for the few short hours of sleep allowed by the guide.

The modern camper should take into the wilderness those pieces of equipment needed for him to travel with some comfort. But there are limits imposed by the carrying capacity of the canoe and by the traveler's willingness to portage. Every tripper travels on his stomach, so he needs supplies and the wherewithal to prepare them. Pemmican fed the voyageur, but the recreational traveler should at least achieve greater variety in his diet, if not more nutrition.

Finally—outside the scope of this volume—the canoeist is exposed to wilderness experiences during the comparatively short duration of his trip to be remembered, relived, and treasured for years. Some may be pure recreational; some perhaps educational.

Nature probably created the waterways over which the canoe glides. But how about the portage trails around the impossible areas? Maybe there is the opportunity for the city dweller to observe how people who have known the wilderness most of their lives cope with their environment—maybe a visit to an abandoned tiny log cabin or lean-to of the trapper, or perhaps the winter camp of natives of the area. Then, a glimpse of a very different life-style may be obtained by visiting an active native summer camp.

Perhaps the scuba diver could investigate the foot of a particularly difficult stretch of white water, where the pools below hold the sunken cargos of old fur-trade canoes that failed to navigate the run successfully.

Fortunate is the canoeist who escapes the pollution of civilization and can dip a cup of cool, clear water by reaching over the gunwale. And the photographer or artist can record a scene where

Bivouac of a Canoe Party, an oil painting by Mrs. Francis A. Hopkins. (*Courtesy Public Archives of Canada*)

the water sparkles blue or green in the sunlight, framed by a green forest background, or maybe a rock-covered shore unmarked by man's intrusion. And, somehow, no sunset or dawn seems so vivid as those over the lonely lake.

The naturalist or ornithologist has ample opportunity to observe and explore. The animals of the forest are shy and avoid man—the intruder; but along the trail are the droppings of the various animals, deserted beds and dens are often found, the trees show the rubs of the antlered animals, and the beaver impoundments are a marvel of construction. Water fowl are likely rearing their young, while back in the forest the land-based birds are seen and heard, while the eagle, osprey, or owl soars overhead.

The amateur geologist has a ready-made laboratory as he glances down into the shallows to see the glitter of iron pyrites. Then the rocky exposed point on which he camps reveals granite, quartz, and other igneous deposits. And maybe a limestone area abounds in fossils.

Then there is the forest behind the campsite or through which the portage trail winds. The stately red pine towers over the smooth, level tent site, lightly covered with dry needles; the jackpine stand shades a smooth, slightly sandy campsite. Across the rocks of the portage leads the trail etched by many passing feet, while to either side are lichens and mosses rarely seen in civilized walks. Beside the trail spring up the vividly colored delicate wild flowers, while the Labrador tea reaches out to scratch uncovered legs—plants to identify, photograph, and maybe gather and press for preservation. And then there is always the patch of blueberries to sample coming back for the second portage load.

The quiet of evening descends over the campsite as the birds have settled in for the night, and only the crackling of the fire breaks the silence as the stars twinkle above to be observed as it never seemed possible in the backyard at home. The evening fire dies, and the path to the tent is lit by a full moon just peeking over the trees, casting its soft, warm light over the campground; or, as the tent is reached, one final glance to the northern sky, and the northern lights start their play—maybe first with streaks of white, and then the colors appear, stabbing and flickering across the sky.

TRAVEL ROUTINE

Daily adjustment in the travel routine of the canoe trip can be made to handle unusual situations; but without an established procedure from the time the party rises until all is secure for the night, there will be confusion and considerable wasted labor.

Mechanics on the water and portage trail are important, but more hours are actually spent on and around campsites. Camp should be broken in the morning and established again in the evening with a minimum of wasted time and effort. A couple of days of disorganization could be endured while learning, but if confusion persists, tripping becomes a chore.

The party also travels on its stomach to some degree, and while meals can be simple—or fancy—the kitchen department must rise to the occasion and put out attractive meals with some dispatch.

DAILY SCHEDULE

Experienced trippers are on the water early in the morning, accomplish the bulk of the day's travel by noon, and quit in midafternoon. The voyageurs set a timetable that the vacationer will not copy, but it ate up the miles day after day. The guide roused his crews at three A.M. or so. Camp was broken perhaps after a pot of tea, and the canoes were on the water with the gray of false dawn. Around nine o'clock a halt was made for breakfast. Every hour or two there was a pause in the lee of a point or island for a "pipe"—in midafternoon, perhaps a longer stop for another meal. And then with darkness already well advanced, camp was made for the night.

A more relaxed timetable is in order, but still the best hours for travel are early in the day. The winds rise as the sun gets higher. The miles slip by effortlessly before noon, but the same distance covered after midday seems interminable.

Breaking Camp

Few parties can cook breakfast and break camp in less than an hour and a half from the moment the fire is laid. A more realistic estimate runs to two hours. The guide would probably rather travel in daylight, and photographers prefer having the sun at least a couple hours in the sky. Rising between five and six should put the party on the water between six-thirty and eight. Fog or mist often shroud the water after a cool night and should be allowed to burn off. Such conditions invariably exist along rivers—particularly near fast water—and frequently it is unsafe to leave a river campsite until eight or nine.

Sometimes the evening fire not only boiled the rubbaboo for dinner, but also heated gum for canoe patching. *View of a Canoe Party Round a Camp Fire,* an oil painting by Mrs. Francis A. Hopkins. (*Courtesy Public Archives of Canada*)

The mechanics of getting off with dispatch vary, but the cooks should rise first. The fire should be laid quickly from tinder stored under cover the previous evening, and any pots of water that must be heated should be assembled first.

When breakfast preparations are reasonably well advanced, the cooks can rouse the others. A pair of cooks can work together efficiently, but extras standing around the fire waiting for water to boil just waste time. While the cooks tend to breakfast, the rest can wash up, maybe take a morning dip, and assemble and pack personal gear.

The cooks can wash up while their water boils, and then continue with breakfast preparation. It should be pretty well in hand when the others arrive ready to travel. While the kitchen equipment is being cleaned, the cooks can roll their own gear. Extra hands can secure the supplies and community baggage.

Last items packed should be tents and fly, giving the canvas a chance to dry after the dew.

Rolling wet canvas should be avoided; the shelter is likely to leak when pitched at the next site, and, occasionally, departure should be delayed a few minutes to let the morning sun do its job.

Loads for the various canoes should be moved to the loading area. As soon as all the baggage for a particular canoe is assembled, it should be loaded and paddled out from the landing to give the laggards room.

Rests

During the day, brief rest breaks should be taken at least every hour; more frequently at the start of the trip. Pick the lee of a point or island in adverse wind; or let the canoe drift with wind or current and "take ten"—about long enough to smoke a cigarette in peace. The break may seem unnecessary early in the day, but the paddlers tire less quickly later on. At the end of a portage, definitely take a pause—maybe on shore after the loads are across, or on the water if bugs are troublesome; perhaps unlimber the fishing rod for a few casts—anything to break the paddle-portage routine.

16

Lunch

Occasionally a cold lunch eaten while the canoes drift along saves time and covers water: sandwiches made the previous night or at breakfast, or a piece of bannock or a biscuit or two and some cold luncheon meat and cheese; pemmican, if the voyageur's diet were available; or maybe one of the compressed energy foods of the backpacker. Perhaps if the wind is right and the canoes are sailing, a cold floating lunch is welcome. But on any trip of more than a couple days the party travels better if a halt is made, offering a chance to land and stretch. Cook a simple, hot meal— perhaps not too filling for older groups, lest they get loggy on the paddle and portages during the afternoon. But it is amazing what a youngster can put away after a morning's work! The Canadian guide traditionally brews a pot of tea—liberally laced with sugar—for his afternoon pick-me-up.

If possible, lunch stops are best taken at portages—it saves unloading some of the gear an extra time. Take a trip across and cook on the far side so that while the meal is being prepared the subsequent loads can come over. Just leave someone to start lunch while the rest return for their second loads. The first one across can relieve the cook, so he can make his other trip while final preparations are made. Eating at the start of the trail is less satisfactory; the final loads have to be packed across before the meal has any chance to settle.

Prior planning makes the lunch break go smoothly. Supplies should be grouped so that only the kitchen equipment and a single food container need be opened; pawing through all the loads to find supplies makes the meal a major production. Only the canoe carrying the kitchen and lunch wannigan need be unloaded. The loads in the others should not have to be disturbed.

The lakeside lunchsite need not be spacious— preferably in the lee of a point or island, so the fire is protected from wind. The canoes also need shelter so that wind or current will not make it necessary to haul each canoe out of the water.

Carelessness at a lunchsite probably causes more canoe wear than any other part of the travel day. If the canoes will float free, simply tying them to a tree with a bit of the bowline is most expedient. If they must be beached to prevent them from drifting off or rubbing against obstacles, be sure that waves will not rock the canoe on the beach, thereby wearing the skin. At a sand or rock landing, the simple precaution of putting a paddle or log under the keel as the canoe is drawn up will protect the bottom. The canoes should be kept in sight so that any change in their position can be observed and then adjusted.

While the cooks start the meal, the photographers and fishermen may find entertainment. Conditions may be right for a quick swim or bath before lunch, even though towels are packed away and the sun has to accomplish the drying off. Then sometimes nothing beats just relaxing in the warm sun.

Locating a Campsite

Toward three o'clock, start thinking of the night. Maybe there is an established site for which to aim, but what if another party is already there? There are some regions where camping and/or fire building are permitted only at certain locations—in which case there is little choice but to head for one of these spots—but in most wilderness areas, the canoeist has freedom of choice.

The party in unfamiliar territory may have to cut a site or stumble onto one by accident. Anyway, about two hours after lunch, start casting about for a suitable location. For the next hour, be selective and take only a well-suited site. After four o'clock, lower the requirements and take the first acceptable site. The canoes should be landed between four and five at the latest. With reasonable dispatch, camp will be made and dinner out of the way before seven, leaving a couple hours for fishing and other interests.

SELECTING A CAMPSITE

If the party counts on using previously cleared sites, remember that Indians and trappers locate camps with slightly different motives than the sportsman. The Indian moves in spring and fall, not midsummer. He needs protection that the summer traveler finds unnecessary. The water in front of the Indian site is used only as a landing area; he is more likely to select a gently sloping sand, gravel, or grassy shore than hard rock. He draws water only for cooking and drinking, and has little interest in swimming and bathing, so his landing is likely shallow.

His site is most likely located in a bay, or at least along an even shore. He rarely pitches on an exposed point. His camp often faces south or in the direction from which the less-violent storms come. Study the prevailing winds; the native site is located for protection.

His fire and tent area are often inland from the

Lunch equipment came from canoe to left, as canoes are tied for lunch stop.

Paddle placed under bow prevents canoe from rubbing on a sand beach.

Line from stern to stake driven into sandy bottom keeps canoe from swinging broadside to beach when using an unsheltered landing.

An Indian summer campsite could be used by a canoe party.

shore and hard to see clearly from the water. Perhaps he left his tent poles standing; maybe he blazed a tree or left some other sign pointing to his camp.

If either end of a portage would make a campground, it has probably been so used. The tent area may be as much as fifty yards inland from the water, however, or equally far to the side of the trail on a better piece of ground. If there is a well-used campground at a portage, it is unlikely that there will be another native site for the next couple miles—the native will camp at the portage rather than reload and move a couple miles down the lake only to unload and make camp.

An exception is territory where the native sets up summer fishing camps. Traveling camps are located at portages; fishing camps where the stay

The Cree winter site is worth a visit, but the land is not attractive for summer camping.

will be of some duration are located down the lake at a smooth landing.

Winter camps are located with much the same geography in mind, although perhaps more protection is sought, but a winter camp may be an impossible summer location. The ground is often quite rough for summer tenting; snow will have smoothed the rolling terrain.

Sites previously used by sportsmen tend to be more obvious and more acceptable to summer canoe parties. An exposed rock point, a sparse stand of jackpine, or a grove of birch are all used by vacationers more than by natives. In northern areas where winged insects are a problem the breeze across the exposed point helps. In spite of the bugs, the sportsman may have camped on fast water; the Indian almost never does unless at a portage.

It goes without saying that it must be possible to land and unload the canoes safely at a prospective site. Rock cliffs make an impossible location. And the shallow area where the canoes will not float at the landing makes unloading and loading difficult.

2

COMMUNITY EQUIPMENT

But first, what about the camping equipment about to be unloaded for the evening? Assume the trip has progressed beyond the dreaming stage. Canoes, paddles, and motors are available. Decisions have been made about packs, duffels, or wannigans in which to stuff the other equipment for the inevitable portages. The transportation part of what might be called the community equipment is ready—now to the camping equipment.

The major needs include shelters and cooking equipment, which may also be suitable for other kinds of camping and already available. But the canoe and the kind of country through which the trip is to be made should influence the selection of camping equipment.

If an outfitter has been engaged to supply the canoes and their accessories, he might be asked to provide the remainder. His equipment has been tested and proved satisfactory for the area in which he operates, and his suggestions and experience may save many headaches caused by forgotten items, inappropriate equipment, and just plain inexperience.

However, sooner or later anyone bitten by the wilderness canoeing bug will develop his own outfit.

SHELTERS

The voyageurs built a roaring fire and then rolled up in their blankets; some slept under ca-noes tipped on their sides. Their brigades carried tents only for ladies or dignitaries who rode as passengers.

Anyone who really wants to relive the past can emulate them, but even the modern Indian does not travel with such austerity.

Sleeping Under the Stars

Open-air sleeping sounds romantic and nostalgic, but it is downright uncomfortable in all but the best weather. There is no way to waterproof a bare sleeping bag. Some cheap bags come equipped with a flap attached to the underside of the bag. It is useful for securing the bag after it is rolled, but the advertisements always picture this flap rigged as a small tent over the sleeper's head. The pictures look intriguing, but the flap is worthless. It is not waterproof in the first place, and it just collects water—either dripping through or waiting until a sizeable puddle collects when the whole rig collapses on the sleeper's head.

Covering the bag with a waterproof tarp laid directly on it is folly. Whether it rains or not is academic—the bag will be soaked in the morning. A sleeping bag must breathe; if not, moisture collects as the warmth of the sleeper's body meets the outside air, and the bag therefore sweats. It will have to be dried out before packing, just as if it had been left out in the rain.

Shelters Made Using the Canoe

If economics are of prime concern and the area

21

Canoe shelters: A) simple rig with tarp stretched over canoe and staked out; B) be sure tarp covers enough of canoe so water will run down backside; C) introduction of a single ridge braced on the ground provides more space; D) or a single ridge may be rigged parallel to the ground; E) multiple ridges leave pockets to collect water; F) however, if center ridge is elevated more than sides, runoff will improve.

to be traveled is relatively bug-free, a reasonable shelter from rain can be constructed using a canoe tipped on its side as a base and stretching a tarp or fly over it. Ponchos, sheets of polyethylene, rubberized tarps, and those of coated nylon, ripstop nylon, or canvas are equally adaptable to such rigs.

The canoe should be placed so that its bottom offers protection from the prevailing weather. Depending on the curvature of its stems, the top gunwale may have to be propped up so the sleepers' heads will fit under the canoe as they lie perpendicular to the canoe. Their bodies and feet are protected by the tarp. The canoe alone will serve a single person who spreads his bed under it, but his partner must then find a spot under the stars.

There are an infinite number of ways to rig the covering, but many prove ineffective in inclement weather. The tarp should extend over the canoe far enough so that water dripping off it will not run down between the canoe and the covering and onto the sleepers. It should either be staked out behind the canoe or tied securely to the lower gunwale. If there is concern that water will run under this gunwale, a small trench can be dug behind the canoe to channel the runoff from the canoe.

The covering is stretched over the sleeping area, and the opposite side of the tarp is staked out and drawn taut. Crawling into bed if this edge angles toward the ground does not make for a very commodious entrance. So, the tarp is often raised off the ground by propping stakes under the corners making the tarp almost parallel to the ground. Should rain come, it becomes an excellent water basin, and no matter how waterproof the tarp, eventually water either seeps through or the whole rig collapses under the weight!

There must be some provision to prevent this pool from collecting; water must naturally run off. The easiest addition is a ridge, longer than the tarp, laid with one end on the canoe and the other angled to the ground beyond the foot of the sleeping quarters—or perhaps lashed to a tree or upright stake to allow more space underneath. The free corners of the tarp are then staked down so the tarp will slope as it comes off the ridge. Avoid several ridges; the tarp sags between them in a storm with the same result as though no ridge were used.

Unfortunately, sleeping under canoes is common practice in summer camps where tripping is only a minor part of the program, and Junior may

have returned from camp convinced that this is proper procedure. When questioned, he will probably recall that his sleeping bag was soaked every time it rained, and for a couple days back in base camp his bag was hung over the rafters of the lodge to dry!

Jungle Hammocks

A small group of canoesmen advocate using jungle hammocks, although obviously not originally conceived for canoe country.

Like any hammock, it is secured between two convenient trees; but the jungle hammock also has a roof that is pitched over it, from which hang down several feet of bug netting attached to the hammock, so the sleeper climbs into his hammock and zips himself inside so his netting protects him from bugs and the roof keeps out rain.

The same outfit can be pitched so that what was intended as a hammock rests on the ground, while the top still serves as a roof.

The end result produces a cross between a ca-

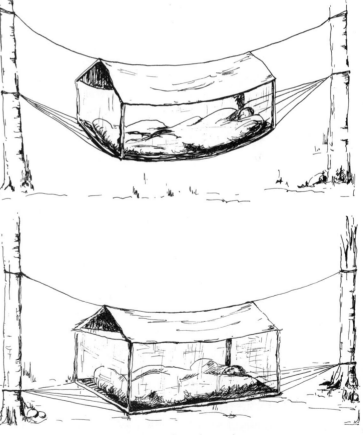

Jungle hammocks: A) may be slung between two trees as intended; B) or pitched so that hammock rests on ground with roof and netting in place.

noe shelter and a tent—with most of the problems of both. If the hammock is pitched as intended, there is practically no way to prevent sag, forcing anyone using it to sleep on his back. And all too often a sleeper thrashes around enough to tip the rig over, making an unbelievable mess from which it is difficult to get disentangled. Sometimes a playful companion even initiates the confusion!

Pitched on the ground, this problem is avoided, but space is limited and confining during a period of inclement weather—plus the fact that expense, time of erection, and bulk carried would all indicate that more comfort could be achieved by turning to a tent in the first place!

TENTS

The family camping boom has caused tent manufacturers to expand their lines to such a point that it is impossible to list all makes and models. If taking a wilderness trip as an experiment to see if it will be enjoyable enough to try again, do not buy tents immediately. Rent them from an outfitter or from a supplier near home; many large outdoors supply houses will rent tents, often applying the rental fee as a down payment if a purchase is made.

In selecting tents, however, cost should not be the deciding factor. Tents, like canoes, represent a long-term investment. The cheaper the tent, by and large, the less likely it is either to last or to perform adequately. On the other hand, the most expensive may have so many extras that it would be unsuitable. Before assessing cost, determine the features that must be included for the intended kind of tripping.

Material and Waterproofing

It goes without saying that a tent that lets water through freely is not very useful, but no tent is absolutely perfect, and all must be pitched correctly and cared for.

Perhaps due to the influence of backpackers and their concern regarding weight, a majority of the quality smaller tents suitable for a traveling camp are now made of nylon. The fibers in nylon cloth can be woven very tightly making a water-resistant material. To be completely waterproofed, the cloth must then be coated. However, a coated nylon tent could not breathe. If sealed shut for the night by the occupants, moisture naturally given off by the sleepers would condense on the

inside walls through which it could not escape—and the campers would find themselves rained upon. Therefore, a suitable nylon tent is either double-roofed or has an external fly of coated nylon that is pitched over the tent. The weight of a nylon tent—including its fly—will be less than half that of the same canvas tent, and the cost will be greater.

Unlike nylon, canvas expands and shrinks as it alternately dries and becomes wet. Cotton cloth has tiny pores, and when moisture hits it the threads expand, contracting the tent and sealing the cloth. In the first moments of a heavy rain, dry canvas allows a fine spray to enter, which should cease relatively soon. Tent canvas comes in various "weights." The six- or eight-ounce weights are preferable to a lighter four-ounce drill.

Introducing the coating needed to waterproof nylon is a manufacturing project. The manufacturer of a canvas tent introduced a waterproofing agent, which may have to be renewed by the owner as the tent ages—maybe every season under heavy usage. Most manufacturers also retail a waterproofing agent that should be sprayed, painted, or soaked through the canvas, and works better at less of a safety hazard than old paraffin-dissolved-in-gasoline home waterproofing solution.

Size

The shape of the erected tent makes little difference. Size is determined by floor space and head room. Floor space is the first consideration; an adult should have an area about seven feet long and three feet wide for his sleeping bag and personal gear. He can get by with less.

Next, determine how many people the tent will accommodate—and of what ages. A tent large enough for two adults will probably house three youngsters up to about twelve or thirteen years of age.

Avoid sleeping a large number of people in a single tent. Large tents may be satisfactory on cleared sites, but in the bush, suitable, flat, level ground may be difficult to find, and an area more than ten feet by ten feet which is free from brush, rocks, and roots cannot be expected at many wilderness campsites.

Height and head room should next be considered. The Army pup tent is fine for the purpose for which it is intended, but it is almost impossible to dress in a pup tent, even if one of the occupants waits outside until his partner finishes. Besides, should inclement weather set in, spending a day in a tent in a prone position becomes wearing.

Consider the head room available after pitching the tent. Erected on the salesroom floor the tent will seem more spacious than when pitched correctly in the wilderness. Most literature lists the height as the distance from the ground to the highest point of the tent—that height is reached only at one very small spot in some models. In general, most canoe trippers would at least like to sit up in bed without brushing the tent with their heads.

Some tents have a slope or pitch so they are higher in one spot—front, middle, or rear; check the maximum height, but pay more attention to the minimum. Often if the sleeping arrangements will be such that the feet will be under the lower part of the tent, such rigs are perfectly adequate; others will be cramped.

The slope from ground to peak should also be investigated. For instance, the wedge tent and the wall tent look similar at first glance, but the wedge tent's wall starts sloping inward at the ground, while the wall tent does not start sloping until the top of the wall—most likely two feet or maybe even three feet (although when pitched, the tent wall is never as tall as advertised). Other kinds of tents—maybe the umbrella—have walls that rise almost perpendicular to the ground, making for more cubic feet of space inside for the same floor area.

Means of Erection

Some tents require special poles and equipment. Some require a structure internal to the tent; others external. Some have complicated telescoping poles secured with springs, bolts, clamps, and various other pieces of hardware. The mechanics of erection should be relatively simple and such that in an emergency, should a pole or clamp be lost or misplaced, the tent will still be usable by substituting something drawn from the bush.

As various camping decisions are made, ecological factors come into consideration. What to do about tent poles is one such issue: carry them; or cut new ones from the forest at every site? Maybe the issue is academic—the trip goes into the barren lands of Canada; there may well not be any trees near the campsite large enough to serve. Maybe the trip travels in an area where it is illegal to cut green wood. But more than likely none of these extreme situations will be encountered.

Some ecology-minded camping schools cry out against cutting any trees at all for any purpose— quite appropriate in areas where man has already made serious scars in the forest, but not every

piece of canoe country fits this category. Even if the route is well traveled, if the canoeist has freedom to select where he camps, the forest around the site could well benefit from some sensible harvesting. Left to itself, any forest will do its own pruning. By no means will every sapling grow into a mature tree—the mortality rate is high in nature, and many canoe areas could actually profit from discretionary tent-pole cutting.

Does the tent have to be staked out? Most soil in canoe country is shallow, making it sometimes difficult to drive stakes. If rock will substitute for stakes, there is probably no problem. Rarely would a canoesman carry stakes, except thin aluminum pins. Small pickets can certainly be cut that will serve the same purpose as wooden stakes—and heavy metal ones add weight without offering any advantage.

Then, how long and how many people are required to erect the tent? The more complicated the rig, the more problems. And on a trip the tent will be struck most every day only to be put back up later the same day. The tent suitable for prolonged occupancy that requires some time to erect becomes a nuisance on a daily basis.

Floors

The desirability of a floor is a matter of choice. A sewn-in floor certainly increases the cleanliness of the interior up to a point, but it must be swept out occasionally to remain that way. Without a floor, every time the tent is moved, the floor at least changes! A floor also increases the waterproofing and bug proofing by sealing off those edges where tent and ground meet. However, the floor should not be considered a substitute for a ground cloth to be placed under each sleeping bag. It just provides more protection.

Many wilderness sites are uneven and rough. Once a floored tent is pitched, it is difficult to reach under and pull out that twig, stone, or root that was overlooked. Comfort aside, unless these inconveniences are removed, the floor may be punctured. If the ground is uneven, often the logical corrective action is to fill the dips with spruce or balsam boughs; such leveling must be done before pitching the tent.

Most salesmen will advise a floor as an absolute necessity; the Indian never has a floor in his tent —maybe because the salesman never got out of the store to convince him.

Bug Netting

The Indian does not have any bug protection

on his tent either, which just proves that he is not infallible. Netting for a wilderness trip is an absolute necessity for the part-time traveler. The blackfly season may be over, and the mosquitoes may be few at the time, but there are other winged insects—houseflies, deerflies, horseflies, no-see-ums, sandflies, the list goes on. Perhaps they are no bother on the water or around the campsite, but when the tent is occupied for the night the presence of even a couple bugs makes getting comfortable difficult. The netting can normally be tied off and stowed out of the way if unnecessary, but just having the door adequately covered offers security. Also, when camp is pitched near fast water, no matter how bug-free the rest of the country, they will be there—and a campsite at fast water is often dictated by the group's fishermen.

Although creating slight problems in entrance and exit, a netting that stretches solidly across the door, loose enough so that it is lifted to enter the tent, offers more protection and lasts longer than a netting split down the center and then secured with ties or zippers. Avoid the tent whose netting stretches taut when pitched on the sales-room floor; the tent rarely pitches exactly that way in the bush. Most manufacturers sell separate nettings to fit their tents, so a worn netting can be replaced or one added.

Windows

Windows are not really needed in a traveling tent, but they could provide ventilation without which it might be impossible to occupy the tent on a warm day. Just be sure they are adequately provided with bug netting; and be sure they will close securely in the event of storm.

Weight

To the canoesman, weight is not vital. If the heavier tent provides size, durability, and protection, there is no need to sacrifice comfort for a few pounds. However, on portages the tent is normally tossed on top of a load and should not be so heavy as to constitute a load in itself—as might be true of the larger-sized tents. Two small tents would be better.

Tents designed for backpacking must be extremely light; there is no reason why they cannot also be right for canoeing, but their size usually is more restrictive than the canoesman desires.

Tent weight varies, but when rolled, a tent weighing from ten to twenty pounds is acceptable, though a carrier would not object if it were lighter! Just do not sacrifice other features for the sake of pure weight.

Perhaps more important, the tent should make a compact bundle when rolled. And poles indigenous to the tent should be included in the bundle. Maybe a package eighteen inches long, and no more than ten inches by ten inches on the other two dimensions would be about maximum.

Color

Color makes little difference. However, a white tent will reflect sun better than the darker colors and be cooler on the warm day, but few trippers elect to spend much time in the tent on a sunny day anyway, and white of course shows dirt quickly.

Traditional colors would be green and khaki, but manufacturers now offer a great variety—some of which are perhaps more photogenic than the traditional choices.

Style

Here follow some tent styles that might be considered. Few manufacturers offer all of them, so if a particular style is desired, some shopping may have to be done, or some manufacturers will produce a tent on special order.

Quality

Quality is the most important ingredient. In general, from a reputable company the buyer can almost equate quality with price when comparing two tents offering the same features. After listing the requirements regarding size, material, style, etc., which the user regards as essential, buy the best that can be afforded.

Without field testing the various options—which is one argument in favor of renting before buying—there are a few features that the novice can look for to select quality.

The stitching along the seams should be straight and uniform without loose threads dangling from the finished tent. The best seams are what are called "lap-felled"—instead of just placing one piece of cloth on top of its neighbor and sewing the two together, the free end of each piece is doubled over and hooked into a similar fold on the other piece; as a result, the sewing is done through four layers of cloth rather than two, and there are no free edges to fray or pull loose.

The waterproofing in canvas should be such that when the tent is rubbed, none of the color

Tent styles: A) Wall; B) Wedge; C) Umbrella; D) Pop tent; E) Draw-tite; F) Baker or Lean-to; G) Miner's; H) Pup tent with sides staked out; I) Mountain tent (normally used for backpacking); J) Nylon Pup tent with external fly

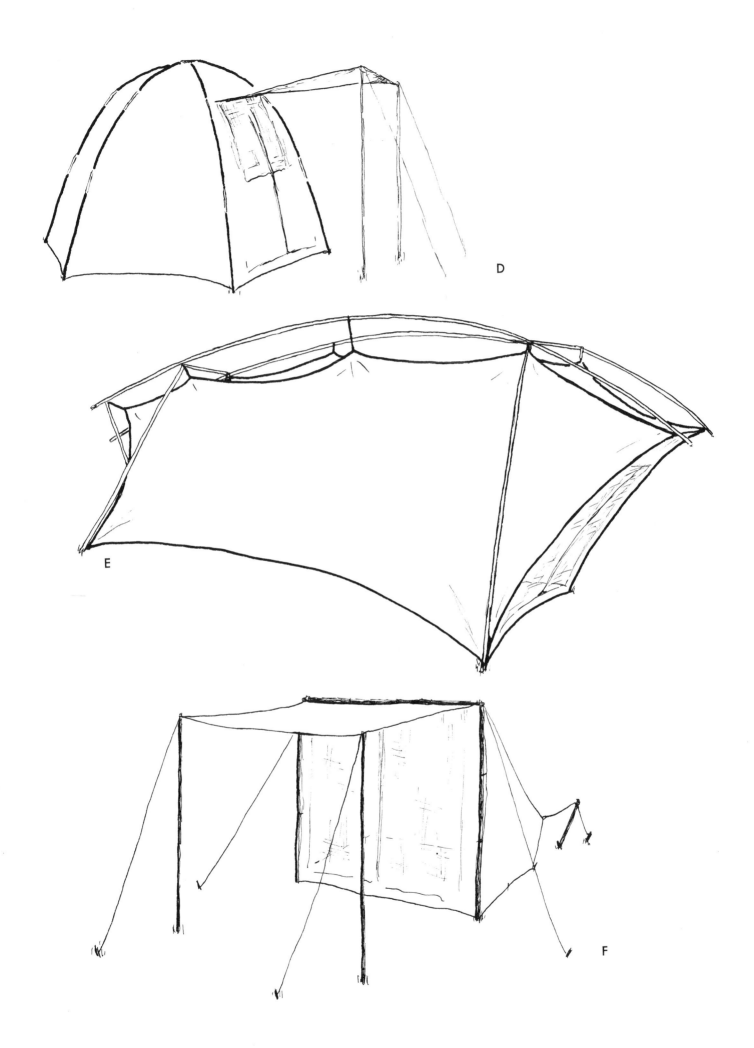

D

E

F

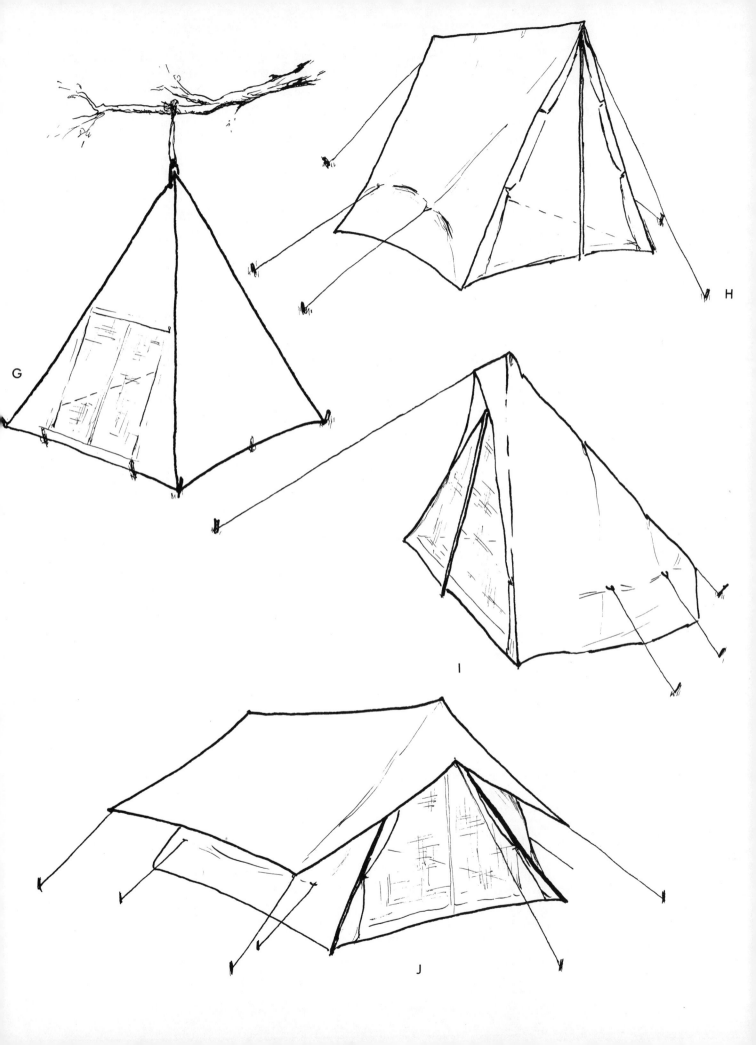

G

H

I

J

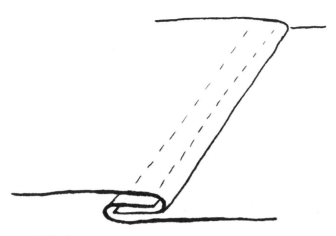

Lap-felled seam

comes off. Beware of the tent with a "waxy" feel.

Grommets should be heavy, secure, and placed in reinforced areas of cloth and set well in from the edges.

The floor should be sewn in without wrinkles, and the entire tent surface should be smooth and uniform when pitched. Nettings, doors, windows, and screens should be adequate, well secured, and have ample material for closure.

Ropes and stake loops—even if they are not to be used—should be of good quality, well secured, and of commodious length—not that they cannot be replaced easily; just that if a manufacturer skimps on small items, the rest of the product may also be inferior. The same holds true of stakes, even if they are not to be used—the tent with wooden stakes these days has disappeared from the quality market. Do not make final judgments on ropes and stakes alone, however; anyone can do right by small items and still have marketed a shoddy product with respect to that which counts.

TARPS AND FLIES

Each party should carry a canvas, coated nylon, or ripstop nylon fly large enough to cover the supplies when stored near the fireplace at night, and large enough to be pitched over the kitchen area to provide a dry working area for the chefs in inclement weather.

For the two-canoe party, a fly eight feet by six feet would be sufficient. A larger party should go to eight by twelve, or ten by fourteen. The weight of a fly is not excessive and its uses numerous enough that it should be a must. It need not be pitched at every campsite, but it should be thrown over the provisions at night and rocked down if high winds threaten.

A single fly or tarp is sufficient for effective covering of the kitchen, but a second fly might be carried to pitch over the fire itself in poor weather if the main covering is not sufficiently large to cover both kitchen and fire.

The same injunctions about quality already offered regarding tents apply to a fly. Extra consideration should be given to placement and reinforcement of grommets, for great stress is placed on the fly when pitched in a high wind. Plastics and rubberized fabrics make for good, light covers, but do not have the strength of canvas or nylon when pitched and subjected to the stress of wind and rain.

Ripstop nylon has additional threads woven into the cloth, making it stronger than coated nylon of the corresponding weight. Unlike nylon tent cloth, that used for a fly should be waterproof. The larger flies are often manufactured by sewing together several panels. Be sure the holes created by the stitching have been filled; otherwise, the seams leak. A coated nylon fly has probably been properly sealed; a ripstop nylon one may not. There are sealers available commercially to fill such seams at home. It should be further noted that, while waterproof canvas is highly flammable, even the smallest spark which comes in contact with nylon will burn a hole almost immediately. Much greater care must be exercised in pitching and using a nylon kitchen fly than with a canvas one.

The fly can double as a sail while traveling, and maybe as an emergency covering to throw over the cargo; or as a quickly erected shelter when the canoes are driven ashore by an unexpected summer thunderstorm.

STOVES

As the wilderness diminishes and the urge to use what remains increases, so does agitation against the campfire. Some maintain that the scars left by the cooking fire are unsightly; certainly the forest fire started by failure to extinguish one is a much greater scar. There are areas where an open fire is prohibited, or there is nothing suitable to burn north of the tree line, so stoves are a necessity.

Stoves for canoe parties have two distinct disadvantages: carrying their fuel is the minor one; the number of burners and therefore the number of pots that can be heated is the major.

Camping stoves can be gasoline fueled and are available in sizes from one to three burners. Use naptha or white gas for fuel if unwilling to pay the price for stove fuel. There are also models that use packaged cylinders. An oven that sits on top of a burner is also marketed.

Other types use propane or even butane cylinders for fuel. Then the backpacker uses a lightweight Svea stove.

COOKERY

If stoves are employed for cooking, some of the equipment in this section needs modification, but kitchen needs vary only slightly with the number of people in the group; and while the canoeist should look to weight, he need not travel with the austerity of the backpacker. There are certain constants, so that it actually requires little more in the way of pots, pans, and other basic necessities for six than for two.

With a group of more than six, the basic elements of the cookery—kitchen or jewelry, depending on what title is used—remain the same, but the size of individual pots and pans must be increased.

The entire cookery should be available without

B

C

Kitchen wannigans: A) Cookery for four. Pots fit into compartment under tray. Reflector fits into thin rectangular area. Remainder of space is available for supplies. B) Also designed for four, but easily expandable for more C) Larger jewelry for ten to twelve people

A

unfastening each portage load. Spreading equipment through various packs makes for inefficiency. Besides, if cooking on wood fires, pots and pans become blackened and must then be bagged or wrapped to keep them from other items in a pack. Therefore, the "kitchen wannigan" has a definite place as a part of the equipment. The wannigan's size and construction depend on individual preference and inventiveness, and many veteran trippers have ingeniously devised compartmentalized boxes for their equipment. In designing the wannigan, keep the black pots away from eating uten-

31

sils and materials that do not come in contact with the fire.[1]

After every use the pot black can be removed; however, black conducts heat better than shiny, bright metal, and aside from the labor involved, removing the pot black reduces the cooking efficiency. The loose black that accumulates can be rubbed off every time a sandy area is used for camping, to reduce that which gets transferred to the cook's hands—but the skilled cook soon learns to handle his equipment and still keep clean. Only when the outfit is stored at the end of the season need the pots be cleaned completely to present their natural, shiny appearance for the first use of the next expedition. Lacquer thinner or paint remover does a good job; make sure the work is done in an adequately ventilated area.

Some trippers feel each person should carry his own "mess kit" and prepare his own meals. Ideal as the philosophy may be for inculcating culinary skills, such arrangements involve a traveling party in a wasteful, time-consuming division of labor. Rotating cooking duties is better. Perhaps the "cook-for-a-day" will not be the accomplished chef of the Ritz, but he will improve with practice, and the community cooking and subsequent cleanup offers economy in time, effort, and use of supplies.

Pots

Many items in the jewelry can be supplied from home or from the household department of a local store, except for the jewelry's most basic ingredient: a set of nesting pots—these should probably be purchased from a camping-supply house.

Starting with perhaps a ten-quart pot and ranging downward in size to about two quarts, there should be a minimum of four pots to the unit, and each should be equipped with a sturdy bail. Most saucepans used at home have handles making nesting impossible, and cooking with them over an open fire where the flame licks up around the handles is difficult. Various possible sets of nesting pots are shown along with the kitchen wannigans in illustration on page 31. Frame A shows a set suitable for four, containing three pots, a coffeepot, plates, cups, and two fry pans with detachable handles, the larger of which serves as the cover for the set. Frame B shows a set also suitable for four. Plates, pannikins, and fry pan are added to the basic unit. Frame C

depicts a set suitable for a group of ten to twelve. Nesting is done in two units.

Lids are not an absolute necessity, although meal preparation is easier if at least one pot has a lid, if for no other purpose than to drain water off certain foods. Then, a covered pot will boil more quickly than an uncovered one.

Skillet

At least one skillet should be included, large enough to handle bacon, fish, and pancakes. One of about ten-inch diameter should be about minimum for a small party.

Some are made with collapsible handles, and if a complete camping outfit is purchased, often the lid of one of the larger nesting pots is designed as a fry pan. However, if space permits, a skillet with its metal handle firmly attached will prove more satisfactory. A removable handle always seems to disengage at inopportune times no matter what the construction. Be sure the handle in any event is metal and not wood or plastic, which might burn or melt as the open fire licks upward.

If space permits, two skillets are better than one; perhaps one slightly larger than the other. A luxury to consider would be a flat, rectangular grill, ideal for pancakes and the like, but if it comes down to a grill or a second skillet, the skillet is more versatile.

Dutch Oven

A more useful luxury is a Dutch oven, or "bean pot." The best ones are made of cast iron and are therefore heavy; lighter ones are made of heavy aluminum. Such an additional pot has many uses

Heavy aluminum Dutch oven

1. For a full discussion of wannigan construction, see *Canoeing Wilderness Waters,* pp. 163–66.

over and above its intended use as a baker—simmering meats and stews particularly. A close-fitting metal lid is a must, especially if baking under hot sand is done.

Coffeepot or Tea Pail

These two possible additional pots could be added to the outfit. If perked coffee is a must, a separate coffeepot should be carried. Most trippers boil coffee, and so avoid carrying the insides of a special pot.

A tea pail is not really a good description of its intended uses, unless tea is made by pouring hot water over the tea and then letting it steep without heating. A small pot that never gets on the fire has numerous uses, such as mixing powdered milk, making puddings that do not require boiling, and becoming the inside of a double boiler in situations where one must be created—as in making an icing or frosting.

Reflector

On a trip of any duration—more than a day or two where the supply of fresh bread will disappear—a reflector baker becomes not a luxury but a real asset. The uses of a reflector are limitless—from biscuits, to cakes, to pies, to rolls, to bread, to fish and meats. The old trapper lumps all of

Open-sided reflector is not as efficient as those shown as parts of kitchen wannigans in the illustration on page 31. Frame A of that illustration contains a reflector whose pan is supported on rails. Frame B illustrates one whose pan rests on a shelf. Both are sizable enough for a party of four. Frame C shows a reflector suitable for ten to twelve people.

his baking products made with baking powder under the title of "bannock," and while a bannock can be made in a fry pan, the reflector is a more versatile cooking aid.

Since their use in the family camping area is not general, only a few of the major camping-supply houses offer reflectors, so some investigation may be necessary to find a suitable one. In general, the reflector consists of a baking pan fixed by various means between two angled reflecting surfaces, so when the pan is placed between them, and the baker positioned in front of the fire, heat is reflected on the pan from both top and bottom. Some inferior models have open ends, but ones with reflecting surfaces also at the ends bake better and are more durable.

While heat cannot be regulated with such precision as on a home range, an experienced baker can reasonably approximate cookbook temperatures from 200° to 450° by moving the oven closer or farther from the fire.

Most are made of aluminum so their reflecting surfaces can be kept shiny. They normally fold into a thin rectangular package that can be fitted easily into plans for the jewelry wannigan.

A reflector whose baking pan is about thirteen inches by seven inches makes a convenient size for the four- to six-man party. Larger models are available from a more limited number of manufacturers.

Cooking Utensils

A couple of large serving and/or cooking spoons are necessary. At least one should be perforated for straining vegetables and other foods. A long-handled fork, preferably with only two tines, is needed for turning fish and bacon. A spatula should be included for pancakes and eggs; the professional cooks seem to prefer ones with holes to those that are solid. A dipper or ladle for serving soup, cocoa, tea, or coffee should be brought along.

Utensils with solid metal handles can have their upper ends bent over to make them double as pot hooks to avoid the danger of grabbing the bail of a hot pot with a bare hand. They are most likely located from a restaurant-supply house.

Knives

A couple of quality butcher knives that will hold an edge are indispensable. One should have a blade thin and flexible enough to fillet fish, and there is no shortcut here with regard to quality.

The thick, wide hunter's sheath knife is no substitute for a good butcher's knife at least six to eight inches long.

A small paring knife also has uses, as does a lightweight potato peeler if fresh potatoes are to be included.

Can Opener

One of the most forgotten but necessary items is the can opener! Opening cans with the ax or hunting knife can be messy. It does no harm to carry two. Best are those that operate by twirling a handle; the youngsters will be baffled by those that cut with an up-and-down pry—plus the fact that they leave a ragged edge. For emergencies, one of the tiny surplus can openers supplied with Army "C Rations" can be tucked in a pack out of the way to be used when the others are lost or broken. Those built into pocketknives never seem to work.

Plates

A plate for each person plus a couple of spares are needed, not only to protect against loss, but for use around the cooking area for storage and serving purposes.

Many cooking outfits include plates along with the nesting pots. Most are made of aluminum and are excellent and also fit the rest of the outfit. Usually in a set designed for four people, there are exactly four plates, but more should be added.

If plates are purchased separately, a shallow aluminum pie plate is an excellent trip plate; and it could be used to bake a pie also. Unbreakable plastic plates could be used, although they will not double as baking dishes.

Cups

Cups are also often supplied in a basic camping outfit. Be sure they will nest, however, if purchased separately. Plastic cups are best; those made of aluminum look sturdy and equally acceptable, but aluminum conducts heat rapidly, and the hot drink in such a cup cannot be touched until the metal rim cools—by then the liquid is only tepid at best. There is a metal Sierra cup available that solves this problem.

As a substitute for, or in addition to, plastic cups, there is a Northwoods replacement known as a *pannikin*. It is just a bowl, without a handle, with a capacity of two measuring cups. As such it serves wonderfully not only for beverages but

also as a soup bowl, cereal dish, or deep plate for stew or chowder. It also makes a convenient sugar bowl, ladle, or serving implement.

There are now plastic pannikins, but the old ones were made of either tin or aluminum. Those of tin will rust, and they turn a little black when used for tea; and many woodsmen would not be without tea. Aluminum pannikins have the same deficiency as aluminum cups when used for warm foods. The rust and discoloration will come out of tin pannikins with a little steel wool, and if dried thoroughly after washing are infinitely more satisfactory.

Pannikins beside a plastic cup, which will nest with other similar cups

Silverware

Silverware is usually not included with the basic cooking outfit and can be supplied from home or purchased at the local household department. Each person should have a fork and a spoon, plus a few extra of each for cooking and serving. Tablespoons are slightly preferable to teaspoons, but a couple of the latter for measuring are advisable. Table knives have fewer uses, but about one per pair of people should be included. Sharper knives for the odd occasion where they are needed should be supplied by an individual's pocketknife.

Dishpan

It may not fit into the jewelry and may have to be carried tied outside, or maybe stuffed in the stern of a canoe, but a light plastic or metal dishpan should be available. Dishes should not be washed in a cooking pot; the danger of leaving a soap residue is great. Either a rectangular or circular plastic pan, available at any household counter, makes an excellent dishpan—and the expense is such that is can be replaced each season. Just be sure no one inadvertently drops a butcher knife into it, and keep it away from the actual fire —the plastic melts! (On-the-spot small cracks can be sealed by rubbing a warm nail along the crack.)

Mixing Bowl

If baking is contemplated, a plastic mixing bowl large enough to fit in the jewelry is an asset, not just a luxury. The dishpan can double as such a bowl, or a pot can be used—subject to the previous comments about soap in the first case and pot black in the second.

Walloping Pot

A walloping pot is not a necessity either, but dishwater must be heated in something, and dishes should be rinsed before drying. The largest cooking pot can be used, but care must be exercised to avoid soap deposits—better if there is a special large pot for heating the water. Pour half in the dishpan, and leave half for rinsing, and the pot should be reserved for this use.

Walloping Accessories

While not a permanent part of the jewelry, since they are replaced when necessary, washing and scouring equipment should be stored in the jewelry. First, the dishwasher needs soap—either liquid or bar. A sponge or swab for washing should be included.

A couple of dish towels should be available so that when one becomes too damp it can be dried while the other is being used. It is assumed that they will be washed out when necessary. Otherwise, spares should be carried and the soiled towels disposed of periodically.

For the pots and pans, a scouring pad with soap built in is needed, and the more difficult pots will be handled best with a copper scouring pad to remove anything stuck to the bottom of the pot. A soap pad will last a couple meals; the scouring pad maybe twice as many, assuming it is not used to remove pot black.

If a reflector is carried, soap pads will do a fair job of keeping the reflecting surfaces shiny. (The harsher scouring pad will scratch the soft metal, harming the reflecting surfaces.) A cake or can of scouring powder is better; or best, a container of a pumice-based cleaner, normally sold as a hand cleaner and used by mechanics who must wash off grease each day.

Mittens

Quite useful in handling warm pots and pans, and especially a hot reflector pan, is a pair of household cooking mitts. Those with an asbestos palm are infinitely superior to those of cotton. A pair of heavy work gloves could substitute, but the thin cotton variety are worthless; avoid leather—it conducts heat too readily.

Condiments and Spices

Space in the jewelry should be provided for both salt and pepper shakers; the best of each being those whose tops can be covered with screw-on lids so that the contents do not spill in transit. The necessity of placing a piece of foil or paper between the shaker and the cap after every use is a pain.

Other common spices should also be carried in the kitchen—maybe cinnamon, ginger, and others, depending on the preferences of the cooks.

Fire Starters

Last, but by no means least, should be matches! While it is fine to carry some other fire-starting equipment—such as cigarette lighters—there is no quick substitute for a box of common, strike-anywhere matches. It is not necessary to waterproof them; just have a box there. Should they get wet, throw them away, but somewhere in the outfit should be emergency waterproof equipment. A simple expedient for waterproofing matches is to melt a bar of paraffin and pour it directly into the box. Then as needed a dry match is just pulled out of the paraffin.

Another valuable aid on the wet, rainy day when the dry wood refuses to burn is a can of lighter fluid. It does not sound very woodsy, but a little fluid squirted on reluctant shavings has saved many a day. And it can be used to refill everyone's pocket lighter. Less versatile would be a tube of commercial fire starter.

FIRE IRONS

Various methods for laying a wood cooking fire will be discussed in chapter 4, but the experienced canoesman carries something to lay over his fire to support his pots—be it a grill, grate, or a pair of "fire irons," which are only a pair of pieces of pipe laid over the fire like parallel rails. Whatever rig is selected, it probably must be carried outside the jewelry wannigan, but it belongs to the community equipment. It probably needs a covering to keep the inevitable black of the open fire from rubbing off on everyone.

AXES AND SAWS

Each canoe or every other canoe should carry a lightweight single-bitted ax. A head of 2¼ or 2½ pounds is sufficiently heavy for camp purposes and for any work that must be done in cutting trails.

An ax file or two should be carried for sharpening purposes, and the files must be protected from moisture—they rust quickly.

Another useful asset is the camp saw—a buck saw with perhaps a thirty-inch blade or less. The saw can safely be used by youngsters who might not be skilled with an ax. Normally one saw is enough—plus an extra blade.

The ax should be portaged by the sternsman with his canoe.[2] The saw can be carried on the back of a pack, tied into a canoe, or on top of a wannigan, so neither poses great problems at the portage. A more complete treatment of both ax and saw is included in chapter 5.

CANOE REPAIR KIT

A canoe repair kit should also be a permanent part of the community equipment; contents depend on the kind of craft used.[3]

FIRST AID KIT

The first aid kit should not be bulky but should be waterproof and must contain sufficient supplies to meet logical medical problems. A treatment is contained in chapter 6.

2. For portaging procedures involving the ax, see *Canoeing Wilderness Waters*, pp. 146–49.

3. For discussion of the contents of a canoe repair kit, see *Canoeing Wilderness Waters*, pp. 170–96.

3

PERSONAL EQUIPMENT

Personal equipment obviously depends on the individual, the duration of the trip, and anticipated weather, but a canoe tripper can pack sufficient gear to be comfortable—particularly while sleeping.

To a large degree, comfort is measured by the ability to stay warm and dry. If the weather proves mild, extra clothing is easy to remove but quite difficult to supplement if nothing is available. Rain gear may never be used, but there is no substitute when needed.

SLEEPING BAGS

Long gone is the era when campers took wool blankets, folded them into an intricate pattern, and fastened the contraption together with blanket pins. Even the expense of a bag is now less than an adequate number of blankets.

Bags are available in various shapes and sizes; comfortable to varying temperatures; constructed in numerous ways; filled with different materials. Any bag should be tagged to explain its design, size, kind of fill, and temperatures for which it is recommended. Beware of the bag that fails to supply this information, and the salesman offering such equipment probably cannot answer all the questions that should be asked. Consistent with the budget, buy the best bag that meets the conditions under which it will be used. It is a long-range investment in comfort.

Temperature Range

Any reliable manufacturer will indicate the temperature range for his bag. There is no point in buying a bag rated for below zero if it is to be used only for canoeing; it would be so warm that it would be uncomfortable. In general, the farther north the tripping area, the lower the temperature is expected to drop at night, and it would not be unusual in northern Canada for the thermometer to dip below freezing occasionally, even during midsummer. Sleeper's cold tolerances vary, but estimate the lowest temperatures that might be encountered, and buy a bag rated at least that low. For canoeing, a bag rated to 30° or maybe 20° would normally be adequate.

Filling

The price depends first on the filler. In descending order of efficiency, and price, are goose down, duck down, Dacron, followed by an infinite variety of polyester fibers, each having its own trade name.

The downs provide the best insulations, with goose down rated at one hundred percent and the other fillers decreasing in efficiency. Look at the tag that advises the weight of filler used, not the weight of the entire bag. Six pounds of goose down are used in bags rated to 60° below. One and a half or two pounds is adequate for canoeing weather. Dacron filling for similar protection is about twice as heavy.

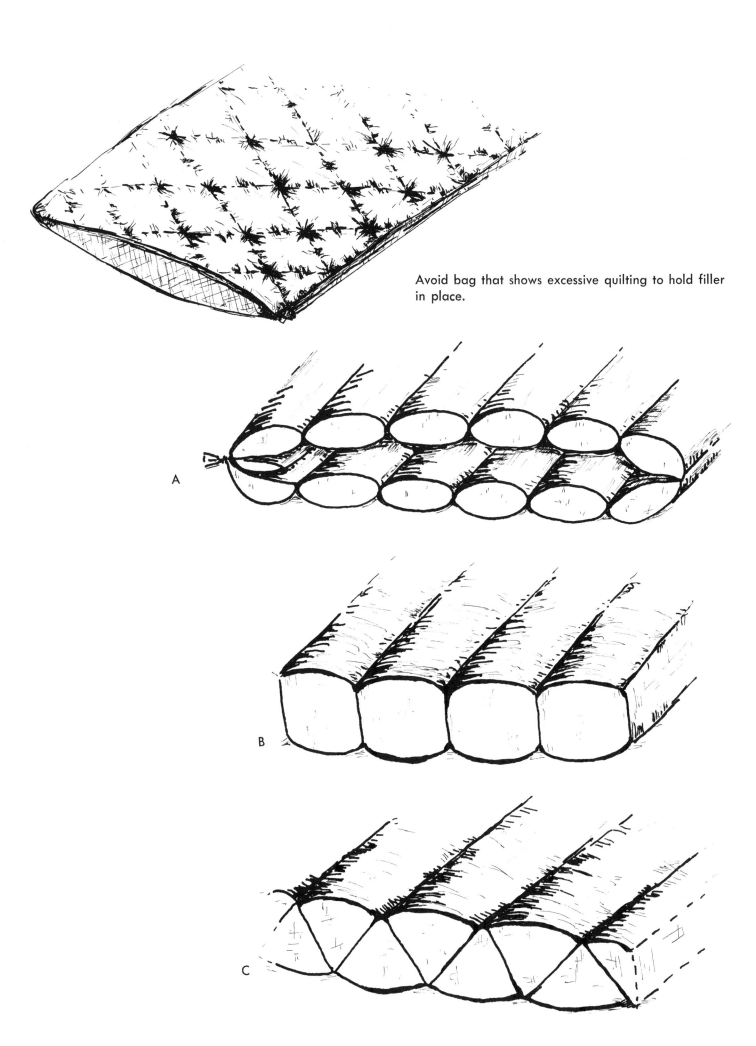

Avoid bag that shows excessive quilting to hold filler in place.

A

B

C

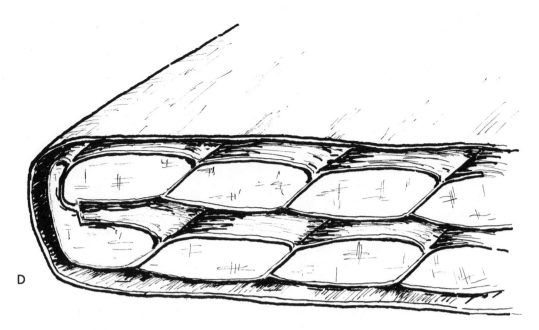

Size and Shape

Bags are made rectangular or "mummy" style with some tapered to offer a happy medium. Unless weight is important, most sleepers prefer a rectangular bag. Mummy construction allows little space in which to turn over. So the sleeper and bag roll together, which, unless accustomed to it, can be confining.

Rectangular bags come in various sizes. Look for the dimensions of the closed bag. Widths vary from about thirty-two inches up to forty inches—lengths, from about seventy inches up to eighty-four inches; some extra-large models range up to ninety inches. Buy a large enough bag. Most sleepers like to stretch out full length, and even occasionally draw the bag up over their heads—on a cool night breathing into the bag for a few minutes can warm it considerably. For the average adult, a size about thirty-four inches by eighty-two inches would probably be most suitable.

Some bags have built-in pockets for air mattresses. They are not absolutely necessary, but they can prevent rolling off the mattress, while also making the bed more restrictive. Some bags have pockets on both sides, making it possible to position the zipper on either side.

Construction

The manner in which the insulation is kept in place will be particularly important in determining warmth and life expectancy.

The cheaper bags are elaborately quilted—

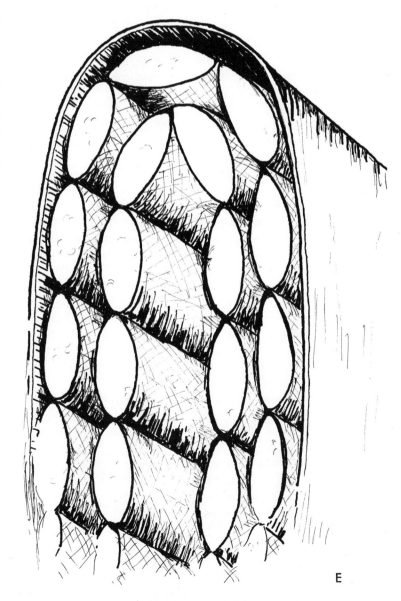

Various arrangements for confining filler: A) parallel tubes, but with little filler at seams; B) parallel tubes, but with better insulation at seams; C) **V**-shaped construction; D) overlapping tubular arrangement; E) double series of parallel tubes, used in bags rated for extreme cold sewed seams throughout the covering—to hold the filler in place and to reduce bunching, thereby giving one area all the insulation while there is little but the outside cover in other spots. Avoid such a bag; there is no filler between the lining and the cover along each seam, and while there may be thick insulation elsewhere, each seam is a cold area.

The better bags have the filler arranged in tubes inside the bag. A parallel V-shaped tubular arrangement offers fewer seams and better overall insulation than quilting. The best are made with overlapping tubes to prevent cold spots where no filler is present at the seams. The manufacturer using either V-shaped or tubular methods for packing the filler will so advertise. The one employing some less-efficient method may avoid the issue.

Use and constant packing compress the filler of any bag. The better ones just need to be shaken out, or fluffed up occasionally to recover their insulating properties, for insulation depends on trapped air between the sleeper and the outside world.

Liners

Flannel is the most likely material used for the lining, but ripstop nylon is gaining acceptance. The weight of the lining does not indicate the quality of the bag; a heavy lining may just disguise an inadequate filler. Just be sure that the user is not allergic to the lining.

Quality manufacturers also sell a removable flannel liner that is purchased separately and made specifically to fit a particular bag. The additional liner can improve the temperature range of the bag by as much as 10°. It can be removed and cleaned independent of the bag itself. It adds weight, and so, unless needed for warmth and cleanliness, it is not universally used.

For the sleeper who wants to pretend he is in his bed at home, it is possible to line any bag with an ordinary linen sheet.

Outer Covering

The better bags have a nylon outer covering, usually ripstop nylon. It is tough, lightweight, easily kept clean, and provides some slight waterproofing because of the closeness of the weave.

Avoid the bag with a rubberized bottom that claims to be waterproof. It soon cracks and peels, and such a bag can neither be satisfactorily washed nor dry-cleaned—and most campers will want their bags cleaned at the end of the season. (If dry-cleaned, be absolutely sure all the solvent is removed by thorough airing before using again.)

No one wants a waterproof bag anyway. A bag so made could not breathe, and the moisture collected inside would make it at least clammy and damp, if not downright wet!

Pay no attention to any flap attached to the top of the bag to be used as a tent or shelter. Except for securing the bag in a compact roll, such flaps have no use, and the better ones offer no such extra cloth. Some, however, offer a detachable hood for the sleeper who wants a head covering for cold weather.

Openings

The rectangular bag should be equipped with a heavy-duty full-length zipper with pull tabs on both inside and outside. It should be possible to open the bag completely to be aired flat so the zipper extends down one side and across the bottom.

The mummy bag usually has a shorter zipper, but it should be possible to turn it inside-out for airing.

The rectangular bags of the major manufacturers usually have zippers so constructed that a pair of similar bags can be joined to make a double bed, which may appeal to family campers.

The better bags have a flap built into their lining, to at least partially stop the breeze that seeps through even the best zipper, and also to keep the sleeper from striking the cold metal zipper. The heat loss through the zipper is not normally a factor outweighing the presence of the full-length zipper in a canoeing bag.

Total Weight

The weight of the entire bag is not of prime consideration to the canoesman, but there is no point in buying a heavy, bulky bag that will not roll compactly and will be a burden to portage. So, perhaps lastly, the entire weight and bulk might be considered, although there are few excessively heavy bags on the market.

The old surplus Army officer's bedroll with heavy canvas cover was excessively heavy even when in vogue. It is better to buy a new, lighter bag than to resurrect the old one lying around the attic.

GROUND CLOTH

Many tents have a waterproof floor, but each tripper should use a ground cloth. When set for the night, the ground cloths of the tentmates should overlap generously, completely cover the floor, and still have some material left along the rear and sides of the tent. A ground cloth about seven feet by five feet is generous for most situations.

Unless it is to double as a fly or canoe sail, the ground cloth does not need careful grommet placement or reinforced corners and edges; but, otherwise, the qualities that make for a good fly or tarp are those of the ground cloth. Above all it must keep moisture from seeping in from below and should be rugged enough to withstand the punishment of being pressed against the forest floor by the sleeper and his movements.

Materials used are canvas, coated nylon, ripstop nylon, and rubberized cloth. Waterproof canvas is least likely to puncture when laid inadvertently over small stones, sticks, and twigs, but canvas has an open weave; used on sites already wet when the bed is laid, or in situations where the weather requires long occupancy of the tent, moisture from below will eventually seep up through. While a canvas ground cloth can be rewaterproofed like tent canvas, the problem of water that soaks through from below is never completely solved.

Treated nylon cloth is light, tough, and less likely to let moisture up through its weave. It is more expensive than canvas, and perhaps more likely to be punctured if laid on sharp objects. With extended use the waterproof coating will start to crack, and rewaterproofing is never entirely satisfactory. Ripstop nylon is quite similar but is less likely to puncture than coated nylon of the same weight.

Rubberized cloth makes an inexpensive ground cloth. It will peel and crack after a season or two, but costs about a third as much as nylon. It suffers from the same shortcomings with regard to puncture as nylon but is almost completely waterproof. When the rubberized side is laid on the ground, it is likely to sweat, as the heat of the sleeper's body presses down on the cold ground. Before packing for the day, the ground cloth should often be aired and dried in the sun for fifteen or twenty minutes. To a slightly lesser degree the same condition exists when using a coated nylon ground cloth.

Avoid using ponchos as ground cloths; their possible dual use as rain gear sounds attractive.

Somehow the opening in the center never closes completely; plus the closure creates a bunching of material in the center of the bed. Besides, the tripper often needs rain gear and a ground cloth simultaneously.

In addition to protecting the sleeper from damp ground, the ground cloth should also be used to roll or help waterproof the individual pack during travel.

AIR MATTRESSES OR FOAM PADS

Once upon a time only the sissy or tenderfoot carried an air mattress or foam pad. True, they add weight and take up space, but these problems are minor compared with increased comfort.

A mattress raises the sleeper off the damp ground, and, while he still uses a ground cloth, the mattress provides more protection from surface moisture. The mattress also reduces the cold that seeps up into a sleeping bag in direct contact with the cold ground, and the bed will be warmer due to the cushion of air. Then there is the tripper who inflates the air mattress only if camped on wet or uneven ground; otherwise it is just laid deflated under the sleeping bag.

Air mattresses come with different constructions and are made of various materials. Construction is either tubular, I-beamed, or tufted—in ascending order of price and probably comfort. The most common is tubular, and in general the greater the number of tubes, the more comfortable and expensive the mattress. Five tubes are a minimum.

I-beam construction at first glance looks the same in many mattresses, but the tubes will retain more or less the same size so that the sleeper's weight does not drive one tube right to the ground while the neighbors swell.

Tufted mattresses look something like that on the bed at home and eliminate the valleys of the tubular or I-beam mattress—and the price reflects this.

Materials also vary. Plastics are used in cheaper mattresses. They may be adequate for a season or two, but will soon crack. Nylon backed with a rubberized coating is more durable, reasonably light, and more expensive. Those of rubber or rubber-backed canvas are heavier but even more durable and most expensive, but are normally a worthwhile long-term investment if weight is not of prime concern.

When selecting a mattress, be sure the seams are well sealed and generous; if buying plastic,

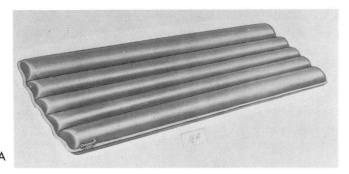

A

flating the mattress. Most trippers pull the plugs when they wake and lie there while the mattress goes down, flattening itself, before climbing out of bed.

The standard measure for correct inflation is the position where the sleeper's hips are just lifted off the ground. Lie on the mattress during inflation, and the pressure is right when the body rises off the ground. Some prefer a more firm mattress.

B

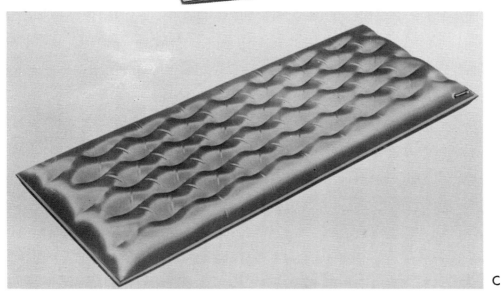

C

Air mattresses: A) normal parallel-tube arrangement; B) ladder design with raised siderails and attached pillow; C) tufted construction (Courtesy Stebco Industries, Inc.)

look for a heavy-duty mattress. Watch the inflated size—all mattresses are larger when deflated than when used.

Then there is the tripper who is concerned about weight. There is a three-quarter-length mattress designed for the backpacker; it is equally reasonable for the canoesman. Comfort depends on supporting the body from hips to shoulders, and support for the legs is not really necessary.

Packing for the day's travel first requires de-

But in any event, avoid kneeling or otherwise putting excess pressure on a small area; the mattress was designed to have weight spread equally over it. Then there is the tripper who would avoid the nightly expenditure of lung power to inflate the mattress. There are available small pumps that operate by foot or hand power.

The valve is a possible source of trouble. If it is a screw-on cap or rubber plug, carry a spare. And make sure a detachable element does not get mislaid while traveling. Some tie a plug to the mattress; others carry it in their pants' watch pocket. Perhaps a screw cap is less likely to work loose during the night than a plug, but on the other hand it is easier to manufacture an emergency plug from the bush should those carried be lost. While not from nature, an empty 30/30 shell makes a good emergency plug. The best closure is probably one that is not detachable and opens and closes by rotating an element of the valve.

Patching materials should be carried; ordinary glue becomes brittle when dry and cracks, and something like adhesive tape is porous. Some people even prefer a mattress that gradually sinks during the night. When they hit rock bottom, it is time to get up and begin the day.

Should a small leak develop that defies detection, taking the inflated mattress into the water will locate the leak by the small string of air bubbles; the mattress, however, was not intended as a swimming raft or float. If the youngsters want such entertainment, carry an inexpensive plastic spare which is expendable.

Some mattresses have an attached pillow; most do not. The pillow is normally inflated separately, so the sleeper can adjust bed and pillow individually. Separate air pillows can be purchased, although spare clothing makes a perfectly acceptable pillow.

The restless sleeper sometimes finds he cannot keep himself on his mattress through the night. Proper inflation will give him a hollow into which he will naturally rest. Others prefer using a sleeping bag equipped with a pocket into which the mattress fits. And some mattresses are built so the outside tubes inflate slightly higher than the center ones, making for a small rail.

The foam pad, either full or three-quarter length, is another possibility. Although apparently

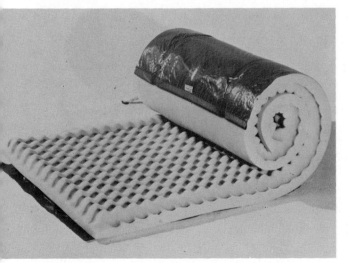

Foam pad will compress for packing. (Courtesy L. L. Bean, Inc.)

quite bulky, it will compress considerably for packing, and the weight is less than that of a quality air mattress. As a result, it has met an enthusiastic response from the backpacker. For the canoeist, the only drawback is bulk; it will not deflate during the night, does not have to be blown up each night, has no plugs or valve to lose or break, and cannot leak.

FOOTWEAR

Footwear requires serious consideration, and two pairs of shoes should be included.

Boots

Most canoeists lean toward a lightweight boot of ankle or higher length—the eight- or ten-inch height being most common. The boot provides ankle support on uneven portage trails as well as protection from muskeg, clay, and wet trails. A composition sole that is less slippery on logs and rocks is preferred.

A leather upper can be made reasonably water-repellent by applying a leather conditioner to the dry boot. Dubbin is the most common waterproofing agent, but mink oil has its devotees. A satisfactory substitute is bacon fat or even lard or shortening.

Be sure the boot is tightly stitched if it is to be at all waterproof, and the sole that lets go cannot easily be repaired in the bush. As with most camping products, quality is normally reflected in price. Boots bought from a reputable outlet are likely more satisfactory than those from the local surplus store. Naturally, be sure of the size. Many mail-order companies suggest tracing the foot. Follow instructions; the street shoe size may not be exactly that of an adequate boot. Do not hesitate to return them if a different size is necessary. In buying boots more than ten inches high, the circumference of the calf is also needed for proper fit.

There are also hunting boots that have a rubber shoe to which a leather upper is attached. They are lightweight and offer greater waterproofing than leather boots. In warm climates, however, the foot cannot breathe, and feet become excessively hot. The difficulty can partially be alleviated by lacing the boots only partway up. However, they do not provide the support of a leather boot. They are available in standard weight—which is only slightly less heavy than a leather boot—or in

Featherweight rubber-soled boots with leather uppers

"featherweight," which is considerably lighter.

Northern Indians wear black rubber boots all summer, allowing them to wade through muskeg and swamp and out into shallow water with impunity. It is unlikely that the vacationing canoeist wishes to emulate them; the Indians admit that learning to walk in them is an acquired skill—the boots have almost no support, and the feet sweat excessively in warm weather.

Sneakers

As a second pair of shoes to be worn around the campsite and where necessary to wade in the water, a pair of either high or low sneakers makes a good second shoe. They are light and will dry more quickly than leather boots. The fisherman who plans to wade will find them adequate; waders are too cumbersome to be practical.

Northern Indians wear rubber boots in the summer.

44

Moccasins

Moccasins with or without rubberized soles also make a good second shoe, although those with soles are frequently slippery on the pine needles of the forest floor. But neither is good for portaging. In spite of all lacing attempts, they provide little or no support, and it is too easy to step out of them on the trail. The ability to walk out of them also makes them poor for wading. But as a comfortable, relaxing shoe around the evening fire they are fine.

There is also a canoe moccasin with a rubber bottom, like the rubber bottom of the hunting boot. As a second pair, they are hard to equal, particularly in the early morning when the bush is wet with dew. In warm climates the foot will not breathe as it will with sneakers or leather moccasins, but in cooler climates, this problem is not noticeable unless worn all day in the hot sun. Sneakers worn around the breakfast fire are usually damp from dew when packed for travel; rubber canoe moccasins will be dry.

Socks

Almost as important as shoes are socks. High-quality wool socks are the only really acceptable ones. Wool allows the foot to breathe as will no other material; it absorbs sweat, and even if wet it provides a nonchafing cushion.

At least two extra pairs of wool socks should be included in every pack—more for the long trip.

If possible, socks should be rinsed out every evening, and a cleaned pair donned in the morning. If the rinsed pair has not dried before camp is broken, they can be slipped under a carrying strap of a portage load and allowed to dry in the canoe—even stuffed in a pocket when the portage is reached.

For the occasional tripper who objects to the feel of wool, a thin pair of cotton socks can be worn under the wool. And, occasionally, using such a lining helps reduce blisters if considerable walking or portaging is necessary.

Color in socks makes little difference to their serviceability, but white might be avoided. Muskeg stains socks badly, and if a boot gets wet, the dye from the leather also stains. The socks may be perfectly clean, but the stains will not come out, and if the socks were originally gray or a darker hue, at least they will not look as dirty.

Socks should reach higher than the boot. A standard Northwoods procedure for protection from winged insects involves tucking the pants cuffs into the tops of the socks when low-cut sneakers or moccasins are worn, for which the longer sock is an asset.

RAIN GEAR

Beware of the bargain-priced rain gear. It looks waterproof in the store, but soaks through quickly in the rain—being only "water-resistant" and not water-repellent or proof. It tears easily, and the seams part quickly under travel conditions.

A rain suit—both pants and jacket—provides the only really satisfactory protection. Sitting in the canoe, paddling along in the shower, pants are a necessity, and many other uses can be found for them—such as on the portage still damp from the morning dew, or going into the wet bush on a rainy day after dry wood.

The jacket—and pants—serves as a windbreak on cold, windy days. Jackets come in waist, hip, and knee lengths. Most come with hood and are normally preferred for canoeing to those without. Some come with full zippers; others with quarter-length zippers. The zipper should be backed with a generous protective flap; otherwise, water drips through. If the jacket is worn while exercising—as is often the case when travel must be accomplished in inclement weather—the wearer's body must breathe, for sweat collected under the jacket is just as damp and chilling as rain, so a full zipper is often preferred, and the front of the jacket can be left open varying degrees depending on the weather. There are also jackets whose fronts close with buttons, although the market prefers zippers.

The cuffs, waist, and hood are normally drawn tight by elastic or draw strings—sometimes by straps. But some method of closure is desirable.

A jacket should be sufficiently large to fit easily over any clothing combination, and should be amply cut so the wearer can move easily while paddling, portaging, or performing camp chores without applying undue strain on the material or seams. The pants are usually sized more to leg length, and the short-legged tripper who may need a large jacket could well want pants of a smaller size.

A poncho is a poor substitute for the rain suit. It works fine standing around the campsite, but is almost impossible when working. It shows off its worst features when paddling into a rainy headwind. The wearer might just as well have rigged a sail to carry the canoe in reverse.

45

The pack should contain a complete change of outer clothing, perhaps more if the trip is exceptionally long; although, unless clothing is so ancient that it is not expected to tough the trip, one change of everything but socks and underwear usually suffices. In selecting color of outer clothing, it might be noted that the darker hues attract more attention from winged insects, while white and lighter colors show dirt and stains quickly. So perhaps red, green, or khaki are preferable to blue, black, or white.

For pants and shirts the ability to withstand punishment is important. A good-quality dungaree, jean, or chino pant is desirable. Both shirt and pants should be loose fitting for freedom of movement. The tapered pants leg found in tight-fitting jeans makes getting in and out difficult. Leg length on pants should be measured to the top of low-cut shoes—any longer, the cuffs will catch on twigs and bushes; shorter, every bug will find the bare skin above the boot.

At least one shirt in the outfit should be long-sleeved for protection from various bugs.

Shorts are comfortable for paddling or loafing around the campsite, but unsatisfactory on all but the clearest of portage trails.

Bandana handkerchiefs are preferable to smaller linen pocketsize. They are useful not only for the purpose intended, but the four corners can be tied to make a serviceable hat, small sections make good canoe patches, and then a potholder is often needed to remove something warm from the fire.

A hat for protection from sun and rain should be available, particularly early in the trip when the reflection off the water can be particularly burning. The standard is the old, battered, felt hat with a broad brim.

A warm jacket is a must for cool evenings and inclement weather—those of wool slightly longer than waist length are preferred by most woodsmen for their versatility. Heavy wool provides some protection in a light rain, and even if soaked through still provides warmth. The superior jackets have an extra flap that covers the shoulder area for greater warmth and protection in the drizzle. A jacket is more versatile than a sweater. If nothing else, the front can be left open to give varying degrees of warmth.

Underwear from the bureau drawer is normally fine. Carry a couple of extra pairs of shorts—they weigh nothing—and plan to rinse them out fre-

Extra flap over the shoulders of a wool jacket

quently. Then the youngster who wears new blue jeans will find after a couple wettings that his shorts have been dyed a lovely shade of blue that he cannot wash out.

T-shirts are light and make an excellent second shirt to wear under the long-sleeved shirt. It is better to buy a high-grade shirt intended to be an outer garment—and, again, white shirts will appear soiled in a short time.

Some canoesmen pack a pair of long johns for those extra-cold days. A suit of open-net underwear might be considered. In cold weather the open-net holds clothing away from the body, forming a layer of warm, insulating dead air. On warm days, the shirt worn alone will cool the skin.

Pajamas are often overlooked or considered sissified. Woodsmen are traditionally supposed to shuck their boots and crawl into their sleeping bags. Few actually do. If the canoesman must display his rugged nature by sleeping in the clothes he wore all day, at least empty the pockets of hard objects, loosen or, perhaps better, remove the belt. But if cleanliness and comfort mean anything, loose-fitting pajamas are really just as warm as traveling clothes, infinitely more comfortable, and the sleeping bag stays cleaner. Flannel pajamas are desirable in cool weather, perhaps; long sleeves may be preferable to short ones. If the night is extremely cool, maybe a clean pair of wool socks will keep the toes warm, and a wool skull cap does wonders for warmth in preference to pulling the bag up over the head. At least use a clean T-shirt and shorts for pajamas. Then when the sleeping gear gets soiled, the shirt and shorts can revert to the clothes supply to be worn during the day.

Avoid the temptation to use all the clothes in the pack equally. Usually one outfit is best reserved for traveling, while the second set of clothing is worn only at the campsite after cleaning up a little. Do not rush to the pack to pull out dry clothes every time the traveling outfit gets damp. Packing wet clothes the next day becomes a real problem, and clothes dry better when worn than they will in the tent or stuffed in the pack.

Attire in the bush does not really vary with sex or age, and female canoeists will want about the same equipment as the men; maybe with some concessions to style and appearance. But loose-fitting clothing is much more comfortable. For the youngsters, this may be the right occasion to wear out those things they will outgrow in the near future.

OTHER PERSONAL ITEMS

Swimming Suit
Average Size Towel—Avoid white.
Wash Cloth—Surprisingly useful for that sponge bath before bed.
Soap—In suitable container; one of light metal being preferable to a more easily broken plastic. However, bar soap carried in the jewelry can double for bathing for all but the most fastidious. A small scrub brush is most helpful in doing laundry, but one is sufficient for the whole group.
Tooth Brush and Tooth Powder—Unless protected, toothpaste tubes have a habit of bursting in the pack, making an unbelievable mess.
Pocket Comb
Shaving Equipment and Other Toilet Articles—

Canoes make good scrubbing boards for laundry day.

Including a small flat, metal mirror. Maybe suntan lotion and Chapstick.
Pocketknife—A Swiss Army knife is particularly attractive because of its various blades. The youngsters and those who have done little tripping will insist on large sheath knives—the bigger the better. The thick-bladed knife has practically no uses on a canoe trip. A small pocketknife will serve almost every purpose. Cleaning fish is best done with the thin butcher knife in the jewelry, but the fisherman may want his own knife; but it will not be the thick hunting knife. A pocketknife can be sharpened with the ax file, but a small sharpening stone is better.
Pocket Watch—Certainly not a necessity, and the timelessness of the wilderness is often desirable, but there should be one in the party. If nothing else, when the sun will not help, it is possible to judge how much daylight remains. It also helps in estimating distances traveled both on water and on the portage. A pocket watch is preferred to a wristwatch; the hands are in the water so often while tripping that the wristwatch gets immersed on occasion. Better to carry an inexpensive watch even if not waterproof. Some prefer the smaller wristwatch to the larger pocket watch, but carry it in the watch pocket of the pants anyway.
Compass—There should be two in the party. Relatively inexpensive ones are entirely adequate.
Waterproof Match Container—Or matches whose heads are dipped in paraffin for emergency use.
Cigarette Lighter, Fluid, and Spare Flints—Even though the tripper does not smoke; again for emergency situations and fire starting. To keep flints from being misplaced, tape the package to the side or bottom of the can of fluid. Most lighters have a depression in the cotton packing for storage of one spare flint. While many a cigarette lighter has started a fire in an emergency, doing so directly with the lighter is difficult—better ignite a piece of tinder; birch bark is best—and then start the fire as with a match. After burning for a couple minutes, most lighters need time to draw more fluid up from the body of the lighter; they will not burn indefinitely. If the lighter is dropped into the water wetting the packing, it probably will not light at all until the packing is dried and resaturated with fluid. Or maybe a butane lighter, or a couple of disposable ones.
Glasses—A spare pair, hopefully nonbreakable, if needed. Equally important for the person who uses contact lenses—if not more so. A pair of sunglasses might be considered. Paddling under the

glaring sun can be a strain, particularly when it is necessary to look ahead constantly for landmarks or obstacles. Running rapids into a morning or late afternoon sun can be easier with them.

Flashlight—One of the batteries in a two-cell light should be reversed when rolled in the pack to prevent accidental tripping of the switch. Multi-celled lights are too cumbersome, and the light will not be used that often. When darkness comes, it is time to turn in. Carry a spare bulb and set of batteries if the light is intended for more than emergencies. If used sparingly, starting with a new bulb and batteries will make spares unnecessary, but even lighter is a disposable flashlight under these circumstances.

Candles—Some illumination is probably desirable in the tent, even if only for retiring after the sun goes down. A six-inch candle, carefully used, will provide better lighting and will allow the flashlight to be reserved for emergencies. In the small tent the candle provides enough lighting for reading and writing. Rarely would a tent use more than a couple a week.

Bug Dope—Both that to use directly on the skin for personal protection and a spray to be used in the tent. Each tent needs only a single can, so only one person in the tent need include a bug bomb in his roll.

Sewing Kit—Heavy linen thread, an assortment of needles, maybe a couple of miscellaneous buttons, and a small pair of scissors—the folding variety being particularly adaptable. Also store in the same container a spare set of laces for each pair of shoes that requires them. While cord from the canoe repair equipment will serve, anyone who swears by leather laces will be critical of a substitute.

Photographic Equipment—Keeping cameras available during travel poses problems.[1] A new roll of film should be with the camera, but other film is more protected if rolled in the personal pack—wet film is worthless. If using 35 mm film, the cans supplied by the manufacturer are reasonably waterproof.

If concerned about water damage, insure the outfit; or maybe it is already covered by a household policy. But carry a cheap camera in preference to none at all. Not all the pictures will be perfect, but many is the tripper who regretted the lack of a record of the trip and many the photographer who realized afterwards he should have

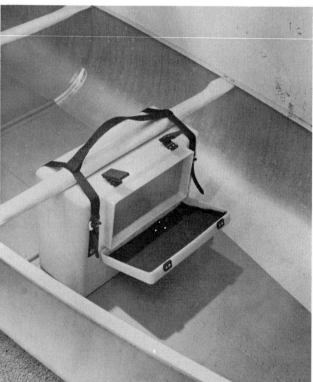

Methods of camera protection: A) *left to right*: flotation bag, rubber bag, ammunition box; B) Sport-Safe. (B, Courtesy Recreation Creations, Inc.)

taken twice as many pictures. Many of the cameras on the market today do all the work except aiming it and pressing a single button, and produce good results even for the absolute novice.

Fishing Lures and Equipment—Packaged in small containers; metal ones that will not break are preferred over plastic.

Writing Materials—A small notebook, maybe six inches by four inches, makes an excellent diary to

---

1. For a fuller treatment of camera protection, see *Canoeing Wilderness Waters*, pp. 138–39.

Map cases—could be used to waterproof papers carried in pack. Zipper cases also come in larger sizes.

preserve for posterity. It also provides a ready place to record notes for future reference—locations of portages, campsites, interesting scraps of information should the trip be repeated or should someone ask for advice. A ballpoint pen is preferable to a pencil. Storage is best accomplished with a small "zipper pocket," which also makes a good map case.[2] Such cases can be used to store maps and trip information not currently being used, and could give protection to the wallet that will not be needed during the trip. If letter writing is anticipated, stamps will stick together unless purchased in book form or backed by waxed paper. The flaps of envelopes react the same unless the self-closing type is carried or a piece of waxed paper is slipped under each flap.

2. For more information regarding map storage, see *Canoeing Wilderness Waters*, pp. 69–70.

A Paperback Book—For entertainment on rainy days; perhaps a deck of cards.

Transistor Radio—There are many lightweight, compact models. In the wilderness, stations probably cannot be picked up well except at night, and even then the reception will vary depending on atmospheric conditions and on the height of surrounding hills; it may be necessary to string an extra antenna. Unfortunately the quiet of many a still evening on a calm lake has been shattered by some of the sounds that contact with the woods hopes to avoid. Still, some people like to maintain contact with the outside, even if all the news is not pleasant.

Tobacco—Tailor-made cigarettes are bulky; a pipe and tobacco take less room. Canadian guides roll their own and in some forest areas all cigarettes are supposed to be roll-your-owns, since the tailor-mades when cast aside continue burning, and the roll-your-owns go out. A woodsman addicted to

A

Rolling the pack: A) equipment is laid flat on the sleeping bag; B) ground cloth is folded over and rolling starts at the foot; C) nearing head, flap of ground cloth is turned back; D) roll is forced into envelope formed by folded ground cloth; E) in theory, the roll is secure, but tying it with cord will help; F) roll is slipped into duffel; G) rain gear and other articles needed during the day go on top; H) the throat of the duffel is tied off.

C

B

D

E

G

F

H

tobacco who is in short supply is a trial to the party, however.

Roll of Toilet Paper (*Bumwad*)—Should be carried by each individual and a spare roll or two made available in the community equipment to be used in situations where the individual packs are rolled.

ROLLING THE PERSONAL PACK

Whatever method is employed, each individual pack should be as waterproof as humanly possible. There is nothing more disagreeable than the prospect of crawling into a wet sleeping bag. Everything else may be soaked through, but if the sleeping bag is dry, the night is endurable.

The time-honored method of waterproofing is to roll everything into the ground cloth, making a cylindrical roll, which is then fitted into a duffel.

The ground cloth is laid flat, and the sleeping bag, air mattress, and other large objects are laid in the center, leaving a foot and a half of ground

cloth free at the top. The sleeping bag is folded over at the foot if it projects past the ground cloth. Clothes and smaller items are evenly distributed on the bag with nonbendable items like shoes laid parallel to the direction of the roll. The sides of the ground cloth are folded in, and the entire pack is rolled as tightly as possible When the head of the bag is reached, the flap of ground cloth left free is folded back, and the roll is continued into the envelope thus formed by rolling over the lower edges of the ground cloth and into the envelope. The cylinder is then secured with a couple of tie strings or straps, although the envelope alone is supposed to be sufficiently binding.

Then the roll is slipped into the duffel. Before rolling, anything wet from the previous day should be left out, as should rain gear, perhaps the towel, and maybe the warm jacket. They are stuffed in on top of the roll so they can be reached without unrolling completely—the rain gear being the last item added, partially to help waterproof the throat of the duffel and also for availability.

51

The use of waterproof stuff bags to organize personal gear would be recommended. Small ones of the five-inch-by-seven-inch size make good containers for toilet articles, film, sewing kit, and the like, so that small items of a particular nature can be grouped together. Small cotton bags can be used, but waterproof bags of either rubberized cloth or nylon are preferable.

Instead of the envelope roll, the pack can further be organized by using several larger waterproof bags—perhaps one bag for clothing, another for the sleeping bag and air mattress. The larger bags are then placed in the duffel in any order desired, and on reaching the campsite only the equipment immediately needed gets unpacked, leaving the rest protected from rain and dirt.

This method of organization resembles a "lumberjack" roll—just taking a duffel bag and stuffing it with whatever comes to hand. As such, the roll is absolutely nonwaterproof, but this problem is solved by using waterproof stuff bags for the various classifications of articles. Problems in organization are also solved by the compartmentalized nature of the pack.

The next difficulty is the problem of packing for the portage. If the pack sack is used for an individual's equipment, the problem is solved by placing the softer stuff bags next to the carrier's back—like the bag containing the sleeping bag. If each individual uses a cylindrical duffel and several duffels are tumped together to make a portage load, the stuff bag containing the sleeping bag is placed in the center of the duffel so that it will be the area against the carrier's back.[3]

Actually, when tumping two duffels, only one side of the duffel need be soft, and if the carrier uses a little care in tumping so the soft side is positioned correctly, an individual can pack the rest of his equipment as he sees fit.

The traditionally rolled pack allows items that should not be squashed to be protected by the roll; the lumberjack method seems to lack such protection. However, if items that will suffer when compressed are rolled inside the sleeping bag, protection is adequate, and in fact improved. Most users of tailor-made cigarettes will be interested in such protection. Do not roll the toothpaste in the center of the sleeping bag, however. It makes an unbelievable mess when squashed. Use tooth powder anyway, or at least get an

Nylon stuff bags are available in many sizes—some are rectangular in shape; others are cylindrical with circular bottoms.

aluminum case in which it might be protected.

The only item that might not fit into this organizational method is the telescoping fishing rod, which could be rolled in the center of the traditional pack. It should be carried, as longer rods are, lashed under the gunwale of the canoe.[4]

The traditional roll is much easier to organize on the spur of the moment, and it is the approach taught by many canoeing organizations. The lum-

Fishing rod lashed to canoe gunwale for travel. Reel is positioned under bow seat to prevent it from swinging below the gunwale during portage. Reel is also protected by a bag to minimize introduction of sand and dirt.

3. For a description of tumping duffels to make a portage load, see *Canoeing Wilderness Waters,* pp. 161–62.

4. For more discussion of portaging fishing rods, see *Canoeing Wilderness Waters,* pp. 152–53.

Voyageur Bags—polyethylene liner goes into reinforced outer bag and is then secured with a cylindrical tube.

berjack method, to be effective and waterproof, demands more prior planning in determining how many and what size stuff bags or liners to use, but after the preliminary organizing is done, proves much more convenient.

The canoeist will have to devise a means of portaging, but perhaps the most effective waterproof bag is one advertised as a "Voyageur Bag." It consists of a polyethylene plastic inner liner and an outer ripstop nylon bag to be secured with a cylindrical closer. The liner is placed in the outer

bag, the bag loaded, and then the top of the double bag is folded over and the locking cylinder slips over the fold so that a solid center rail is under the fold while the outer cylinder has a slit down its length, through which the folded bag slides. The bags and liners come in two sizes: the smaller twenty-two inches by thirty-six inches; and a larger seventeen inches by forty inches. The cylindrical sealer makes the closed bag somewhat unwieldy and difficult to fit into standard portaging methods, but the bags themselves make excellent stuff bags for lining duffels, even if only tied off at the top with a piece of cord.

4

CAMPSITES

The time has come to stop for the day. A possible camping area lies near at hand, but there is still plenty of time left for travel, and the guide can be selective about the site. He lands to investigate. Maybe he is looking over a piece of ground used by other parties; maybe a virgin camping area; but no matter, he should be casting about looking for the same requirements before accepting the location.

Naturally the canoe landing must be considered first; the preliminary investigation would not have been undertaken were the landing inappropriate. Now on shore, in order of necessity, the guide looks for: (1) a suitable kitchen; (2) respectable tentsites; (3) a source of dry wood; and (4) water for cooking and washing. Everything is rarely perfect. There will be some sites more attractive than others, but the requirements for the fire, tents, wood, and water have to be met before other considerations.

KITCHEN AREA

The kitchen arrangements, organization, and requirements vary from group to group and should be flexible, but there must be some routine or all will be chaos, resulting in undue effort and time just performing the mechanics of feeding the party.

Fires

If a stove is carried with its own fuel, logical rules of safety and efficiency dictate how it will be set up and used.

If cooking is done on an open fire, safety precautions must be observed. The best fire area is flat, level, bare rock. A clay base is safe but in rainy weather quickly becomes a gooey, slippery kitchen. A level, safe fire area is easy to create in sand, but unless the food preparation and dining area is located off the beach, the stuff works into the food with amazing certainty. The only advantage is the opportunity to bake in hot sand; but it is normally wiser to create a special "baking hole" on the beach and locate the main cooking fire elsewhere.

With more effort the safety of sand can be secured while avoiding its disadvantages by creating a "box" about six inches deep, most easily done by enclosing a rectangular area with six-inch logs and then filling the box with sand. Such is a common arrangement in Cree wigwam tents where a circular fire box is located in the center of the tepee (he uses old wash tubs to make his retaining wall), and the fire is laid on this box. (If he has no sand, the Indian achieves equal safety by placing large flat slabs of stone in the middle of his wigwam.)

If no other base is available, good, solid, mineral earth can be acceptable. All surface material

Cree sand fire box around which his tepee is pitched

such as pine needles and grass must first be scraped away so the fire cannot spread. Such an area should be free of roots and other such underground channels, which might trap and retain the fire.

The means for supporting pots over the fire will dictate to some degree how it should be located. Any camping text will suggest a dozen ways of arranging the fire and the pots—many of which are novel and interesting—but they boil down to two basic ideas: either hang the pots over the fire or support them from underneath.

If pots are to be suspended, there are two basic procedures. First, the butt of a green stick of nonresinous wood is sharpened, and then is driven into the ground so that it is angled over the fire. A log or stone is then wedged underneath for support. If the butt cannot be driven into the

Hanging pot from a pole driven into the ground

Rail supported by **Y**-shaped stakes from which pots are hung

ground, a rock cairn is built around it. The stick is angled so that a pot hangs the appropriate distance over the fire, prevented from slipping down the stick by leaving a small stub of a branch against which the bail rests. The Cree Indian often cooks this way. He normally uses only a single pot, sometimes only for tea, and the remainder of the meal is cooked by roasting or other means.

The second method, and much more commodious procedure of suspending the pots, is to create a bar over the fire, parallel to the ground from which to hang the pots. The bar can be placed in the crotches of two forked sticks driven into the ground at either end of the fire. Or a three- or four-pole tepee can be erected over the fire with rails joining the legs of the tepee. Poles laid across these crossbars will offer convenient rails from which to hang pots. Such rigs are usually made by Canadian Indians for smoking fish or game, and cooking pots can be hung below the smoking rack. No matter how the bar from

Three-pole tripod to support rail for pots

Four-pole tepee. Dingle sticks are employed so each pot hangs individually.

which the pots are hung is positioned, after the scaffolding is erected, each pot is best hung individually using a pot hook, or "dingle stick," of either wood or metal. Each pot can then be removed without disturbing the others, and its height can be adjusted by shortening or lenthening its hanger.

Pots can be supported from underneath either by arranging rocks or logs on the ground around the fire, or by running rails across the fire. Wooden rails must be placed far above the fire so that heat comes slowly, or there is danger of their burning through and dumping the soup. Rails of green hardwood are best, though it is well to have a spare set nearby to replace those on which the meal is started.

Since a canoe trip is neither a test of survival techniques nor a situation where all comforts must be sacrificed to reduce weight, most canoeists carry a portable grate. A more versatile rig,

Nemiscau Indian frame for smoking fish

however, consists of a pair of "irons" or rails. The irons are just lengths of pipe of sufficient diameter not to bend when heated. Normal iron pipe of three-fourths-inch to one-inch diameter is entirely adequate. The ends of each iron should be flattened so that the rails will not roll when positioned. Their length depends on the size of the cookery. Irons three feet long are sufficient for the normal four- to six-man set of pots. Irons up to four feet long are better should the nesting pots be larger. The pots might be arranged in imaginary fashion for a meal to determine the ideal length.

Fire irons call for a long, narrow fireplace so that heat rises between the parallel irons, spaced four to six inches apart. The flattened ends are placed on stones at either end of the fireplace so they will be level and solid. Irons placed too high require an inordinate amount of fuel, while irons placed too low prevent the fire from breathing. A height somewhere between seven and ten inches is average. Naturally, heat at either end of the fire will not equal that in the center, so pots to be simmered or warmed are placed on the ends, while those that must boil take the center.

When locating the fireplace, consideration should be given to the prevailing wind. The fire laid on the exposed rocky point is a delight if the heat rises straight up, but in a heavy wind where the flames are driven from the pots, it becomes impossible. On a one-night stand, in the calm evening, wind has little effect, and at breakfast it will probably be no stronger. Should the stay be longer, however, the fireplace may have to be moved in the event of a stiff breeze. Whether a reflector baker is used or not, the fire will be more efficient if a back wall is built to reflect the heat. A stone wall, just in back of the fire is best —perhaps six to ten inches behind the back iron. Within reason, the higher the wall, the better. One about twice the height of the irons is quite efficient. If made of smooth stone, surfaces are available where the cook can store items needed near the fire. A small flat stone placed across the ends of the irons will maintain their spacing and also offer a shelf. If a reflector is used, the back wall is not an absolute necessity, but it throws heat back into the oven, baking about half again as quickly as it would if there were no rear wall.

The breeze should blow in against the back wall. If it blows into the reflector, so will the fire, creating uneven heat as the flames lick back and forth.

When a reflector is used, consideration should

A

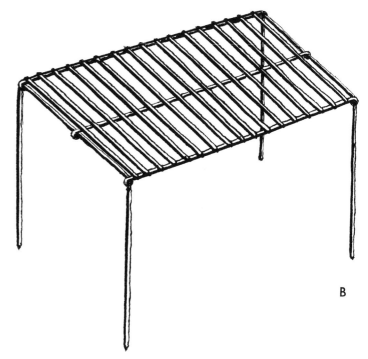

B

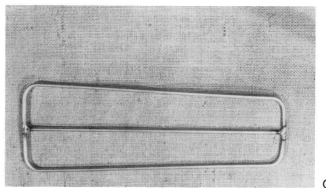

C

Various equipment to be carried for supporting pots over the fire: A) irons; B) folding grill, feet are driven into the ground; C) backpacker's grill, to be supported on rocks or logs. (C, Courtesy L.L. Bean, Inc.)

58

An unusually fine stone fireplace

be given to the evenness of the ground. If there must be a slope, it is preferable that the reflector sit lower than the fire. It can always be raised with small stones or chips of wood. A properly designed reflector distributes the heat so that some bakes from the underside and some from the top; and a reflector placed so that most of the heat enters the underside results in burning the bottom long before the top sets. If the slope of the fire area places the reflector below the fire, at least the cook can see the top and adjust the reflector.

If baking is not contemplated, a breeze that blows the length of the irons may be acceptable, though there will be hot and cold ends. It is easy to keep fuel at the hot end, but difficult to draw the fire back toward the cool end. Perhaps on a windy lunchsite, when only a pot or two is used, building so the breeze blows the length of

the irons is better than perpendicular to the irons —assuming it is too much trouble to build an adequate rear wall.

If there is no rock available to support the irons, a couple of blocks of green wood will do. If there is the danger that such blocks might roll, dropping the irons, their undersides should be flattened slightly with the ax and small notches cut in their upper sides; or small pickets (stakes) can be driven beside them to keep them stable. The back wall can also be made of logs—green wood being better. But a wooden back wall may burn out before the stay at a site is terminated. If no single log provides a sufficiently high wall, a couple can be laid one on top of the other and made stable by driving pickets on either side of the wall, keeping the inside pickets at the ends of the fire where they are less likely to burn. The reflecting surface so arranged is almost as efficient

59

Flattening and notching side blocks to prevent rolling

Fireplace made with wooden side rails and back logs. Pickets are driven as shown to hold back logs in place. Green wood would have been preferable.

as one made of rock. When the site is vacated, logs used for the fireplace should be dunked in the lake to be certain no fire remains in them, but not just tossed into the water so as to create navigational hazards.

Sometimes the fireplace can be built with a natural stone backing, but never lay the fire against a fallen tree; the fire it holds is difficult to extinguish.

The cook would prefer the kitchen reasonably close to the water supply. But if the water must be some distance away—particularly true in campgrounds located at the ends of portages—every time someone goes down to wash up or wallop a pot, he might draw a pail of water.

If the kitchen is located inland, remember that a fire must breathe. Protection cannot be carried to such an extreme that no air stirs, or, even worse, that air drives down on the fire. Fires laid in hollows draw poorly, and fires laid backwards so that the breeze drives against the rear of the fireplace may look protected until the pots are put on the irons, when no satisfactory means of forcing the fire to burn—other than by creating an artificial draft by blowing on it—can be found. If it is necessary to blow on a campfire, something is wrong! The wood is wet; it was green to start with (or punky); or the fireplace is laid wrong. The latter cause is most often the problem, and the last one admitted.

There will be occasions when a gale is blowing, driving heat from under the pots. Maybe the fireplace should be located in a more protected area, or an artificial windbreak should be created out of brush, logs, or the fly, but the normal evening fire built in calm weather draws better if open toward the water, off which a light breeze is likely to come. Later in the evening, there may be a land breeze, but by that time the meal should be completed.

There are many other ways to build satisfactory cooking fires, and every woodsman has his favorite, but the canoe party that does not carry something on which to rest the pots is making a needless sacrifice to "roughing" it. Of course, the irons, or grill, become blackened by the fire and should have a covering to protect whoever portages them. A piece of canvas, a foot longer than the irons and a foot to eighteen inches wide, offers an easy, quick wrapping, which can then be tied with a piece of cord so that it will not unroll in transit. The irons are normally portaged as part of the load of the person who carries the cookery; they are too long to fit into a wannigan and are either laid on top or hand-carried on bushy trails.

Rest of Kitchen Area

After locating the fireplace, a "wannigan line" should be designated near the fire, and the crew of each canoe should deliver its part of the commissary to the area. On a one-canoe trip, there is little difficulty, but as the number of canoes rises, so does the problem of collecting and arranging the kitchen each night; so there should be a predetermined arrangement of the wannigans. The jewelry should be within easy reach of the cook, and so should the supplies that he is most likely to use. Personal items should be kept away from the kitchen; the cook who must first paw through a couple jackets, a fishing rod, and two or three

Wannigan line for a large party

cameras before reaching the flour soon becomes weary of the job.

Whether the fly is automatically pitched at every campsite, or sometimes just tossed over the supplies at night in fair weather, is optional, but the kitchen should be arranged so that when and if the fly is raised, the equipment will not have to be rearranged.

The normal pitch for the fly is a lean-to arrangement, whereby it is stretched across a ridge and the corners tied out so that the rear slopes toward the ground while the front is higher. In fair weather, the front usually faces the water, letting the breeze enter, but under adverse conditions the pitch should be such that the lower rear side of the fly takes the brunt of the weather.

Whether pitched immediately or not, where the fly will go should be planned as the wannigan line is established. If there are a couple of con-

venient trees between which the ridge can be located so that additional poles will not be needed for scissors on the side, the line might well be located between them. Or maybe there is one such tree, eliminating one of the scissors.

The fly can be positioned over the fire if large enough; just be sure that water dripping off the fly will fall behind the fire and not into it. A fire faced in toward the fly will let the cook move around under cover; one that faces out forces him to keep his rain suit on while cooking. Actually, if camp were pitched under fair skies and a storm were to come up later, there would likely have to be some minor adjustments, depending on its severity and the direction.

The front corners of the fly can be elevated to allow access, but when the party retires, these corners should be dropped. A shift in wind might drive a storm in under the fly during the night.

61

Fly pitched to cover fire so that the cook has protection. Front poles would be lowered at night.

When the cook gets up to make breakfast, he can raise them again. Supplies should be left secured in their normal packs or wannigans used for travel, even when under the fly and theoretically protected by it. There is actually better all-around protection if the fly is just tossed over the wannigan line and rocked down so no gust of wind can lift it off. And the party can sleep in confidence when the storm comes up, knowing the fly cannot collapse or rain be driven under it.

A couple more arguments can be presented in opposition to pitching the fly automatically at every camp, in addition to the labor involved in erecting it. The farther north the trip goes, the more likely mosquitoes and blackflies will be present all summer; if camp is made near fast water, they will be present even farther south, and the fly becomes a haven for every bug within miles. When the wind blows correctly, smoke gets trapped under the fly, reducing the bug population, but creating its own discomforts. Lastly, the fly has to slope to allow rain to run off, and to pitch it high enough for the cook to stand erect means lashing the ridge at an absurd height such that the fly is most likely to be carried away by the wind.

CANOE STORAGE

After the canoes are emptied, they should be removed from the water, carried in from shore out of the way of traffic, and stored for the night.

They should be tipped bottom-side up, with the bottom facing the prevailing wind—particularly in an exposed area. If possible, tip them so the open area of the canoe is tight against protective rocks, trees, or brush, so a sudden wind will not sweep

Wannigan line covered with fly and rocked down for the night

Open side of the canoe faced inland for the night

under and carry it off the site, or throw it against an unyielding object.

A canoe should not be left right-side up for the night. Moisture seeps into the wood of the canvas canoe, making it heavier the next day. Aluminum and fiberglass models do not have this problem, but the canoe left right-side up is much more likely to be blown about during a storm.

Occasionally, circumstances indicate that it would be safe to partially beach the canoe, leave it upright, and let part or all of the canoe remain in the water. Occasionally, the native's freighter is so heavily laden that unloading becomes a chore, and he will cover the load with a waterproof tarp, draw it up on shore far enough so that any rain water collects in the stern, and leave it for the night. The vacationer normally needs most of his cargo, so nothing remains in the canoe anyway, and a canoe left this way makes for an uneasy night, knowing that a storm can endanger it. At least make sure the bowline is securely tied to an immovable object. Searching for the canoe that floated off during the night due to a storm or a rise in water level provides unnecessary excitement.

Sand beaches offer poor storage for a canvas canoe. As soon as the canoe is tipped over, the lower gunwale digs into the sand, and the particles work down between the sheeting and canvas and add weight that cannot be removed without recanvasing. The Indian always lays spruce boughs on his sand beach before pulling up his canoe. The tripper should either store his canoe inland off the beach, or should lay protective boughs or logs under the lower gunwale to raise

it off the sand. Aluminum and fiberglass models do not need such careful handling, but there is no point in adding sand to them either.

Care should also be taken when boarding a canoe off a sand beach. Equipment should be moved from the campsite directly to the canoe without setting packs and wannigans down in the sand. And then the paddlers should rinse off the boots before boarding the canoe. Clean white sand looks picturesque and harmless, but the grains get imbedded in everything—canoe, packs, and cooking utensils—and never get out.

The paddles should be slipped under their own canoes so they are not misplaced, and out of the sun. The damp wooden paddle left in the sun warps quickly.

If a fisherman removes his rod from the canoe during the evening, he should replace it that same evening, even though darkness is approaching and the bugs are troublesome. Rods lying around the site are invariably damaged; lures that are left attached are dangerous; and moving come morning is delayed appreciably should someone still have to collect his equipment and replace his rod before loading the canoe.

TENTSITES AND PREPARATION

The wilderness trip will be a one-shot adventure without a good night's rest. So the tent must be carefully located and pitched. The day's travel may have been difficult; the weather may not have cooperated; but the problems and discomforts of the day cannot only be endured, but even enjoyed, provided that once the tent is occupied,

Canvas canoe stored on a sand beach should have logs or brush placed under lower gunwale.

the camper can look forward to a night which is (1) dry, (2) warm, and (3) bug free.

It goes without saying that the tents should be in good condition and waterproof. Nylon or canvas must be treated with respect. Tossing the folded tent onto rocks soon results in a cut; dropping a canvas tent into the water inevitably results in pitching a wet tent that will leak if it cannot dry before rain sets in; and packing a tent still wet from the previous rain will frequently result in a leaky one the next night.

Selecting the Site

Avoid pitching on sand; a sandy sleeping bag will be most uncomfortable. Avoid the naturally hollowed out bowl; water collects under the tent no matter how much ditching is done or how waterproof are the ground cloths. Beware of moss

or other spongy surfaces; they soak up moisture only to release it when compressed by the weight of the sleepers. Reindeer moss can be an exception, provided it covers firm soil. Otherwise, this gray white moss makes attractive trees for a model railroad or chinks a log cabin wall, but makes a chancy bed.

Choose a relatively level site. If there is a slope, pitch the tent so that the heads of the sleepers will be on the higher ground; sleeping with feet higher than the head is uncomfortable. A tent with a side-hill slope causes trouble, as the person on the higher side always rolls onto his companion. Too much slope, even from head to toe, is also undesirable, particularly on cool nights when the sleeper snuggles down in the bag, and gradually works the whole bag down the slope and out of the tent.

If there is concern that surface water will run

under the tent, dig a small ditch around it on the uphill side with the butt of the ax. A ditch three or four inches deep is adequate, but be sure the ditch drains into an area where no damage will be done. If the ground is reasonably level and firm, a ditch is unnecessary—the forest floor will soak up any moisture that is likely to fall during one evening. Then, if the rain continues, maybe the ditch can be added the next morning.

How smooth the ground must be depends on the occupants. The important area is that to be covered by the sleeper's body from shoulders to knees; he can pillow his head, and his lower legs will not notice uneven ground. Nevertheless, the site should be cleared of stones, sticks, pinecones, roots, and other protrusions that might cut the tent floor or ground cloths—particularly after weight is placed on them. Be sure small bushes are cut off below ground level. The stumps of blueberry or laurel bushes make tiny punctures in the ground cloth; it is often better just to bend them over. A camper with a mattress has less clearing and leveling to do than his companion without one, but still he wants to protect his air mattress from puncture.

Locate the tent to offer some protection from a storm or heavy wind. The exposed, breezy point is inviting under warm, sunny skies; the breeze drives off the bugs and the view is enchanting; but come the storm and wind, the site loses much of its appeal. Striking the tent and repitching it is usually impractical at that point; if nothing else, it is the middle of the night. Native tentsites are often impossible to see from the water; there is at least a thin line of trees protecting them. Storms that rise inland are less trouble; the forest breaks their force. Sites frequented by unthinking sports often lack this protective line of trees; they have been cut for firewood, or tent poles, or just to improve the view.

It is pleasant to pitch so the tent door faces the water; if nothing else, on waking in the morning, a quick glance out will answer the weather question. Also the strong storm comes off the water, and one end or the other of the tent—where the cloth is approximately perpendicular to the ground—offers better protection against driving rain than does the sloping side.

Drawing Poles

The ecological reasons for using tents with the necessary poles included have already been mentioned under the discussion of tent selection. However, if poles are a nightly necessity, cut them

behind the site, not between it and the water unless there is an absolute wall between the tents and water so no air will filter through. If camped at the end of a portage, perhaps cut beside the trail doing a little trail improvement in the process (just do not leave the trimmed branches in the middle of the trail for the next traveler to trip over). Cut in an area where the forest needs thinning anyway. Take one from an area of tightly packed trees; the next from another clump where all would not grow to maturity anyway.

Poles should be reasonably straight, strong, and neither too long nor short. Spruce makes the most acceptable pole. Jackpine rates high, and birch or poplar can be good. Avoid the twisted misshapened pole; alder, for instance, makes an inferior crooked pole. Except in dire emergency avoid balsam and other resinous woods; it is impossible to pitch the tent without getting covered with gum. Leave the pines, maples, and other trees generally considered more valuable and attractive. Poles should be carefully trimmed of branches that might snag the tent. The ridge demands special attention—the straighter the better for this one. Select poles that are strong enough, but remember it is only a tent that is being erected, and heavy logs are unnecessary and difficult to work with.

At the end of the stay, stack the poles against a convenient tree. Someone else may use the same camp and the poles left behind will be appreciated. Poles thrown down on the ground rot quickly; those left standing will be dry and useful for years.

Pitching

An improperly pitched tent will not keep out the wet. The fabric should be stretched tight and smooth, and there should be considerable slope to sides so that water will roll down. Creased or wrinkled cloth leaks; tents stretched loosely will have pockets where water collects and drips through.

A hard, driving rain causes a very fine spray to filter through canvas, though as the pores fill, the spray will disappear after the first couple of minutes. Rubbing the canvas with hands, or anything else, causes water to drip through, and during the storm care should be taken not to rub or brush the tent. If a leak appears, there is little that can be done—assuming the tent is properly pitched—during the storm. Seams are likely to leak first. If lucky, the drips will run down the inside instead of dripping on the equipment.

Wet canvas and ropes shrink. The tent should be inspected before turning in. Ropes and canvas may have dried since the tent was erected and slack shows where there was none when pitched. A moment or two spent tightening lines will pay dividends. On the other hand, the tightly stretched canvas tent should be loosened during rainy weather so that there will not be undue stress on corners and grommets as the canvas shrinks. Pressures on a two- or three-man tent are not likely to be terribly great, but with larger tents the shrinkage could create enough pressure to rip out grommets.

Nylon tents do not react the same since the fabric does not alter shape when wet, but, otherwise, a well-pitched nylon tent is no different. If using tents with special poles, their pitch is already determined, although perhaps some of the following ideas could be helpful. Otherwise the following suggestions are made for pitching a seven-foot-by-seven-foot canvas tent with a two-foot wall, using poles drawn from the bush.

In addition to guy ropes on the corners there are normally additional ropes along the wall, and

Pitching a 7-by-7-foot wall tent: A) poles are carefully trimmed; B) two scissors are lashed together about as high as can be reached comfortably; C) ridge is tied to pole, or pole is run through openings provided; D) scissors are spread so rear and front walls drag on ground when in place; E) ridge is lashed to each scissors and then staked out; F) corners are drawn down and out on each pole; G) wall should be smooth and taut; H) lines from wall are tied out to pickets.

D

E

F

G

H

A

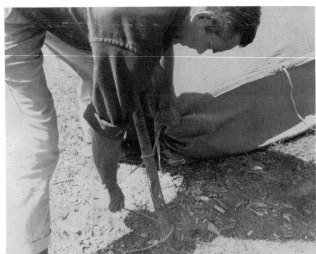

B

C

Corners must be tied down tightly to stretch wall correctly: A) loop corner rope around pole after pulling down as hard as possible; B) pass free line over standing line and reverse direction around pole; C) pass doubled line around standing line and under itself. In the morning, one pull on the free end will release the hitch.

these should be tied out to pickets. If stakes cannot be driven on the campsite, a large rock provides a good anchor—or maybe a tree root—or even a heavy log. Place the anchor so that the rope draws the tent downward as well as outward—at the same angle as the slope of the tent's wall.

Drive pickets with the flat side of the ax. Hitting the elusive top of the stake with the blunt end of the ax requires more exact aim and digs into the top of the picket anyway.

Bough Beds

Consult camping instructions of fifty years ago, and it will seem impossible to be comfortable without a bough bed. Not so, but the Northern Cree always lays a bough floor on the ground of any summer or winter camp to this day.

No responsible camper could advocate harming the forest for the sake of a few boughs, but if traveling country where drawing tent poles at each camp is acceptable, there is no reason not to make a bed with boughs from them. Just drag the unlimbed tree to the site, and do the pruning there. Acceptable beds can be made from spruce or cedar. Balsam is perhaps better, but the resinous poles are an abomination.

The bough bed will cover minor dips and rises in the site, and even make it possible to lay a perfectly comfortable bed on bare rock—if that was the only place to pitch. But if the site is on bare rock, be prepared for the run off of the water; it will not sink in and the tent cannot be ditched. Or maybe the site is slightly damp, or the tent must be pitched on spongy moss, or maybe the sleepers just want a slightly more springy, aromatic bed.

Lay a row of boughs at the head of the bed so that each branch is laid upside down, with the arc of the branch away from the ground. Lay successive rows of boughs, working back toward the foot of the tent so each successive row covers the butts of the previous row with the heavy needles of the row being laid. A couple of layers of boughs will produce a bed several inches thick. Then lay the ground cloths on top. The bed will be softer than bare ground, and will raise the sleeper slightly off damp ground.

Bugs

Early in the season there are usually mosquitoes, blackflies, no-see-ums, and sandflies—not to mention various sizes, shapes, and descriptions of

68

Rocks can be used instead of pickets if the ground is too firm.

flies. Farther north these pests are likely encountered no matter what time of year. If the campsite is near fast water, they are always present.

During the day the tripper learns to live with flying insects. On the water they are normally only a minor problem. On land at portages and campsites the story is likely different. Depending on the season and the locale, mosquitoes are thickest in early morning and late evening. Black-flies arrive about four hours before sundown and cause real aggravation, but they disappear as the sun sinks, to nest in the tops of tall conifers. No-see-ums start a little later but continue after dusk. And sandflies—well, look for sand, and there they are, particularly toward evening.

One of the first acts of the northern traveler is to kindle a fire as soon as he lands. Normally the kitchen will be reasonably habitable, except under the fly. Smoke drives bugs away reasonably well;

Logs can also be used to secure side lines.

A 7-pole pitch is more complicated, but is quite sturdy.

tection. Normally conditions are not so unbearable as to require smudges. But if necessary, punch a few holes around the base of a large can—a number ten can is about right, or maybe a five-pound lard pail. Shovel in some hot coals and stuff in some green brush. Rotten wood and bark off the forest floor work well. The Indian smokes his hides with rotten spruce; it will smolder quite a while.

There are all sorts of commercial insect repellents—sprays, liquids, and pastes. The old woodsman has his own favorite recipe. They all work for varying periods with varying success. Experiment until one is found that works best for a particular individual. They all lose their protection in time, and they all have a greasy feel and some odor. None work all night while trying to sleep. On top of that, the camper who crawls into his sleeping bag coated with bug dope soon has it also coated. The base for most is diethyl-meta-toluarmide or DEET, which researchers claim is particularly effective on mosquitoes.

It is imperative that the tent be equipped with bug netting, and no one should trip in the north

although when using smoke for protection, it may be necessary to stand directly in its path. It is a little choking, and the odor lingers in clothing so that the camper smells something like a well-smoked moose hide for days—but at least bugs dislike it. After dinner a little green brush or damp wood will add to the fire's smoke and pro-

Interior of Cree winter camp. Entire floor is covered with spruce boughs.

70

A

B

C

D

Laying bough bed: A) spruce boughs collected off tent poles; B) first layer laid upside down; C) successive layers cover butts of previous layers; D) finished bed

without it. If the tent is floored, it is probably secure from bugs and other insects along the ground. Otherwise, pitch the tent low so that about six inches of fabric drags on the ground, to be tucked in under the ground cloths to seal off the tent. Then each occupant should lay down a ground cloth so they overlap and cover the flap of tent canvas when folded in.

Most tents are equipped with loops along the lower edges with the intention that the wall will be pegged down. But the nonfloored tent so pegged down can never be insect-proof. If there is fear that a high wind may blow the walls out from under the ground cloths, rock them down on the inside, particularly at the corners.

After unrolling the beds, close the netting.

Carry a spray can of bug dope intended for indoor use, spray the tent liberally, and leave the tent unoccupied for ten to fifteen minutes. It should then be habitable, and if the netting is kept in place, should be livable for the entire night. Bug spray intended for indoor use always instructs the user not to spray himself, although a skin reaction is unusual. The spray is a little choking, however, in tight areas; so it is best to leave the tent unoccupied for awhile.

It is often pleasant to leave the flaps open in fair weather; though some close them as a matter of course. However, the netting should be weighted down if free so there is no opening along the ground—a couple of pairs of boots so laid will do the trick. Using smudges in or near the tent is unpleasant, unnecessary, and dangerous.

Lighting and Heating

A two-cell or disposable flashlight should be

Tents without floors should be pitched low so walls will tuck under to seal out bugs.

carried for emergencies and can be used to light the way to bed, but for reading, writing, or other such purposes a flashlight beam is too concentrated to be satisfactory night after night.

There are small lanterns operated on gasoline, butane, kerosene, propane, or a similar fuel. All provide adequate light but are fragile, difficult to pack, and require special fuel. These problems can be solved with a little thought, but such lights also present dangerous fire hazards. Under no circumstances should they be left burning when the occupants doze off. Lanterns give off considerable heat, particularly upward, and they must never be suspended near tent sides or roof; the tent could go up in seconds. Such lamps might be used safely in larger tents, but are particularly dangerous in the two- to three-man ones.

A simple candle is more practical. It is not without danger, however, and should not be left untended either. Collapsible lanterns can be pur-

chased to hold a candle or one can be made from a tin can, but easier is the simple expedient of sticking the candle on a base that will be stable, nonflammable, and firm. A flat rock works well; or maybe a metal fishing tackle box. A single candle gives plenty of light for a small tent.

A canoe-tripping tent probably does not require heating if the party has reasonable sleeping bags. A candle produces considerable warmth in the confined space—probably enough to warm the tent sufficiently while turning in. There are portable heating units that operate on the same fuel as lanterns, but they have the same fire dangers as lanterns, and many should only be used in well-ventilated areas, and the two-man tent is too small for safe operation.

The Indian heats his tent with a small, metal, wood-burning bush stove, which he sets on four pegs to elevate it about six inches off the ground. Or he places it on a wide, flat rock. He also car-

Wood-burning bush stove used by Indians for tent heat and cooking is normally set on four pegs driven into the ground and notched at the top to hold stove. Passage of stovepipe through tent wall is made safe by an asbestos collar.

ries a stovepipe and an asbestos fitting to pass it through the tent safely without leaking or setting fire to the tent. He uses it in cool weather and as a cooking stove, but for summer canoe tripping it is cumbersome and a definite fire hazard.

Another possible way to warm the tent is to pitch it so the door faces the fireplace a couple yards away. The back of the fireplace is built higher to reflect heat into the tent, and the fire is stoked up for the night with a couple of good-sized logs. There is considerable heat lost to the surrounding bush, so it is neither efficient nor economical, but in dire emergency it might help; assuming sparks from the fire do not burn the tent.

It is much better, however, if the canoe party forgets about artificial heat, refrains from cooking in the tent, and comes provided with seasonally suitable clothing and sleeping bags.

Repairs

Tent repairs are hopefully needed infrequently. If a seam parts, however, before it really opens,

resew it, carrying a heavy needle and linen thread for such repairs—not for the tent alone, of course. A triangular needle for canvas is best, but in an emergency, a normal, round, heavy needle works. If a patch must be applied, waterproof adhesive tape works well on all but very large tears. So will some other waterproof tapes. A strip of tape

Tent repairs: strip of adhesive tape is cut to cover tear and carefully smoothed; second strip is also put on inside.

73

placed on either side of the tear serves. A tear can be sewed, or a patch sewed over the hole, but leaks develop at the needle holes, and sewing together the lips of a tear creates a wrinkle in the fabric. There are exceptional cases when patching will be absolutely necessary, and in such cases rubbing the patch and the needle holes with an ordinary wax candle will do some rewaterproofing. A patch put on with a conventional glue will be unsatisfactory—the glue hardens and cracks as soon as the tent is folded for carrying.

Tenting Arrangements

There are some difficulties that can be encountered in the cooperation needed to live together in a confined area, which can be avoided with a little prior thought, planning, and order. Two or three otherwise good friends can find themselves at each other's throats after a short period in a small tent. The old-time trapper preferred heading into the bush alone for the winter, rather than living with one other person. Partnerships often terminated with neither speaking and each occupying his own half of their living arrangement, having as little as possible to do with the other.

Contact is not for that long, nor so confined on the canoe trip, but perhaps on a smaller scale the same unpleasantness can arise—not from a single event, but from a series of little happenings that if recounted seem so trivial as to be ridiculous.

If there are several canoes in the party, divide the canoe pairs when it comes to tenting. It is an unusual pair that can work together twenty-four hours a day without some friction.

Tenting pairs might change every week or so, but there is some loss of speed and efficiency by having new pairing arrangements where each must relearn the little idiosyncrasies of his partner when it comes to arranging the tent.

If two people share a tent, decide before the first night which side belongs to each and stick with the agreement. One side is always preferable, but it will balance out. A less-satisfactory method is to alternate choice of side each night.

If three people are to live together, the middle area may be drier, but this position is less-desirable in other respects. There should be a rotation of positions with each getting the middle an equal number of times.

In a two-man tent, each person gets half the tent—never take more. Better plan the outfit to use only one-third, leaving a wide no-man's land down the middle. Each should keep his gear on

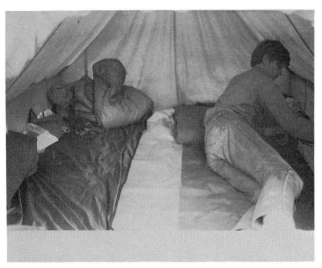

Tent interior should be arranged to provide a no-man's land between partners.

his side without letting odd sweaters and socks float over into the middle. Organize so it is possible to locate equipment without disturbing the other camper. Make a pillow out of extra clothing and equipment—maybe by stuffing them in the pack or stuff bag. Or lay extra gear along the tent wall so no one trips over loose gear getting in and out of the tent. Plan so it will not be necessary to tear everything apart to find a heavy sweater or something like that.

Any camper should keep his clothes and himself clean, neat, and dry. Otherwise, after awhile, even if the owner does not notice, his outfit begins to take on an odor. And to be greeted by a dirty, damp smell every time the tent is entered does not help the good-neighbor policy.

Some people snore; they might try sleeping on their stomachs or sides if a neighbor seems bothered. Avoid rolling toward the center of the tent. Anyone wakes up occasionally through the night and should pull himself back where he belongs. In the morning, only one person can probably roll his pack at a time in the tent. Take turns on who is first, while the other guy clears out and does something else. If rolling first, a ground cloth will have to be pulled out, but otherwise the partner's gear should not be disturbed.

When there are community projects needing doing—or are best done that way—be on hand. Do not run off to fish while the tentmate puts up or takes down the tent alone. Do more than half the work that should be done together.

FIREWOOD

There are few items more vital than dry firewood. Meals should be cooked as effortlessly as possible with some dispatch, and the balky fire makes cooking a chore.

But the selection, drawing, and preparation of dry wood is skill in itself and deserves a fuller treatment in chapter 5.

WATER

If the trip goes far enough into the wilderness, drinking-water poses no problem; it is man who creates pollution. Clarity of water is no test of purity. Water naturally absorbs some color from its surroundings, just as taste varies from one locale to another because of mineral content. Some absolutely safe northern lakes and streams are copper-colored and occasionally even a pure spring is so colored.

Wind, waves, vegetation, and soil along the bank also cause discoloration and create a sediment that will filter out if the pot is allowed to stand unagitated for some few minutes. Just let the foreign matter settle and then pour off the top into another container, leaving the last inch or so to be tossed away. Such sediment will be particularly evident if traveling a clay-banked river or one swollen by recent rains.

Even in virgin territory, the water occasionally has small, almost microscopic animals swimming around in it—wigglers. They do no harm, but most people prefer not to have them in the soup. They occur only near shore in shallow areas. Just slip a canoe into the water and draw the supply farther off shore—usually ten yards is sufficiently far out.

Occasionally the expedient of drawing water from a canoe must be employed in other situations where the water in front of the site is either very shallow or stagnant.

A few trips terminate in saltwater. Arriving at a Hudson's Bay post, just ask or observe the natives. Normally the fresh water of the river that enters James or Hudson bay at the post is powerful enough so that water drawn as the tide is going out is satisfactory. Taking the canoe out on the bay itself is another story, and finding fresh water becomes a problem.

A sudden change in the mineral or salt content of the drinking water may cause stomach disorders that result in a form of twenty-four-hour gripe—diarrhea and vomiting sometimes. Usually the effects wear off in twenty-four hours, uncomfortable as they may be; but the water is not necessarily any less pure.

In areas where contamination might exist, precautions should be taken. Water that bubbles out of the ground is not necessarily pure any more than lake water is.

In case of doubt, drinking-water should be boiled for five minutes or treated as directed with halazone tablets or a similar water purifier. Most cooking where water is used requires that it boil, so water thus used is purified anyway.

Swimming and Bathing

Plenty of soap and water is a good first aid treatment for cuts and abrasions. It is not always possible, but a bath after a long, hard day is something to look forward to. If there are youngsters along, it becomes more of a swim.

The first person to try the water should check carefully for hazards. If the site has been used by others, there may be debris in and around the water—broken glass, old cans, rusty fishhooks. A cut or punctured foot makes portaging a problem, and others have to pick up the slack of the loads that the injured member should be taking.

Be careful wading on smooth rocks; those underwater are lightly coated with an extremely slippery film; one misplaced step and the bather is flat on his back. If there is a rocky swimming area, it is better to choose a spot where the swimmers can dive or slip into the water without wading.

If diving is contemplated, first check carefully. There may be a rock or log just under the surface, and it is unlikely that the water is so clear that every possible threat can be eliminated without inspection by someone in the water.

Canoes are for transportation, not swimming rafts. If a canvas canoe gets wet, the sternsman who carries it will regret it. Nor should any canoes be used for the various games that might be applicable off the cottage dock. Gunwaling, for instance, does the back of the canoe no good.

The same applies to the air mattress, which makes a pleasant swimming raft, provided the owner can dry it out and does not care if it gets punctured.

Swimming activities that are challenging at the cottage have no place in the wilderness. High diving is fun, but a sprained back is not worth it several days from help. And the same holds for any such adventure.

75

All normal safety precautions should be followed—only more so in the wilderness. Swimming is for cleanliness, recreation, and relaxation—not adventure. No one should swim alone, and activity should be restricted to the immediate area. "Swimming across to the island" would be safe if a canoe went with the swimmer, but wilderness water is usually considerably cooler than that back home, and even the best swimmers may tire quickly.

Throw in a bar of soap with the swim. Soap carried in the kitchen is available at lunch when the sun is high. And the long, hot day will go more quickly if occasionally the hourly break becomes a swimming party on a sand beach or an inviting rocky island.

Do not overlook the possibility of a morning dip in the rush to get on the water quickly. Some find it a good way to start the day.

Then there is always a youngster who wants to swim in fast water at a rapid or falls. There are situations where it can be done safely, but, in general, avoid water with a current. The best swimmer cannot fight it, and eddies and falls have currents that an experienced riverman has a difficult time predicting with assurance. Occasionally a canoe upsets in such water, but at least the crew can hold onto it; the swimmer has no such support.

However, there may be emergencies when swimming in white water is necessary. Go with the current, just working to keep the head above water, angling as much as possible toward shore or protection. A breast stroke, side stroke, or even a dog paddle is preferable to a racing stroke.

Naturally the personnel should be able to handle themselves in the water, or they should not have undertaken the trip, but swimming emergencies can be avoided with care and common sense.

Many old-time guides and lumbermen cannot swim a stroke, but keep themselves cleaner in the bush than most vacationers. It would be unusual for the northern guide not to wash up and brush his teeth when he rises in the morning. Few days will pass, in reasonable weather, before he bathes; he just waits for a spot where he can do so without swimming. And before turning in for the night, he will make a trip down to the water to wash up—not to mention the times in between when he pulls the soap out of the jewelry and heads for the lake to wash his hands.

WILDLIFE

The wilderness is approached hoping to observe wildlife, but also frequently with apprehension about such encounters. Except for winged insects, most wildlife prefers to give man a wide berth, and the possibility of unwanted visitors to the campsite will be left to chapter 7.

MISCELLANEOUS CAMPSITE LORE

Walloping

At every meal, as soon as there is space over the fire, a large pot of water should be heated so the dishes can be walloped quickly and well.

Half the water is poured into the dishpan, and the remainder left in the pot to use as rinse water.

Liquid soap in plastic containers makes washing easy. If bar soap is carried, store it in a clean food can after the bottom and lower sides have been punched with holes so the can may be placed in the dishpan and hot water poured into the can. If more suds are needed, agitating the can for a few moments will produce enough. The soap can will find a corner of the kitchen wannigan in which it can be stored.

A sponge or swab makes the washer's job easier, and the drier should have a clean, dry dish towel. A couple should be carried so that when one gets soiled it can be put aside to be boiled and washed.

Plates and cups or pannikins should first be rinsed in the lake to keep the dishwater from becoming dirty. If camped on a sand beach, sand makes a good scouring agent. Or a little clump of moss makes a good sponge to wipe out plates being rinsed.

As the washer cleans each piece, he drops it into the rinse water for the drier. The process works best with two people working together. The rinse pail is probably too small to hold everything at once. Water for both washing and rinsing should be as hot as possible. The fastidious washer carries a pair of rubber gloves to cope with hot water. Plates and silverware sunk in the rinse pot are hard to retrieve, and the drier's job will be easier if he first slips a large spoon or spatula into his pot so plates rest against the spoon rather than sinking to the bottom where he must brave the hot water to retrieve them. Silverware can be sunk to be recovered last and all at once by pouring off the water before reaching into the pot.

Walloping pair at work. Washer drops plates into rinse water for drier.

Beware of sharp knives; they will cut the careless washer, not to mention the plastic dishpan. Only items in the jewelry that do not get placed on the fire should be cleaned by the dish crew; the pot black caused by the fire will not add to the cleanliness of the dishes.

If the party is moving after the meal, the dishwater goes on the fire. The rinse water gets poured into the dishpan to help clean it, and that too goes on the fire. Both dishpan and pot are then rinsed in the lake and brought back full of water to give the fire an extra lick for good measure. If there is still doubt about the fire, a couple more pails are in order. Any side or back logs that might still hold sparks should be dipped in the lake, and charred wood left in the fireplace should be poked around to be sure everything is completely saturated.

After the dishwater has been heated, the irons or grate should be kicked off the fire to cool. If still warm when the time comes to pack, they can be cooled in the lake. Watch dipping hot irons in the lake; as they hit the cool water, they spit back hot water through the open end toward the person immersing them.

Pots and pans used on the fire should be walloped separately. With a small two-man party, it is practical to do them after the dishes in the same hot water. With a large group, it is quicker to wallop them in the lake.

The pot walloper should be supplied with scouring pads; they take little space and are light. Sand, moss, and gravel are good natural scouring agents, but often unavailable. Carrying copper pot cleaners and some abrasive soap pads makes all the difference. The pot cleaners do the heavy work; the soap pads, the finer jobs. Pot cleaners can be brought back to life if coated with grease by burning out the grease over the fire—if the pad burns bluish green, that is copper, not grease, and the pad is past its prime. Or try boiling out the grease.

Most woodsmen scour only the insides of their pots. A black pot absorbs heat better than the bright shiny one. Removing the pot black at each washing ruins a pot cleaner at each meal. If the black must be removed, soap the outside of the shiny pot before putting it over the fire, and the black will come off more readily. If the black is left on, gradually it builds up and starts to peel. Whenever camp is made near sand, rubbing the outside of the pot through the sand a couple times will remove the loose excess.

The obstinate pot or the one coated with grease will wallop easier if first boiled with a little water before being taken to the lake. Fry pans or grills are more easily cleaned if as soon as the surplus fat is poured off, while still hot off the fire, they are quickly immersed in the lake; the film of grease will almost completely release.

If a reflector is used, or any utensil requiring a shiny reflecting surface, it requires special care. A dull reflector will not bake successfully. The inside of the reflector pan should be cleaned without scratching the surface; bannocks will not release from the scarred and dented pan. The reflecting surfaces must be polished without being scratched. Soap pads are acceptable, but never pot cleaners—better is either a powdered or cake household cleanser containing pumice; best are the pastes sold as hand cleaners for mechanics and others who must get grease and grime off their hands. A small tin will go a long way, is easy to

Pots are dried and drained by turning upside down on rock.

carry, and shines the reflector perfectly with little effort.

Normally, pots and reflectors need not be dried, but if the pots are turned upside down on a rock or log after they are walloped, excess water will drain out making them easier to pack, which avoids carrying extra water along to the next campsite.

Latrine

A campsite needs only one latrine. It need not be fancy, just utilitarian and sanitary by bush standards, located well inland of the water. Have everyone pack a roll of toilet paper—bumwad, as it is termed—in his pack. Then put a roll or two in with the community supplies to be available when the packs are rolled.

A fallen log makes a good latrine; birch or a smooth log is preferable to a gummy one! Digging a latrine at each campsite is preferable, but the soil in wilderness sites is often too shallow to make it practical. Perhaps a natural depression in the ground or a crevice between two rocks makes a natural pit in lieu of a man-made one. The log seat laid across such an area at appropriate height is satisfactory.

When traveling in areas where latrines can be dug, a small folding shovel should be carried—available at most surplus stores and quite familiar to the ex-infantryman. Someone should be detailed to dig, and then cover the latrine before departure. Size depends on the party, but a simple slit trench maybe a foot wide—with length and depth depending on use—would serve quite adequately.

After each use and particularly when camp is broken, loose moss or pine needles off the forest floor should be thrown on the latrine. The forest will take care of subsequent decomposition.

Garbage and Kitchen Waste

Some well-traveled canoeing waters have local rules regarding the waste disposal. Maybe a latrine exists; provisions may have already been provided for the disposal of nonburnable waste—containers or a designated dump.

In many areas, trash carried into the area should be carried out to be disposed of after the trip. If so, maybe a plastic bag or two for such trash would help.

However, if traveling in virgin territory or having just occupied a newly established campsite, the following guide lines might be followed.

A

B

Simple campsite furniture: A) a few boards from a nearby abandoned lumber camp help make a table; B) the Indian makes a peg by driving wedge into a tree after first making a slit with his ax; C) a table can be constructed out of small logs by resting the top on rails supported by **Y**'s driven into the ground.

C

79

A

B

C

D

Log seat placed between two trees: A) diagram for construction (do not notch trees too deeply); B) one end of the seat is placed into the notch; C) other end is driven home with the back of the ax; D) completed seat—top side has been flattened with the ax.

Trash that will burn goes on the fire, and most garbage and left-over food burns. Quantities of left-over edibles impractical for burning could within limits be left with the nonburnable refuse. Under no conditions should garbage be scattered or tossed in the water or about the site. Birds, squirrels, chipmunks, whiskey jacks, and their friends will take care of such handouts; but so will a scavenging bear. And a garbage-dump bear can be a formidable opponent. Better such waste be buried in the latrine.

If cans are to be left, open them at both ends, flatten, and burn the cans. When the fire is doused, remove the cans and place in a single can dump or bury in the latrine. Except for aluminum, metal so burned disintegrates more quickly than if not burned. Do not toss waste cans into the water off shore; some swimmer will find them to his misfortune. It is sometimes acceptable to carry cans along in the canoe until over deep water where no one would venture, and sink them.

The remains from cleaning fish should either be burned, buried in the covered latrine, or tossed far out in the water where they will be taken care of by gulls and other scavengers. Never toss fish remains in the bush; the odor created as they decompose will drive everyone else away from the site for a long time to come. Only those fish that can be used should be kept; others should have been put back to grow larger, so the number involved should be manageable. However, there are times when the party's eyes are bigger than their stomachs. *Never* throw a dead fish in the bush—better it be sunk in the lake or buried.

Campsite Furniture

It goes without saying that a campsite should be left in better condition than when occupied. Tent poles should be stacked vertically, latrines closed, cans put in a proper dump, tentsites cleared of refuse, kitchen area policed, and firewood left for the next occupant. Maybe the next visitor will even be the same party in another season.

In addition, if some comforts are added to the site with each visit, soon the campground becomes more than just a place to spend the night. A table or bench, maybe crudely constructed, helps. It is not necessary that additions be expertly constructed; even a log bench set in front of the fire makes the site more comfortable. A couple of nails carried for construction purposes make the job easier; maybe a little copper wire or string for lashing together the pieces of a table.

It is not necessary to hew out boards for the projects, but constructing a little campsite furniture would give the neophyte axeman a useful project on which to practice; there is usually enough sound, already down lumber available near the site, so green trees should be left to grow. And if there are youngsters along, they are often quickly enthusiastic about a building project.

Building a bench near the campfire or doing so for a latrine seat in the following manner will probably kill the trees involved and cannot be recommended. Find two relatively large trees an appropriate distance apart and notch each at seat height. Cut a log seat, maybe beveling the top, slightly longer than the spread between the trees, and taper the ends to fit the notches. Then drive the seat into the notches. With luck, rather than good management, the trees may learn to accept the foreign seat and continue to grow around it as many species of tree grow burls to compensate for disease or foreign matter.

5

AXEMANSHIP AND FIREWOOD

An experienced traveler rarely cooks over a fire built of fallen wood. Most of it is too green or rotten and punky; it may be just the thing to throw on toward dusk to provide a cheerful, warm campfire, but by then the cooking is done and the party just wants the blaze to take the chill off the evening.

Occasionally, dry wood can be found along a beach, tossed there during the spring; and if dry and firm, driftwood burns well. However, the party that expects such a supply at every meal is doomed to disappointment.

Small scraps of dry wood are sometimes found scattered around the forest. The northern guide calls it "squaw wood"—stuff that can be picked up and broken across the knee. Sometimes there is enough lying around for a lunch fire, but rarely can enough be found at an evening camp to cook both dinner and breakfast.

While the person drawing dry wood does not have to be an expert naturalist, it helps if he can recognize trees native to the area and knows something about the burning qualities of the various woods. Even if he cannot name the tree, he should be able to tell if it is dry before dragging it back and trying to cook on it.

Trees dropped by nature are rarely dry, even if obviously dead. A couple of blows with the ax will determine if the downed tree is rotten. Dry, powdery, rotten wood burns, but a fire eats up vast quantities without giving off much heat. Solid dead wood lying on the ground is probably wet—it will have soaked up moisture during the winter and with every rain. Decay may not have started, but it is unlikely to burn.

The northern guide looks for what he calls a *chicot* (pronounced *shee-ko*), which is a standing dead tree from which the bark has dropped. The literal French translation means stump, but the French Canadian means something more than just a stump.

A good, dry chicot is easy to test with the ax—a couple of blows will discover hard, dry wood that has a clear, resonant ring to it with each bite of the ax, and chips will fly as when seasoned lumber is splintered at home.

The ecology of the open fire must be considered by any responsible tripper. Felling chicots does the forest no harm. With rare exceptions, to be noted later, drawing green wood for the fire is senseless, and the camper is only harvesting that which nature has discarded.

If traveling popular country or camping on a well-used site, dry wood can be frustrating in a forest already picked over by others. Frequently, instead of just walking inland, the wise woodsman launches a canoe and paddles off to a more virgin shore. Normally the paddle is not very long. Or if the guide scans the shore before reaching the site, he will locate wood that can be drawn and tossed in the canoes to be carried to the campsite.

The vacationer probably will not camp in a

Chicot is a standing dry tree from which the bark has dropped.

burned area by choice. The northern Indian frequently does, or at least on the edge of a burn; drawing dry wood is so easy. Chicots abound just for the taking, and if such a burn exists near the campsite—that's the place to find firewood!

The most convenient chicots are those maybe six to eight inches in diameter at the base, and one such chicot will provide enough wood for a one-night stand. A couple of smaller chicots will do the job. Anything of larger proportions requires too much labor to draw the wood for the short stay.

The tree should be cut with the saw or ax into relatively short lengths—no more than eighteen to twenty inches—and the logs should be split into convenient sticks no more than two to three inches in diameter. A six-inch log will give four good sticks of firewood. The larger, thicker log makes a pleasant campfire, but has no place on the cooking fire. The finer the wood is split, within reason, the better its contribution to the cooking fire.

Kinds of Wood

In general the hardwoods produce a hotter, more lasting fire than softer ones. Again, in gen-

Indian winter camp on the edge of an old burn with some standing chicots still showing

eral, the harder woods are the deciduous trees—the leaf-bearing ones. Unfortunately in canoe country, stands of hardwood are encountered only in certain areas. Oak, maple, ash, hickory, cherry, and such woods, if encountered, are great.

The hardest woods normally encountered are birch and poplar, and both are excellent if gathered at the right time. Birch chicots are rare. The bark rarely falls off until after the wood rots within, and a dead birch is always wet and punky. It is not even worth testing with the ax—it will not burn. Green birch, however, burns with great heat and produces one of the steadiest baking fires in the Northwoods, but it cannot be used to start the fire. But finely split green birch can be added to the fire already well underway with other starters. As with other hardwoods, birch produces lasting coals throwing off heat at a constant level. The traveling canoeist will not benefit much from laying up firewood for the future unless returning to the same site in another season, but if cut and split while green and then allowed to dry for a season, dry birch makes an excellent cooking fire from every angle.

The poplar, or quaking aspen, sometimes drops its bark when it dies, and dry poplar produces a fine cooking fire. But there is no point in drawing poplar—however dead—with the bark intact. It will be either green or rotten and, in either event, worthless. Dry poplar, when found, is second to birch, however, as a frequently discovered baking wood.

Most likely the canoe tripper must use the conifers for firewood. They are easier to cut and split than the hardwoods; but in general the various pines burn more quickly and erratically than hardwoods. The fire must be fed constantly to avoid radical variations in heat.

Everyone has a favorite wood for one purpose or another. In canoe country, however, of the conifers, the most acceptable for the cooking fire are—in no real order—white pine, red pine, jackpine, tamarack, and spruce. Tamarack does not belong to the list since it is really deciduous; but it looks as though it should be a conifer when encountered in the summer. Much less acceptable for the cookery are cedar and balsam.

White and red pine are normally straight-grained, easy to handle, and a joy to split. Both grow to sizes where they are impossible to handle for the overnight stand. They both burn readily and quickly when dry, giving good heat, but the fire must be replenished frequently to maintain the heat. The bark drops from both quickly when the tree dies, often leaving good standing chicots. Neither grows north of the height of land where the water flow changes from that which flows into the Atlantic or Pacific into that which flows to the Arctic, and looking for either north of that line is a waste of time.

Jackpine looks something like a stunted red pine, but rarely grows to the stately size of the pines, and often looks dwarfed and undernourished. It burns as well or better than the pines but can be twisted and knarred, making it difficult to draw and split. The straight jackpine splits easily, but beware of the twisted tree! In order for it to be dry and acceptable as firewood, the jackpine does not necessarily have to drop its bark. Normally the tree devoid of needles is sufficiently dry—test with the ax; there is a different ring of the dry tree from the indescribable but recognizable "squish" as the ax hits the green tree. If still in doubt, feel the wood exposed as a result of a chip taken out by the ax. But seven out of ten jackpines without needles are dry. Next to birch and poplar, jackpine is probably the best readily found baking wood.

Stands of tamarack, or larch, are rarer, and the tree usually grows in damp areas, and so may appear in places unsuitable for campsites. A dry tamarack will look much like a dry jackpine. The green tree, however, is much less dense and its needles are more widely spaced; its boughs would make a very poor bed. It is lighter in color than spruce or jackpine, and so stands out in the forest. Tamarack burns with an intense heat. The story goes that a winter stove in which tamarack is used consistently will burn out in a year.

Spruce is the most general conifer and the easiest to locate. It usually grows straight and narrow and is easy to draw and split. Like the jackpine, the dry spruce need not drop its bark and become a true chicot to make excellent firewood, and a tree devoid of needles is probably acceptable. But look carefully—spruce reaches straight for the sky and frequently only the very top shows green, while the lower branches are completely dry. Straight-grained spruce is often of uniform diameter, making it one of the most useful woods for purposes other than burning. From it the Indian fashions his paddles, poles for climbing rapids, tent poles, and lumber for his house—if he has a sawmill handy. He builds his winter camp from spruce logs, sometimes splitting them in half with either the ax or chain saw. Jackpine would be his second choice.

Cedar often grows along a lake shore where

there is excess moisture—sometimes a swamp. The shoreline cedar is often twisted and bent into odd shapes; the straighter trees are normally a short way back from shore. Cedar is excellent for many purposes—building and repairing canoes in particular—but it makes poor firewood since it sparks more readily than the other conifers. It gives satisfactory heat, but the sparks make it dangerous—both from the point of view of starting an unwanted fire and from burning the cook.

Balsam, when completely dry, burns quickly with less heat than the others and should be avoided except in emergency. Dry spruce, jack-pine, or tamarack retain their bark and still make suitable firewood. A dead balsam that has not dropped its bark—and most do not become chicots —is almost always rotten and punky. The slightly green balsam is impossible to handle; balsam gum covers the bark, making it difficult to touch without getting hopelessly covered with the sticky stuff. The only practical use of balsam is making an excellent bed from its boughs. From a distance it is often mistaken for spruce, but its needles grow out only on opposite sides of the branch, while spruce needles grow out at every angle. Once close to the tree, however, the bark of the spruce and balsam are quite different and easily distinguishable.

A gum-soaked piece of spruce burns readily with great heat, but the stump of any conifer struck by lightning is a great find. It is surprising how many exist. They are extremely resinous and will go off with the touch of the match and burn with intense heat. Only a few sticks knocked off such a stump will boil water quicker than it takes to tell. The one problem created by resinous wood is its black soot. The bottoms of pots placed above such a fire show the kind of wood used, as does the face of the cook who works too close! Baking is unsatisfactory since the baked goods pick up the black; but there is no doubting the heat thrown off. A lunch fire using wood from a lightning-struck stump boils water in nothing flat. Such wood is difficult to draw with the ax; it feels like rock when attempts are made to chop it, but the effort is normally rewarding since relatively little needs be drawn.

Fire Starters

When the dry wood is laid up, preparation should be made for making the fire spring to life with relatively little effort. The universal fire starter is birch bark, and a little strip will ignite almost any fire. The white birch peels itself, and, with a little help, a fair-sized birch will yield sufficient quantities of its paper-thin skin.

There is a temptation to score the tree parallel to its trunk, and peel off the bark in layers as if building a canoe. The thick sheet burns less well than the paper-thin peelings already falling off, and harms the tree to no purpose.

The next most easily acquired tinder is a bundle of small twigs and branches broken off the base of one of the conifers. As they reach skyward, the lower branches die off, leaving good, dry tinder.

It takes longer, but a small stick of split dry wood can be made into a "fuzz" stick with an ax in a few moments by cutting toward the center of the stick at an angle many times, without completing the cuts, leaving a multisided stick that will ignite quickly.

Of course, finely split shavings will go off more quickly than the thick stick. And usually after drawing and splitting the firewood there are chips lying around.

However, as already suggested, one of the easiest methods for ensuring that the fire will touch off quickly is carrying a can of lighter fluid in the cookery to be used in emergencies when the cook is too lazy or rushed to gather proper tinder; it can also be used to refill lighters! Or maybe carry a tube of fire starter. Ambroid from the canoe repair kit is excellent, but it would be wiser to save it for its intended use.

AXES

The kind of ax carried depends on the user. Heads come in so many shapes, no one can be described as best. The weight of the head and length of the handle are much more important. An ax with a head weighing 2¼ to 2½ pounds is standard. A two-pound head is slightly light for drawing firewood; anything more than 2½ is unnecessarily large for the wood to be cut—plus being heavier to carry. Whether the head is a "Hudson's Bay" head or some other model is relatively immaterial—as long as the user likes it.

A handle about twenty-seven inches long is about right for most people, an inch or two either way for others, but avoid extremes. Whether the handle is straight or curved makes no difference— just that the grain of the wood be straight. Some handles have a finish like sandpaper at the butt to offer a better grip—and create blisters as the ax is used. Keep the handle smooth and learn not to lose one's grip!

Fuzz stick: A) manufactured by shaving with the ax; B) touches off easily

A double-bitted ax may be a lumberman's badge, but it has no place on a canoe trip and is an unnecessary hazard.

Occasionally, someone suggests that a hatchet or machete would be useful. They will cut tent poles, clear campsites, and open portage trails, but neither does any job that an ax cannot do better. If an additional tool is necessary, carry another ax.

After winter storage, the ax head is likely to be loose. Soak the head in a bucket of water, and the handle will normally swell and hold firmly again. If the head starts to slip, hold the ax with the head down and the shaft perpendicular to the ground, and rap the butt of the handle sharply with another ax or hammer. The head will "jump" back on. A hardwood or metal wedge then driven into the head will keep it in position.

Ax Sharpening

The dull ax not only will not do the job but

86

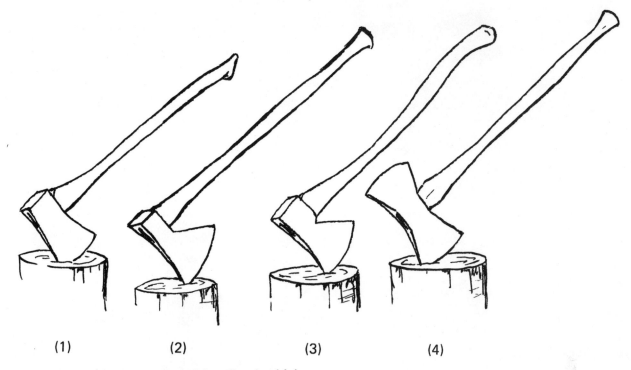

(1)   (2)   (3)   (4)

Shape of both the ax head and handle should be determined by preference of user: A) camper's ax with a relatively straight handle ending with a fawn's foot butt; B) Hudson's Bay head with a straight handle and a square butt; C) modified Hudson's Bay head with a curved handle and a bulblike butt; D) double-bitted head requires a straight handle and a square butt.

is more dangerous than the properly sharpened tool. A sharp ax bites; a dull ax bounces off or deflects and causes more accidents than does the well-honed ax.

The ax file is indispensable. The ax should be touched up every couple of days, under the pressure of normal duties. There should be a couple of files carried in different places. They will rust if they get wet, and a rusted file slips. Most files come without handles, but a handle can easily be made from a piece of wood maybe an inch thick. The butt of the file is driven into the wood, making a handle to protect the user.

The straighter the blade of the sharp ax, within limits, the better its cutting surface. The curved blade slips; the straight blade cuts even if the blow is slightly off target. The heel and toe receive punishment from rocks and other obstacles. It is rarely necessary to sharpen either; they wear down on their own.

Sharpening is done by stroking the file across the blade with pressure on the file and the major stroke directed diagonally across and toward the

blade; be careful of fingers wrapped around the butt of the file. The stroke of the file as it is drawn away from the blade does little sharpening. Every time the ax is sharpened, the file should cut back from the actual blade while it also tapers the cutting edge. Filing just the very edge of the blade may produce a fine cutting edge for the first chop, but it dulls quickly. A new ax has a beveled blade, and with each sharpening some of this bevel should be taken out. Most new axes come with sharpening instructions, which all too frequently say the blade should be sharpened in a wedge. The woodsman will find his ax more serviceable if the blade is more V-shaped than wedge-shaped. The wedge-shaped blade may be fine for the moment, but the edge dulls quickly, and the steel behind is so thick the ax no longer cuts. The V-shaped blade nicks more easily, but the steel behind the nick is thinner and the ax still cuts. The wedge-school will be sharpening axes nightly; the V-school needs to touch up the ax every four or five days.

Both sides of the blade, naturally, should be honed equally. It is normally easier to sharpen one side than the other, and temptation to work harder on one side than the other must be avoided. Holding the ax steady poses a problem that can be solved by selecting a large tree and cutting a V into the trunk so that the back of the V is narrow and slightly thinner than the head of the ax. Then the head of the ax is driven into the V

87

Ax head jumps back on by pounding butt of handle.

A

B

Ax sharpening: A) if only one hand is available for the job—pressure is applied to file; cutting stroke is one that drives toward ax; file is angled across blade as shown; B) more pressure, and therefore a quicker job, can be applied by pressing down on file with other hand—notice bevel of ax is being taken down behind cutting edge. Using either method, be careful of the possibility of cuts to hand gripping the file.

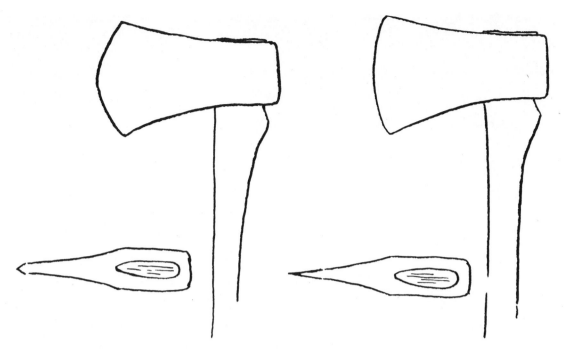

Left: two most common sharpening faults—heel and toe taken down too far, resulting in curved cutting edge; only cutting edge sharpened, leaving thick wedge. *Right*: proper sharpening—blade has only a slight curvature; wedge-shaped cutting edge eliminated by filing back of edge.

Sharpening vise made in tree

so that it is wedged in place. When one side is done, the ax is withdrawn and driven into the V with the other side up. If the tree is large enough, both the tree and the ax vise remain for posterity.

After the rough sharpening with a file, some will want a fine edge, which can then be achieved by using a stone carried primarily for sharpening knives. In such manner, while it has not real use in the bush, the ax can be taken down so fine as to shave with it.

Storing

The ax should be protected with a sheath when not in use. Leather is fine. If no other is available, one can be constructed by bending a tin can around the blade to be secured by a couple of thongs.

The number of axes to be carried varies, but there is no need for more than a maximum of one per canoe; and fewer with a large group. The axes can be passed around if tent poles must be cut. However, remember that if a guide is hired, there is an unwritten law that no one touches the guide's ax—and it is poor etiquette to suggest he loan it, and a sin to borrow it without permission.

If the luxury of having an ax only for splitting can be afforded, a slightly dull ax splits better than a very sharp one. The sharp one sticks in the log more often, while the dull one breaks open the log and releases easier.

An ax is normally portaged with the canoe; portaging by putting it on top of any other load,

Sheath made from a folded tin can attached with thongs

even though protected by a sheath, opens possibilities for running hands against the blade either on the portage or while loading and unloading.

There are numerous dos and don'ts associated with axemanship—mostly safety rules:

Do not use the ax as a tomahawk to be thrown at trees and targets. The ax is a vital tool, and throwing does it no good. There are guides who will demonstrate their skill by splitting and lighting a match with a thrown ax. Someone always wants to copy, and at best succeeds in dulling the ax, but all too often splits the handle.

When not in use, the ax should be stored out of the way. Never stick the ax into a tree at head height; someone will brush against it and drop the ax onto himself. Lay the ax against a tree, wannigan, or tent pole so that the handle sticks up where it will be spotted easily when needed or when camp is broken. Angle the blade toward an

area where no one will step or walk. If it is absolutely necessary to drive the blade into something, do so with the blade close to the ground and the handle sticking up.

Use the ax only for necessary chores, never as a play toy to while away idle hours. Let the novice get his practice in constructive ways, not by going back into the bush to drop trees indiscriminately; wood is valuable, maybe not today, but for the next guy who comes along.

Hanging a Head

Hanging an ax head properly is time-consuming and a labor of love. Make absolutely sure the new handle will be satisfactory before starting; inspect the grain to be sure it is straight and will not break when first used.

A store-bought handle will be thicker than the slot in the ax head into which it fits. Shave down

90

the head of the handle with a knife, another ax, spoke shave, or plane, being careful to take equal wood off both sides. If power tools are available, a disk sander does the job easily. Test frequently by starting the head on the new handle. Setting the head is the same procedure as for setting a loose head. Do not drive the head on.

Make sure the head is lined up straight and true. The blade should be exactly parallel with the handle. If the head starts to angle, and a correction cannot be made by shaving different sides of the handle, start over again with a new handle. To end up with the head skew to the handle makes using the ax dangerous.

When the head is tested, small curls of wood will be created in spots that should be shaved more. Remove the head and take down those areas, being careful not to shave too much off as the project nears completion.

When the head is finally seated, there will be extra wood sticking out—saw it off flush with the top of the head. The handle had a split in the top when purchased. Drive a hardwood wedge into the split. A good wedge can be made from the old ax handle that is being replaced. Then saw the wedge off flush with the top of the ax. Metal wedges of various sizes can also be used and can be purchased for a few cents at any hardware store.

Occasionally when a new handle is needed, the old one defies removal. Saw off below the head, lay the head on a floor, line up a metal or wooden wedge with the top of the handle to be driven out, and strike as sharp a blow as possible with another ax. The shock of the blow should drive the old handle out. Perform the operation in an open area; the ax head occasionally travels some distance. If absolutely necessary in the bush, the old handle can be burned out, but beware of destroying the temper of the steel. Otherwise it should be drilled out.

In a wilderness emergency, a new handle can be blocked from available hardwood—birch, maple, ash, hickory. There is no point in using soft wood. Blocking the handle and hanging the head are time-consuming, and to have the handle break after a couple strokes is discouraging!

SAWS

The Swede saw can be a labor-saver if large amounts of wood are to be laid up. It is often appreciated in well-traveled areas where chicots

Two Swede saws; both having rubber sheaths over the blades

are few and far between. Making up firewood with an ax is wasteful, and blocking with the saw saves several sticks of wood from each tree. It is also infinitely safer than an ax. Often, the axeman can draw the chicot and leave the job of making up the blocks to less-experienced campers who can make them up faster with the saw than with the ax.

The best saws are those made of metal with about a thirty-inch blade, although a smaller saw may be easier to portage. Since the blade normally remains in place during travel, it should be covered with a sheath. One can be made of wood, but the easiest is a split piece of plastic pipe or rubber hose—small garden hose—placed over the blade and lashed on with cord. On the portage the saw is normally tossed on top of a load or hand-carried, although it can be tied to the load if desired.

There are collapsible saws on the market. The small ones cannot handle the size wood normally drawn and are not worth packing. Some of those that make up into a full-sized saw might be considered, but the chore of unfolding the saw for each use is normally not worth the effort—and for canoeing, at least, carrying a full-sized saw is not prohibitive.

A spare blade should be included to safeguard against the possibility of snapping one. Most blades will roll into a cylindrical package maybe five or six inches in diameter and should be wrapped carefully to prevent anyone from inadvertently hitting the bare teeth while reaching into the storage area.

If the saw had a new blade to begin the trip, it will certainly last the run without sharpening. Sharpening can be done with a file, and some guides prefer setting their own saws rather than

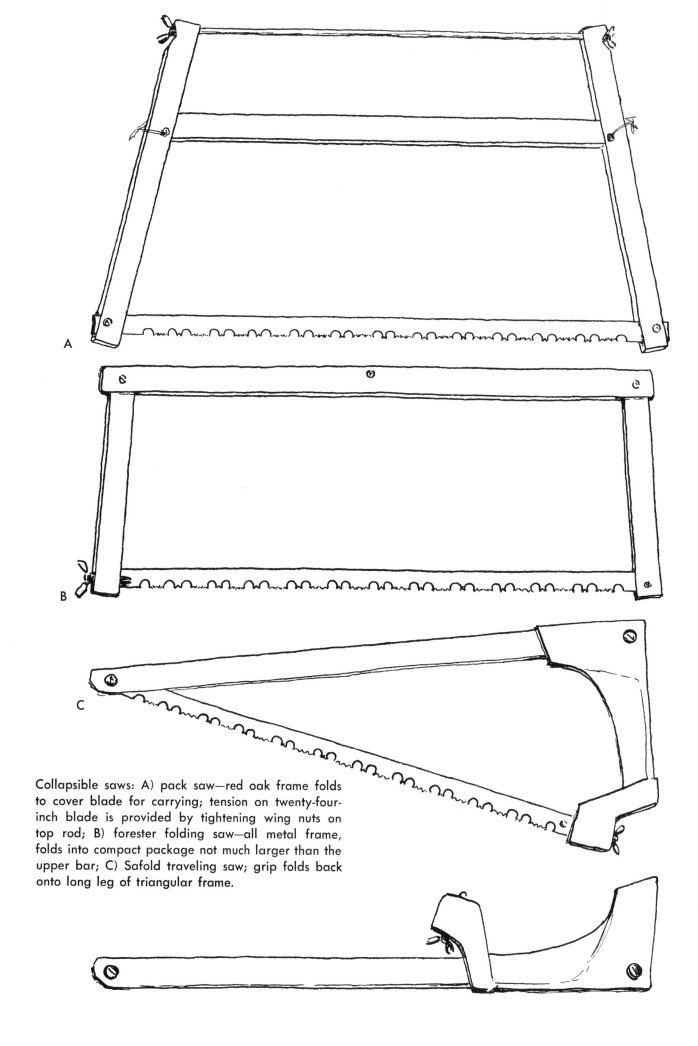

Collapsible saws: A) pack saw—red oak frame folds to cover blade for carrying; tension on twenty-four-inch blade is provided by tightening wing nuts on top rod; B) forester folding saw—all metal frame, folds into compact package not much larger than the upper bar; C) Safold traveling saw; grip folds back onto long leg of triangular frame.

buying a new blade, but it is a time-consuming job that needs a professional touch—and new blades are inexpensive.

AXEMANSHIP

Two of the most frequent serious medical problems are burns and ax cuts; either can spoil the trip not only for the injured person but also for everyone else. An ax must always be treated as a potential weapon; it takes only one moment of carelessness and one misdirected swing.

The novice should admit his lack of experience and seek instruction if he wants to gain skill in using the ax. An ax is a tool—an important one—and not a toy. Youngsters are likely fascinated as they see the chips fly, and fail to appreciate the dangers. The novice should let the best axeman draw the wood from the bush and begin learning his trade back at the campsite after the wood is collected.

Felling

After locating a chicot, clear away underbrush or limbs that could deflect the ax. Choose the area into which the tree is to be dropped—sometimes the tree is canted at such an angle that it is easier to drop in that direction rather than trying to alter nature's arrangements. The lumberman can drop his tree with pinpoint accuracy; it is doubtful if the summer canoesman can do the same. The tree should be far enough from the campsite so that if its fall is miscalculated, it cannot land on anyone—or the canoes or tents or other equipment.

Start cutting on the side toward the direction of fall. A couple of downward strokes at about a forty-five-degree angle to the trunk begin the V of the chop. The downward stroke is easier than the upward, but after a couple of downward strokes, take an upward one to remove a chip. The upward stroke is a more horizontal cut made at an angle of sixty degrees or more. Make the initial cuts wide enough apart so that a sizeable chip is dislodged. Felling a tree where the V being worked is too narrow is difficult. Alternate downward and upward swings, trying to remove a chip with every pair of swings. Keep feet out of the road so that if the ax misses or is deflected it will not strike the user.

As the V deepens and the tree begins to weaken, stop cutting on the side where it is to fall and work on the opposite side starting a new

Felling with an ax: cut first in direction of fall slightly more than halfway through the tree; second cut is made on backside above the first.

V slightly higher than the first one—do not match the V's. If done perfectly, the tree will drop exactly in the direction of the initial V, but most part-time axemen find that pushing the tree when it is ready to topple makes sure of its path.

Trees dropped for firewood are normally considerably less than a foot in diameter, but there is a possibility that the butt of a large tree when freed from its stump will jump backwards as it falls, so stand to the side—not directly behind it. The tree that jumps backwards is one of the hazards of the lumberjack where larger trees are involved.

If a saw is used for felling, greater accuracy can be achieved. With the saw, cut into the tree exactly perpendicular to the direction in which it is to fall, until over one-half of the way through. Remove the saw, and with the ax cut downward until the saw cut is reached to remove a large chip above the cut. Then cut on the opposite side, again perpendicular to the direction of fall and

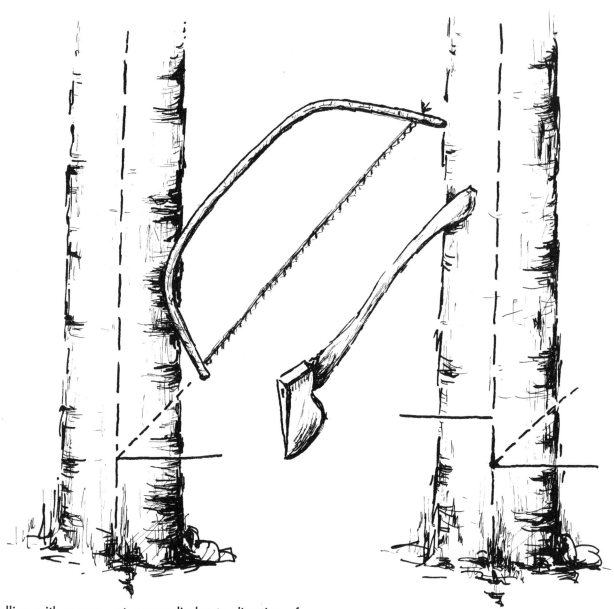

Felling with a saw: cut perpendicular to direction of fall, parallel to ground; remove chip with the ax; make second cut on backside also perpendicular to fall.

just a shade higher than the first cut. The proficient guide drops his tree within a foot of where he planned!

Blocking

If a Swede saw is carried, limb the fallen tree and cut it into convenient lengths to carry back to the site to be cut and split there.

If a saw is not carried, use the ax to block the sections of the tree into firewood lengths before returning to the kitchen, cutting V's about every eighteen inches approximately three-quarters of the way through the log—not all the way—and take the blocked sections back to the campsite.

In blocking the log, sometimes the tree will remain stationary so the cutter can keep his feet well away from being struck by a deflected ax, but often the log must be held in place by bracing it with a foot. With experience it will be discovered that one foot is more comfortable than the other. The foot is placed at least a foot away from the V being cut—eighteen inches is better. The V is cut similar to that used to fell the tree. As the blade is directed away from the holding foot, the tree is struck at about a forty-five-degree angle, the cut coming toward the holding foot, closer to being perpendicular to the tree trunk.

No one should use the ax without some protec-

Dry wood blocked with an ax, each cut about three-quarters of the way through the log

tion on his feet. The ax will slice through even the best boot, but even so the boot offers some protection—and considerably more than sneakers or moccasins, but even these are still better than nothing! The barefooted youngster should never touch the ax! In fact, he should not have been wandering around the campite barefoot anyway. Too many previous users may have dropped glass, cans, or fishhooks, not to mention the hazards placed there by nature.

The tree should be limbed as it is blocked, and limbing is easier if cuts are made starting up the tree from the base. Again this can be dangerous if the axeman is not cautious about foot placement.

After the wood is brought back to the campfire, an area removed from the fire, kitchen, and any other center of population should be used to make up the firewood. It is better to cut up the firewood slightly into the bush rather than on a rocky area; there is no point in asking for unnecessary nicks in the ax if it inadvertently hits the rock. If using a Swede saw, lay the log to be cut across a block off the ground so the section being cut off will drop down as the cut is made.

If the campsite is to be occupied for some time so that a large quantity of wood must be laid up, a homemade sawhorse helps. One can easily be constructed by driving a pair of pickets into the ground solidly so that each pair forms an X, across which the log will rest. Almost any Indian site comes equipped with such an arrangement. The crossed pickets might be wired, nailed, or tied together. Of course a portable rig can be manufactured with more effort.

With the Swede saw—used either by one or two people—the actual cutting is done as the saw is drawn toward the user, and little pressure is put on the stroke away from him. This is particularly so when two people operate the saw—the operator just rides with the stroke as the saw moves away from him. Do not bend the blade; it will snap with careless use, and a bladeless saw is not very valuable! The free end of the tree should be allowed to drop off without resistance under it, or the blade will pinch, making sawing difficult and endangering the blade.

Without a saw the tree should have been blocked into appropriate lengths where it fell. When the blocked log is brought back, it is placed so the row of V's that were previously cut angle toward the axeman and at about a sixty degrees angle toward the ground. Bracing the log with his foot, the axeman starts at the open end of his log and elevates the first stick, and if the tree was well blocked, a single blow at about a forty-five-degree angle away from his restraining foot on the back side of each V knocks off each stick of wood.

Splitting

Split wood burns infinitely better than a solid stick, and each block should now be split—depending on the diameter of the log—into four or more pieces. The stick a couple of inches across burns nicely; the log of greater size takes ages to catch. No one brings in wood of such size that a splitting wedge is needed. The twisted, knarred piece of wood is difficult to split and should have been avoided, so hopefully the blocks have reasonably straight grain.

There are two accepted splitting methods. The safer, saner method should be employed on all wood that has been blocked with an ax, and by all but experienced axemen. A chopping block is laid on the ground in front of the splitter in an area where no one will be walking around him— particularly behind him. The log is laid on the chopping block so the butt of the log rests on

Sawing on campsite horse, made from a pair of pickets lashed together

Previously blocked wood is broken by a blow taken on the backside, cutting away from the axeman's restraining foot.

the ground on the far side of the block. The top of the log is laid so that a section about two to three inches below the top rests solidly against the block. The log is inspected before being positioned to locate the best area for driving the ax. If there is a check in the wood—a crack placed there by nature—the ax should be driven into the check. Otherwise, the best splitting spot is either a knot or a place where a limb was cut off. The ax should be driven into the check, knot, or base of the limb so that the chopping block is directly under the section being struck. The log rarely splits cleanly on the first blow. The ax should be freed and the log struck again in the same place. If the ax sinks into the log without splitting cleanly, there is a temptation to raise the ax with the log attached, and bring both down together on the chopping block—it rarely works! To free the ax for the next blow avoid reaching down with a hand to grab the log and work the ax free—all

Splitting: A) log is positioned so the ax hits the stump of a limb; B) log is struck as many times as necessary in the same place until slit opens.

A) When wood is almost split, ax is driven in deeply; B) Block is lifted off chopping block, turned sideways, and end of block is brought down sharply on chopping block.

too often the hand rubs against the blade and suffers a cut. Even if the hands remain undamaged, the constant stooping and bending to free the ax leaves all but the most youthful exhausted after splitting a couple of logs. Use a foot to brace the log and free the ax, or pick up the ax with log attached and tap the far end of the log on the chopping block to dislodge the ax. And strike again. Make each blow of the ax telling; a little weak stroke is not worth the effort.

When the log is almost but not quite split, with the ax still deep into the log, ax and log can be raised together, and the ax rotated ninety degrees so the blade is parallel to the chopping block. Rapping the log on the block completes the split. Breaking the log apart this way puts pressure on the ax handle that, if undertaken repeatedly—

particularly before the log is ready to drop in two—will twist or warp the handle, or break it. It takes experience to sense when the log is ready to drop apart.

Then there is the log that refuses to split after three or four blows. Try turning it end for end and working on the split from the other end. Or roll the log over and try splitting from the other side directly opposite the split started by the first couple of blows.

Then there is the log that refuses to fall apart even though split through. Avoid the temptation to pick it up and tear the few remaining slivers apart with bare hands; use the ax to finish severing the log.

A

C

B

D

Flicking: A) block is positioned and held with foot; B) as blade strikes wood, blade is rotated fifteen to thirty degrees; C) straight-grained wood drops in two; D) successive blocks are broken off in the same manner.

After the log is halved, divide each half into the appropriate number of sections. Second and subsequent splits are normally easier if done by driving the ax into the outside of the log rather than the open side.

An alternate splitting method should be used *only* on *sawed* wood, and only by experienced axemen. It is quicker and more dramatic, but also extremely dangerous for the novice, who will inevitably want to try it once he sees someone split by flicking the ax. The log is laid on the chopping block so the butt rests on the ground on the side toward the axeman. He then braces the butt with his foot. The ax is aimed for the sawed top of the log, but just before the blade

hits, it is rotated fifteen to thirty degrees, so that the blade is actually "flicked" as it strikes. Straight-grained wood falls apart like match sticks if this method is employed correctly, with seemingly little effort. The experienced Northwoodsman splits his winter stock of wood this way. But beware of the blow that misses; the foot bracing the butt is in the path of the ax, and the flick sometimes makes it bounce off the log!

Woodpile

Stack the split wood near the fireplace where the cook can reach it easily, but also so the breakfast wood will be covered at night by the fly or whatever cover is used for the supplies. Make up enough wood for breakfast when the evening supply is drawn. Toss some kindling on top of the breakfast stack and maybe a couple of strips of birch bark or tinder.

98

Woodpile is laid up for the morning with tinder on top.

Enough wood should be drawn and split so there is no danger of running out halfway through breakfast. Wood for the evening campfire can be trash lying around the site and need not be carefully drawn dry wood. How much should be courteously left for the next party depends on the wilderness nature of the country. It does no good to draw and split large stacks if the site will not be used until next summer. Better leave large sticks of uncut wood leaning against a tree almost perpendicular to the ground, to be blocked and split by next summer's group. However, where others are likely to appear in a day or a week, it is simple courtesy to leave at least enough split, stacked, dry wood to make a meal should they arrive in rough weather.

6

FIRST AID

Every party needs a well-supplied first aid kit and knowledge for using it. A kit can be bought ready packed, but one fabricated to anticipate its most likely uses perhaps serves better.

The kit should include a small booklet on first aid—perhaps a publication of the Red Cross or similar responsible organization. It could provide valuable aid in diagnosis and treatment. However, there are few medical problems where immediate action must be taken. There are only three where a matter of minutes is vital: (1) heart stoppage; (2) stoppage of breathing; and (3) excessive bleeding. But the first aid necessary on a canoe

trip rarely involves such emergencies, and it will invariably turn out that the first aid kit gets opened less frequently than the medicine closet at home. Prevention is much more preferable to first aid, and somehow those entering the wilderness subconsciously exercise greater care than in other situations.

Except for serious emergencies, in case of doubt, be cautious about applying remedies and making quick diagnosis. The patient can sometimes be harmed further by overly solicitous treatment.

The kit to be carried should anticipate the most

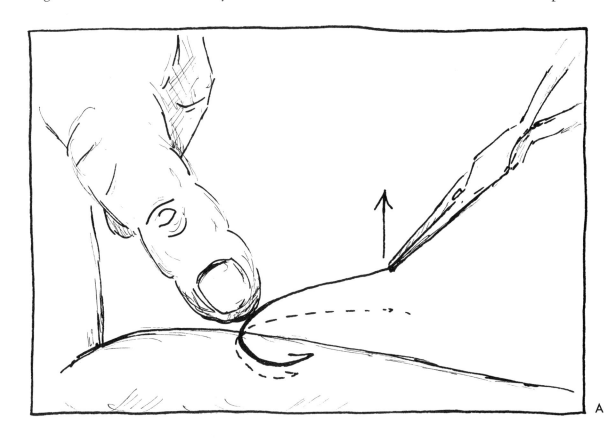

A

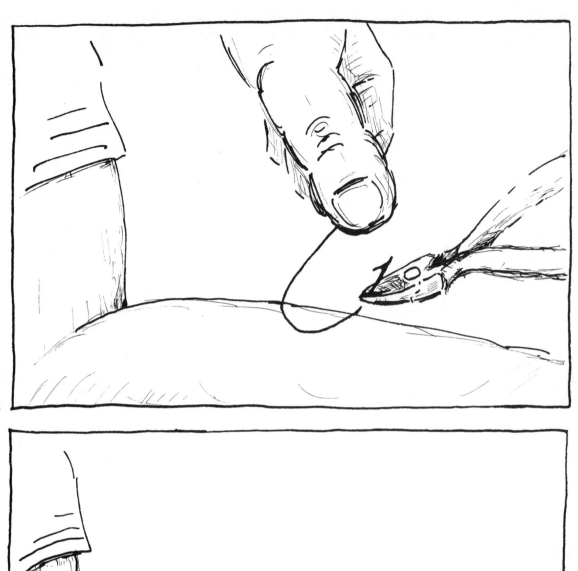

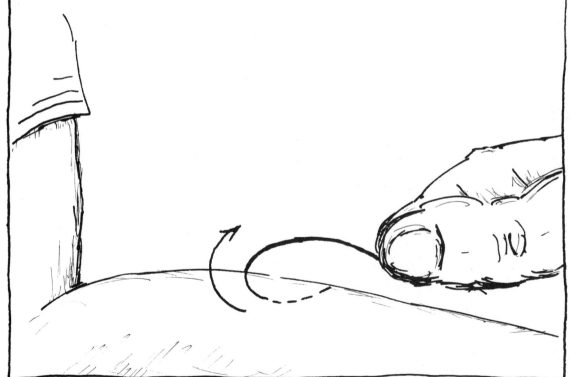

Fishhook extraction: A) after cutting hook from bait, leaving shank as long as possible, pass barb through skin to surface again; B) snip off barb with cutters; C) back bare hook out through skin and treat as a puncture wound.

likely medical problems for the canoe party, which might include the following:

Ax and Knife Cuts—Sterile gauze pads to stop bleeding and provide a dressing. Waterproof adhesive tape to secure the dressing. A provision for closing the wound—either a surgical needle and thread or instruction in the use of butterfly closures. They can be bought at the drugstore, or made from waterproof adhesive tape. Either two-by-two or three-by-three sterile pads are large enough. Adhesive tape in a one-inch width is most utilitarian—remember it might also be used to patch canvas—so have enough.

Burns—Treatment depends on severity, but burns from hot grease are particularly dangerous. No one should be allowed around the fire without protective clothing, particularly shoes. At least some of the danger of burns is reduced. Immediate immersion in cold water reduces the pain and spread of the burn. Soap will cleanse the open wound. A burn ointment will help ease the pain as time goes on.

Fishhooks—A bait should never be left on a fishing line during travel, especially if the rod is lashed into the canoe. Leaving baited rods around a campsite is dangerous. Such a rod should at least be propped up securely away from traffic, and

baits are best removed when not in use. But still occasionally someone runs into one. If the hook is driven in past the barb, just plain backing it out is almost impossible. The first aid equipment should contain a pair of cutting pliers. The embedded hook is snipped from the bait, leaving as long a shank on the hook as possible. The hook is driven through the skin past the barb. The barb is snipped off with the pliers, and the shank is then backed out. Subsequent treatment is then as for a puncture wound.

Occasionally, the hook can be backed out in the same path through which it entered, with knowledge of how to release the barb. Free the hook from the bait as before. Pass a length of fishing line inside the bend of the hook, line the hook up so that the plane of the hook is perpendicular to the skin, press down on the eye of the hook, and pull back on the line around the hook, withdrawing it. Pressing down on the eye in this position can release the barb, enabling it to be withdrawn.

Cuts and Punctures from Nails and Cans—The first aid kit can do no more than supply agents for treating the wound like any other cut. An ointment or antiseptic should be carried to prevent infection—a doctor should be consulted for suggestions. One of the antibiotic ointments may

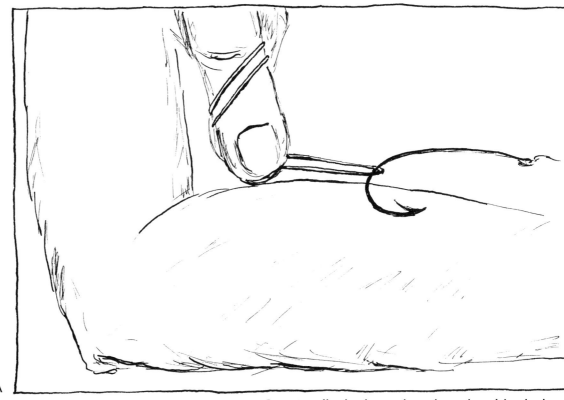

A

Occasionally, barb can be released and backed ou
A) with shank perpendicular to skin, pass line aroun
bend in hook; B) depress eye of the hook, releasin
barb; C) pull on line to back barb out.

102

be best, although they have a shelf life. Otherwise, soap and water are the best deterrents to infection. As a wise precaution, everyone should have had a recent tetanus shot or booster.

Blisters—Hands and feet in particular suffer from activities to which they are not accustomed. Paddling and portaging during the early stages of the trip will strain the Band-Aid supply—not for their antiseptic qualities, but as a pad to keep the offended area from rubbing. Better than a Band-Aid for covering blisters is a plain piece of adhesive tape. Make sure the area is clean, and smooth over it a strip of adhesive tape. Leave the tape in place until it falls off by itself. It provides a cushion between skin and that which causes the chafing. Changing the dressing, as with

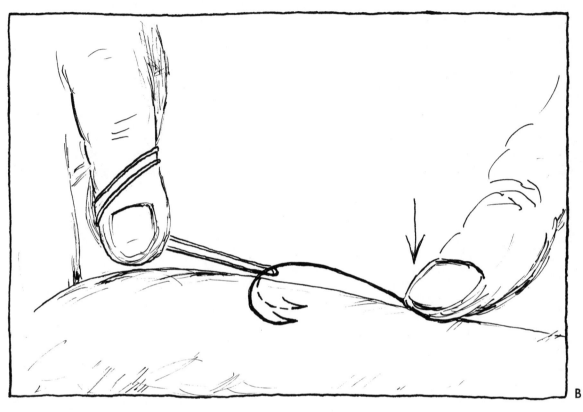

B

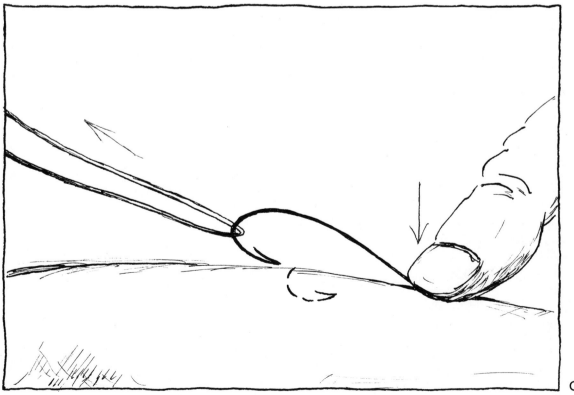

C

a Band-Aid, lifts off the new skin trying to form, and healing must start all over again. Actually, the wound will heal more quickly if left open to the air, but during the first couple of days it will appear that the Band-Aids will never last!

Stomach and Internal Disorders—The wilderness trip changes the diet and water to which most people are accustomed. In addition, the extra physical labor, or even the excitement of the trip, affect some stomachs. Normally after some discomfort, the system adjusts without much help from the first aid kit. However, some medication designed for an upset stomach and/or diarrhea would be valuable. Baking soda could help, maybe a little warm tea or soup. Otherwise, pills are more compact than liquids, easier to carry, but numerous products are available. Constipation may be a complaint for a couple days when the diet is altered, but is normally solved by including prunes and dried fruits in the diet. Of course, stomach complaints can also be signs of more serious ailments—appendicitis being the most feared in the bush—and disorders that continue more than twenty-four hours should not be treated lightly. A thermometer is useful, and high fever for more than twenty-four hours should be regarded seriously.

Sunburn and Sunstroke—The glare off the water possesses far more burning capability than the same sun in one's backyard. At least for the first couple of days everyone should have a broad-brimmed hat; the old, battered, felt hat being the time-honored bush chapeau. A sunburn ointment, maybe Chapstick, can be carried to help relieve pain and soreness; but the best solution is prevention, not cure. Sunstroke is far more serious, but little in the kit will help.

Sprains—Particularly, ankle sprains from slippery rocks and uneven portage trails. They occur much less frequently than might be supposed. The best treatment is immediate immersion in cold water to prevent swelling. Afterwards, wrapping with a two-inch Ace bandage gives some support.

Broken Bones—Slips and falls are frequent on the portage trail, but most trippers are subconsciously aware of the dangers and protect themselves as they fall, and broken bones are uncommon. The most serious injury can occur as a result of a swimmer diving into shallow water with consequent head and neck injuries. Once the danger of drowning is eliminated, moving the injured person can be extremely dangerous.

The best splint is the plastic sleeve inflated by air to be placed around an arm or leg. However, the incidence of its use is rare enough that its value is debatable. Ace bandages and roller gauze from the first aid supplies can help. Otherwise, splints, padding, and binding materials are provided from nature or from clothing.

Pain—Normally, simple aspirin or APC tablets will be enough. In case of a severe injury, where medical assistance will be sought as soon as possible, a slightly stronger pain reliever might be desirable. Normally a doctor's assistance will have to be enlisted for such a suggestion.

Infections—Surprisingly, the bush is relatively free of infection unless brought in by man. Sunlight, soap, and water are excellent deterrents. But occasionally an infection sets in; the most serious being a staph infection. Bush treatment involves the use of an antibiotic ointment—and a doctor should be consulted, although different staph infections react to different treatments. The infection should be dressed frequently and the old dressing burned to prevent spread of the contamination to others. There are some antibiotic pills that can be carried on advice from a physician. A penicillin-based treatment should be avoided; some people react violently, and not all are aware of what their reaction will be. Penicillin is safe in the hands of a doctor near help, but can be dangerous when administered by amateurs in the bush.

Bites from Bees, Wasps, and Hornets—While most people recover quickly with some discomfort and swelling, a few react violently. If so, they probably know of their allergy. For such cases, a few benedril or similar pills should be carried.

Mosquito and Blackfly Bites—A few people seem to attract more than their share. Washing with soap and water provides some relief as will immersion in cold water. The major first aid problem is caused by subsequent rubbing and scratching. Youngsters are sometimes unable to resist. Best first aid is prevention rather than cure. A tent well protected with bug netting, maybe an occasional smudge, and bug dope help. Tripping too early in June or July increases the possibility of encountering swarms of blackflies, and improperly protected campers have been driven from the bush suffering enough to require hospitalization! Wear protective clothing. Long pants, long-sleeved shirts with collars, a hat, and even a head net can be advisable. Blackflies seek exposed ankles, waistlines, necks, and wrists. The shirt should be tucked in, and the old bushman tucks his pants into his socks to protect his ankles.

Snake Bites—The farther north the party travels,

the less likely are poisonous snakes—the harmless garter snake, but no others. The garter snake bites—like other nonpoisonous snakes—and the stricken area shows tooth marks, not fangs. One of the reasons for sealing off the tent at night is to make it bug proof, but it might also include making it snake proof. It would be unusual, but the snake might crawl in during the cool evening to get warm! In poisonous snake country, carry equipment to give first aid for such emergencies.

Ear Infection—Normally caused by getting water in the ear while swimming, which fails to drain out. Such a water bubble can be broken by tilting the head and putting a couple drops of rubbing alcohol in the ear, working the lobe up and down so the alcohol penetrates the bubble, and then draining. Not much can be done for the true earache except the application of a warm oil.

Eye Infection—It is not unusual for a bug to be trapped in the eye causing momentary irritation. Flushing with clean water normally solves the problem if other attempts fail.

Toothache—A mild pain killer, usually oil of cloves, is about all that can be expected. Aspirin may work; then there are some pills that might be supplied by a doctor or dentist. A temporary filling can be made by mixing equal parts of zinc oxide powder and eugenol if absolutely necessary.

Splinters—A good pair of tweezers is valuable. Needles would normally be included with the sewing equipment.

EQUIPMENT FOR KIT

A reasonably well-equipped first aid kit might then contain the following items, quantities of each determined by the number of people, duration of the trip, and the distance from medical assistance. All should be packed in a waterproof container and carried by the person most versed in first aid. Depending on the composition of the party, it is sometimes a wise procedure to allow no one but this person to open the kit.

2 x 2 or 3 x 3 Sterile Gauze Pads
1″ and or 2″ Roller Gauze Bandages
1″ Waterproof Adhesive Tape
Band Aids
2″ Ace Bandage
Butterfly Closures (optional)

Tweezers
Cutting Pliers
Scissors
Thermometer
A Few Safety Pins
Inflatable Splint (optional)

Aspirin
Pain Reliever Stronger than Aspirin
Antiseptic—Ointment Preferably
Small Bottle of Rubbing Alcohol
Medication for Staph Infection (optional)
Benedril or Allergy Pills
Medication for Stomach Upset
Medication for Diarrhea
Burn Ointment
Toothache Supplies (optional)

First Aid Manual
Snake Bite Kit if traveling in poisonous snake country

OBTAINING ASSISTANCE

Unless absolutely necessary, do not move a patient until the extent of the injury is ascertained. Pain and muscle spasm make instant diagnosis of many conditions impossible. Let the patient rest, relax, and take time before acting rashly. Keep him quiet and warm until the proper procedure is clear. Rest and quiet are often the best immediate first aid—as long as heart and breathing are normal and there is no excessive bleeding.

People who have never traveled the wilderness always inquire what is done in case of medical emergency—and the answer, callous as it sounds, is indefinite. The best course of action should help be needed depends on the circumstances—not only the problem of where the party is and what the medical situation is, but also time of day, proximity of help, personnel available, transportation, weather, and a host of other factors.

Almost anyone encountered in the bush will spare no effort or expense to lend assistance. In case of need, any reasonable appeal will be instantly answered.

The first simple precaution is to know the exits from the area—roads and towns. Know the locations of any permanent establishments where help might be secured. Ranger stations and fire-patrol services are located through much canoe country. All are at least equipped with radio

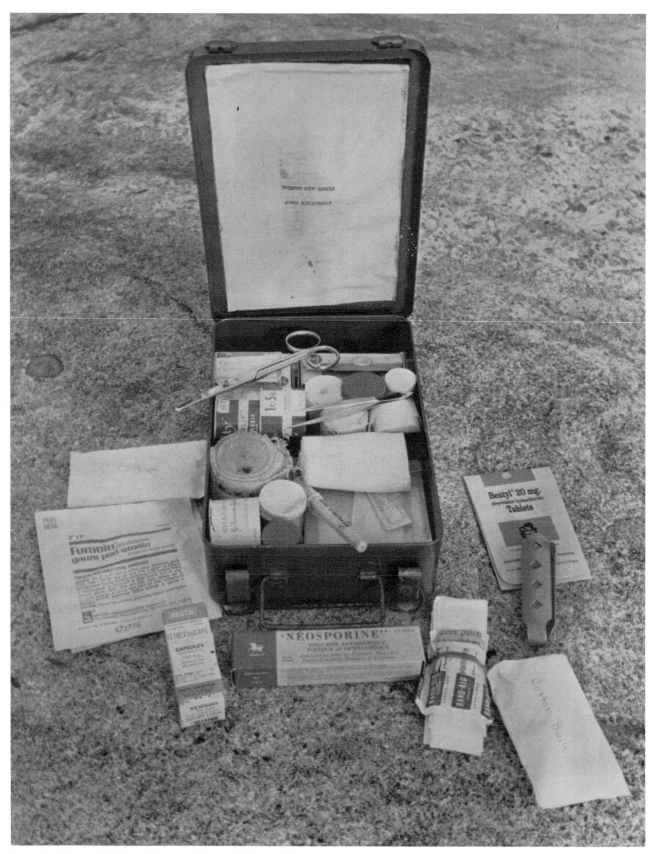

Sample first aid kit with supplies sufficient for a
party of ten for several weeks. Metal box is water-
tight; first aid manual is stored in lid.

communication to a base, in addition to having a means of transportation quicker than the canoe either at hand or on call. Lumber camps and resorts have better facilities than the canoe party. The trading post or Hudson's Bay Company post in the north are ready to help.

Then, in case of necessity, there are three possible courses of action: (1) take the injured person to the nearest place where he can be transported to medical attention; (2) attract the attention of either a passing boat, aircraft, or a ranger fire tower; or (3) send one canoe to the nearest source of help with instructions to procure an aircraft or boat to aid the injured party.

With the ambulatory injured, the first course is probably logical. One canoe can travel faster than several, so the two strongest paddlers should take the injured person and a minimum of equipment and head for help. The departing canoe should be supplied with maps, sleeping gear, and food to get them through. They may be able to travel only in daylight, so they must be prepared for whatever time the trip will take. Probably the injured person cannot help on portages, and loads should be kept to a minimum so the sternsman can take the canoe while the bowman carries the rest in one trip. Make absolutely certain the crew knows what to do to rejoin the party after their trip out. Is the rest of the group going to follow? If so, where do they expect to be on a given day, and what exact route will be followed? Are they going to stay where they are and await the return of the canoe? Anyway, decisions should be made and strictly adhered to.

If it is decided that it is best to try to attract attention from aircraft, passing boats, or fire towers, know a little about the best means of communication. There is an international standard set of ground signals, but a bush pilot will investigate any unusual signal from the ground. Such aircraft usually fly at an altitude such that ground signals can be seen easily. A large signal fire can be prepared, ready to ignite on sound of approaching aircraft. A series of three is better than a single fire, which the pilot might mistake for a campfire. Remember that small float planes usually have no instruments for flying in inclement weather or at night; so signals can be useful only in reasonable weather during daylight. The attention of a fire tower can be attracted by creating a fire which gives off a large volume of smoke. Green brush piled on a large fire on the beach may do the trick. It might be possible to set off a small island, but remember the addi-

tional problems that would occur should it get out of hand. Most fire towers are manned on a schedule, and the tower man will only be on lookout during his working hours. There are few towers manned twenty-four hours a day in all kinds of weather, and in inclement weather, the tower is likely unmanned. The schedule is most usually something like nine to five. Many areas formerly scanned from towers are now patrolled by air, so the chance of attracting a passing plane is greater. Do not overlook the possibility of using a mirror as a signalling device; such patrols fly most often in fair weather when fire danger is great. Even in areas where towers are still active, the findings are reported by radio and then investigated by air.

The third possibility is sending a canoe for help; usually to the nearest radio or means of transportation, and then requesting a plane or boat to assist the patient. However, it may be necessary to move the injured person to a place where a plane can land. The canoe making the trip should know where the plane will find the party. The plane cannot set down on the tiny pond, the rocky or shallow area, or in the midst of fast water. The chances of finding a helicopter that can set down almost anywhere are poor, but survey crews and mining operators in the north are sometimes so equipped and will obviously assist.

Meanwhile, make the injured person as comfortable as possible and wait. Quiet and rest will probably do more for the condition than anything that might be carried in the first aid kit.

Someone invariably asks whether the wilderness party should carry a radio for summoning aid in the event of an emergency. Aside from the legality of operating such a station, transmitting sets capable of reaching the outside are bulky, and their range is quite variable because of weather, time of day, and terrain—many bush pilots cannot communicate with their base until airborne. A few airlines which operate in wilderness areas do have for rent sets which can communicate with their base; usually available only if that airline is contracted to perform other services for the party. There is normally a prearranged schedule for regular communication with the agreement that should the party fail to meet the schedule a search will be made by air—at the expense of the party; which could be quite costly in the event that communication failed because of transmission difficulties.

7

WILDLIFE

The wilderness canoeist expects to encounter wildlife, but unless a determined effort is made, the canoe party is likely to be disappointed. Only very inquisitive animals intentionally have anything to do with man, and often more wildlife is spotted driving isolated highways than encountered in the bush by accident. Try Yellowstone for bear, Algonquin Park for deer, and the Trans-Canada Highway for moose!

Still, magazines frequently carry stories of sensational adventures leaving the inexperienced reader with the impression that encounters with wildlife are frequent and dangerous. Rarely will any animal—large or small—intentionally attack or have anything to do with the canoe party. The greatest source of trouble comes from an interference by man with the animal's young, and most of the large female wild animals possess strong maternal instincts—even if father deserts his family after the mating season. Otherwise, a truly wild animal attacks or fights only if cornered, exceptionally hungry because of a disappearance of his natural foods, or perhaps because of sickness or a hatred of man born of some past contact. More dangerous are those animals who have learned to enjoy the leavings of man; the garbage-dump bear, for instance.

But dangerous encounters during the canoeing season are very rare, and traveling the bush is infinitely safer than the highways! When most mating seasons roll around, the canoesman is off

the water, so there is little danger from the animal whose habits are altered by the rut.

What follows is not an attempt to describe fully the most frequently encountered wildlife—just briefly their relations to the canoe party that is interested in photographing or observing, and perhaps concerned about meetings on the water, portage, or campsite.

MAMMALS

Moose

The moose is the largest, most formidable-looking animal likely to be encountered. He frequents damp, wet, marshy areas in the north. Flies drive him into the water for protection and food. He is a vegetarian and is most normally encountered while rounding a bend in the stream or lake, to be discovered standing knee deep—or more—in water, occasionally dropping his head into the water to feed or drink. He will retreat to higher ground to bed down until the flies drive him back again, and so can be encountered at any hour of the day.

He travels the portage trails—as will any game —if that happens to be the easiest route, but rarely will he be seen along the carry. He practically never stumbles into the canoesman's camp.

His senses of smell and hearing are well developed, though his eyesight is less keen, and a canoe can approach quite close while he is in the water if made from downwind quietly. He will spot movement, but if he neither smells nor hears the canoe, the paddlers can often move closer when he dips his head into the water if the canoe rests quietly, almost motionless, when he looks around. In moose country, travel should be along the shore, and quiet should be maintained, for he may be just around the next bend.

The female travels with her calf, but the bull with the massive rack is a loner and is completely disinterested in the cow except during the rut. After the mating season he drops his horns, to grow another set each year. Occasionally a horn dropped the previous winter is found lying in the bush, but rodents make quick work of them, and only a horn dropped in the water is likely to be found in good condition by the next summer. The horns are shed individually, so a pair is rarely found together, although having rubbed one off on a tree, the bull will try to free the remaining horn as quickly as possible. Early in the canoeing season his rack will still be in velvet—which he rubs off as the spring and summer progress—but when the canoesman hits the water, his rack will be fully developed.

Occasionally, a swimming moose is encountered, or one that can be forced to swim if the canoe gets between him and the forest. He swims like a horse and is almost defenseless in the water. A canoe pair can paddle faster than he swims, and the canoe can be paddled right next to him without danger. Only his massive head will be held above water, and a bowman can hop from the canoe onto the swimming moose for a ride with no danger—except from the flies. The moose's

Swimmer grasps ears or horns to avoid sliding down moose's back.

back will be angled downwards almost 45°, so in leaping aboard, the rider must grasp the ears or horns, or he will slip down the moose's rump. Perhaps there could be some danger if the swimmer dives underwater and encounters sharp hooves, but otherwise the rider is safe. The moose is so intent on keeping his head above water, he can do no damage with either rack or teeth—and will not try. He will tire quickly with a rider, who should obviously slip off before the animal starts to flounder. A calf cannot support the extra load, but the full-grown cow or bull has little trouble.

As soon as the moose catches shore, the ride is definitely over. He will take to the bush with amazing speed and ability to navigate between trees even with his massive rack, and the rider on dry land will not stay in the saddle long.

The frightened moose will be heard pounding back into the bush for a short period, but quiet will soon reign as he picks his way through the forest. His memory is short, and as soon as the flies become unbearable, he will be back in the water again, often in exactly the same area.

As the mating season approaches, the bull becomes a different animal. His horns become weapons to win from other bulls his cow or cows, and man may also become an enemy. The likelihood of his charging or even approaching man during the summer is negligible, but come fall, his search for the cow and willingness to fight for his right could make a chance encounter on the portage trail or campsite dangerous.

Bear

Canoe country is often black bear country—maybe the grizzly in the far remote Northwest —other varieties being less likely. The bear is essentially a vegetarian, getting most of his summer food from berries. He is also a little bit of a fisherman and a large part scavenger. He will settle down to dinner at any garbage dump he can find, and so may approach the campsite—particularly a well-used one where previous parties have carelessly disposed of their waste, leaving an attractive feeding area, which accounts for ninety-five percent of the adventure stories involving meetings with bears.

He is inquisitive and equipped with an excellent sense of smell. He finds bacon, for instance, particularly attractive. But he will also visit just for the sake of seeing what is there. He can puncture unopened cans with his claws, crushing the can as he does so, and often will just leave his spoils without feeding. He might find a canoe turned over on shore and rip out the bottom to see what is under it, whereas he might leave the canoe alone that is turned right-side up where he can see there is nothing of interest. He will be attracted by fats—lard and the like—and by sugar in particular, and it is not unusual for him to break into cabins and other structures in search of food —or seemingly often just for the sport of it.

However, the bear who has not learned to feed off man's leavings who intentionally visits the campsite where the smell of man lingers is unusual. Protective measures are rarely necessary around the wilderness campsite; he is much more of a threat on the well-traveled route around frequently used sites.

An intricate early warning system can be rigged by circling the tent area by a string to which cans are attached so that when the bear stumbles on the trip wire the clatter set up by the cans will arouse the sleepers and drive him off. The construction of such a trap will entertain the youngsters for awhile, but insistence on such a rig imparts to them an unnecessary fear of bears.

There are some old-timers who place their axes in easy reach when they retire, but light and noise usually drive him off—either an open fire or a flashlight.

Provisions having smells that might attract him to the campsite—of which side bacon is the most attractive—are best sealed. If bear visits are a threat, hang supplies from a tree limb high enough above the ground so the bear cannot reach the prize. Pick a limb too small to support his weight and removed from the tent area so the bear will head there rather than toward the sleepers.

The bear is occasionally found swimming a river or lake. He can move rapidly in water, though he takes to deep water only to travel. While paddlers can sometimes overtake him, close approach is ill-advised—he can do a vicious job on the canoe with one swipe of his claws.

Encounters on land are more likely. There is no likelihood of outrunning him; he moves with amazing speed with a rocking gait as his rump rises higher than his head. He is most often observed from the water as he meanders along shore, picking his way over rocks and through bush, apparently completely oblivious to the canoe lying off shore; knowing he can escape any time he wants. And the really wild bear has been known to stop and stare at those strange objects out on the water until the canoes close in and his nose tells him he better retreat.

The wild bear is partial to country where he can find fruit—berries and other delicacies. As such, burned-over or logged areas where blueberries and raspberries grow in the open spaces are his most likely habitat. He will walk the shore of the lake or river for water and maybe fish, or just because it is the easiest path in search of food.

He travels the forest trail of least resistance, which might include the portage trail. But he probably will not stay around once alerted to the presence of man. Only when the traveler finds himself between a sow and her young is there serious cause for alarm. At first sign of danger she will gather up the cubs and head them for safety, often having them tree nearby. Avoid the attraction offered by the cubs—herein lies the second greatest threat posed by the bear: she may attack to protect them!

Occasionally, someone decides a cub would be an interesting pet. He is just a cute, cuddly teddy bear when a couple months old. But beware when he grows; he has claws that will rip the bottom of the canoe to shreds in seconds. But more important, should her cub be carried off, the sow will follow as long as she can pick up his scent—which could be days. She will go to almost any extreme to get him back.

Caribou

In the far north there is the possibility of an encounter with woodland caribou—the barren land variety north of the tree line. The latter type is a migratory herd animal whose movements still defy explanation even to the northern native who in the past used to rely on the caribou to such an extent that when the herd failed to appear, starvation likely resulted.

Encounters with the woodland variety are slightly more likely, but he lives north of the moose, and the trip is now close to the Canadian tree line. He is smaller than a moose with a rack that is more delicate and without the heavy flat boards of the moose. He might be standing in the water as the bend is rounded, but is more likely on land having come down only for a drink. He will retreat when he discovers man, moving through the forest with great ease in spite of his massive rack. More likely than a sighting is the discovery of an unfamiliar rack at some abandoned northern Indian hunting camp—one which might otherwise seem to be that of a deer.

Deer

The canoesman expecting to sight deer is much

farther south, but is frequently disappointed. Unlike the moose, deer come down to the shore only for water and then head back to higher, dry ground during the day. The canoesman will have greatest luck early in the morning or in the evening along quiet water.

Occasionally, one is encountered swimming, like the moose or bear, but again these occasions are rare. Encounters on portage trails are more likely during normal traveling hours, though the startled deer will probably hide or leave too quickly to be observed.

His visits to the campground are negligible, and even should he appear, his presence carries no threat to the party. He will not attack or invade the supplies anyway—at least in canoe season.

Wolves

Very rare is the sighting of a wolf, but occasionally in the evenings his calls back and forth across the hills provide entertainment. As one family starts baying at the moon from a distant hill, other wolves will answer from around the lake, until a chorus echoes through the still evening.

There is little danger of the wolf approaching camp, though he may observe from a distance, and perhaps his tracks can be discovered in the morning. The savagery of the legendary wolf pack has been considerably dispelled by better research —thus, a summer traveler should have no fear.

Lynx

This tawny cat is a rarity, but if a whiskered creature with long legs and short tail disappears from the shoreline, the paddlers had a brief glimpse of a lynx.

An unusual encounter with a swimming lynx

Wolverine

An equally unlikely encounter. He is the robber of the north and steals with great cunning. Tales of the carcajou outwitting the winter trapper can be entertaining and fascinating—except to the man involved.

Fox

Much more likely to be encountered than the wolf, the wild fox is almost as timid. Be very suspicious of the fox that approaches the campsite —usually in a well-traveled area—much like a lost pet dog. He may well be sick, and his bite could be dangerous as a result.

Beaver

The beaver is probably the most frequently encountered aquatic animal. He makes his home along the bank or in a mound in the center of a pond.

He feeds on the bark and shoots of poplar and birch by choice, and near the house he may have felled trees of amazing size. His work is often nocturnal, and occasionally the sound of the falling tree in the quiet evening denotes the beaver at work.

Like humans, the beaver differs greatly in his industry. The bank beaver along the lake or river just draws his food from the nearby shore. The pond beaver works harder, erecting dams to flood areas so he can reach food and float it down to his house. He often impounds large areas, frequently turning the small stream into a veritable swamp in a short time.

His work may be a boon to travel, but more often creates obstacles, flooding out campsites and portages and generally altering the proportion of water and land designed by nature. Breaking his dams performs no long-range service; he quickly senses the change of water level in his house, and repairs will be underway quickly.

His house is entered underwater, but his living quarters are above water; usually a two-room dwelling with one room for drying his fur at water level, and a second living room at a higher, drier level. The kits remain at home for a year, and whole families are often observed—usually early in the morning or toward evening.

The mature beaver, with his broad tail, is sometimes sighted swimming along, nose just above water. On approach, the tail rises and descends on the water with the traditional resounding "thwack," warning others of danger; where-

Beaver house built along the lake shore

upon, he dives immediately. He may surface several times before gaining the safety of his home or other protection, and gliding along, the canoesman can watch his steady progress toward safety.

The beaver poses no threat to the campsite, though his nocturnal labors may be undertaken close by. He rarely enters man's habitat and takes little interest in man's equipment—though his teeth make it possible for him to chew through wood with amazing speed—but the incidence of his approaching canoes and paddles with a gleam in his eye is almost unknown.

Otter

The otter is the most playful and inquisitive of the aquatic animals. He slips and slides through mud and down chutes into the water just for the sport of it, and sometimes can be surprised at play. More often the canoesman sights his whiskered face elevated above water as he watches the approaching canoes; he looks much like a seal. He will watch awhile, dive, swim away, surface again, and take another look before disappearing. If the canoes get close enough, the paddlers will hear the otter talking to them—or maybe he is spitting at them!

His only threat to the canoe party comes from his interest in fish. The Indian loses some from his net to the otter; the canoesman lacks a net, but the otter has been known to steal fish left on a stringer in the water overnight.

Muskrats, Fishers, Mink, Weasels (Ermine in the winter)

These animals are occasionally sighted, but

none will approach man intentionally, though they may be somewhat inquisitive about the passing canoe. None will invade the campground.

Skunk

The wood pussy is first a scavenger, has little fear of man, and possesses a natural inquisitiveness that allows him to invade the campsite, meaning no harm, but fully prepared to protect himself.

He can be encountered along the forest trail, but is just as likely to come visiting. He will be attracted by uncovered food and may be difficult to discourage from staying around until his desires are satisfied.

He rarely defends himself unless startled or attacked, and he can usually be convinced to go his own way with gentle urging and a display of quiet activity and light. The unexcited skunk rarely damages the outfit, but trying to rush his departure could be unwise.

Speaking quietly to him and exposure to a flashlight normally convince him he is unwanted, and he will waddle off at his own speed. Children and dogs pose the greatest threats to a calm, quiet approach to the visitor.

Beware of the skunk who turns his face to look back at a viewer as he raises his tail toward his enemy. His discharge can be injurious to the eyes, as well as unpleasant. The family dog is most often the victim in such situations.

Should he let go with his powerful scent, it takes a lot of washing to remove traces of his presence; discarding clothes permeated with his odor may be easier. Wash clothes, humans or pets in tomato juice, or a fifty-fifty solution of white vinegar and water may work. Baking soda dissolved in water might help.

Porcupine

Porky travels at about the same leisurely pace as the skunk. He is primarily attracted to the campsite by salt, which he discovers on paddle shafts, ax handles, tump lines, and carrying straps where sweat has left a salt residue. He can, and does, do a job on sweat-soaked wood, gnawing away not with the speed and spectacular results of the beaver but with effectiveness.

Paddles stored under the canoe at night are usually relatively safe. The ax should be propped so the handle is above ground where the porcupine is less likely to discover it.

The porcupine cannot throw his quills, contrary to popular belief, but transfers them to anyone who contacts him. Each quill is equipped with tiny barbs and, if not removed, will work deeply into the flesh. His quills can gradually pass completely through a fleshy area, to appear opposite their point of entry much later.

Painful as the process may be, they should be removed immediately using a pair of pliers to pull them out without snapping the quill. Removal can be aided by prior application of a baking-soda solution. The family dog may not understand the service being done for him, so holding him may be a task; made easier if his head can be covered with a piece of cloth, or at least his eyes covered.

Like the skunk, the porcupine can usually be urged to depart quietly. Avoid getting too close, but he can be pressured more firmly than the skunk—though under pressure he tends to stop, sit, and bristle his quills, waiting for his enemy to make contact.

Raccoons, Squirrels, Chipmunks, and Rodents

These animals all make inquisitive visits to the campsite, but cause little trouble provided foods are secured to prevent looting. Given no openings, they cannot quickly enter packs, wooden, or metal containers. Occasionally they will be attracted by salt and will chew on salty leather.

Squirrels and chipmunks in areas frequently used for campsites become quite tame and sassy and scamper through the area looking for handouts. Many can be enticed into posing by offering bannock or corn bread crumbs left out for them a short distance from traffic of the party. Some can even perhaps be drawn in to accept offerings by hand. The red squirrel in particular can become quite demanding in his insistence on attention and handouts.

CACHES

Occasionally a canoeist may need to invent or construct a cache, and wildlife poses the greatest threat to its well-being. True outdoorsmen would never raid a cache, and the native would only disturb such supplies in dire emergency, and then he will go to great lengths to repay that which was borrowed.

Caches of three kinds might be employed: (1) that around the campsite to protect food for the night, or maybe for a day while the party sidetrips; (2) that left for a period of time to be picked up later in the same season; and (3) that which might be stored for considerable periods, perhaps until next year.

Campsite Caches

Storage on the campsite would normally require only the tight closing of the containers used for portaging. The smell of man will usually discourage the larger animals, and the smaller ones find gnawing into the containers too time-consuming.

However, should it be necessary, a pack can be hung from the branch of a tree, high enough so that it cannot be reached, and secured to a branch small enough so as not to bear the weight of large, climbing animals.

Another method would involve bending down a sapling, tying the pack to its top, and then letting it spring back upright. A birch makes the best storage; it will bend without breaking and spring back easily.

Caches for a Period of Time

A party leaving a jump-off spot to return by the same route may want to cache supplies for the last couple of days so that weights do not have to be carried over all the portages only to end up being used on the voyage out.

Leave only supplies that can be protected from moisture. Canned goods are easy; others have to be waterproofed. Do not leave foods whose odors will naturally attract wildlife. A rock hiding area is usually relatively safe; perhaps a small cave or crevice that will be protected from the elements. Block the entrance with large rocks to discourage animals. Logs may have to be employed if rock is unavailable.

Storage in small trees, as in the campsite, is also possible, but more difficult to waterproof.

Permanent Caches

The Indian makes a permanent cache by building a rack six to eight feet above ground. He normally cuts off three or four trees at this height, or sinks posts to stand this tall (obviously harder), and builds a rack of poles on top of his posts. He builds his platform to extend over the uprights, so an animal climbing the posts is blocked by the platform and will have trouble getting over its lip. He further defeats them by topping each post with an upturned metal pail—a lard pail is usual—or he arranges a metal skirt around each pole so the animal cannot climb around the skirt.

Tree cache: rope tossed over branch and pack is then pulled up and rope secured around the trunk.

Indian permanent cache: platform built on tree stumps; tops of posts are often capped with upturned lard pails to prevent invasion of climbing animals.

He places his cache on the platform and lashes a tarp (or in these days, sheets of polyethylene) over it so that it cannot be lifted off by the wind and provides waterproofing. He frequently leaves a canoe used for inland travel cached on a rack, so that he can store supplies under it supported on the thwarts.

The vacationer probably does not want to spend the time and effort to build such an arrangement, but the native would probably not object to having his cache used for a little storage for a week or so.

BIRDS

In the still of early morning or dusk, before or

114

after the breeze rustles the trees, the quiet of the wilderness is punctuated by the winged population. Their presence or absence may not be apparent when other sounds overshadow their calls. In addition to the normal songbirds, which can be identified with pleasure and excitement by the ornithologist, of particular interest for the canoesman are the water fowl.

Loons

The loon is seen most normally on the calm evening lake. His plaintive wail as he swims slowly along, looking for fish, echoes through the calm. On occasions as many as a dozen loons flock together, but normally there are only several birds on a particular section of water. The absence of loons on northern water is said to indicate the water is fished out—an impression open to debate.

The loon does take to the air, but his seemingly continuous swimming and diving provide entertainment. He needs a long runway to become airborne and looks quite clumsy and inept on take off. He prefers to remain on or under the water so far as the canoesman is concerned, and he has a fascinating ability to vary his buoyancy so that sometimes he floats high on the water and at other times submerges so that only a little of his neck shows. He has no rating as a source of food; the recipe for loon requires boiling him in salted water into which a rock has been tossed for several hours, and then discarding the loon and eating the rock. The Indian occasionally does use him, but he is usually hunted by youngsters with slingshots rather than wasting ammunition on him.

Ducks

Early in the season the duck family will entertain as the canoesmen paddle along. There are many varieties, but as the fledglings and their mother are approached, any female will head the youngsters toward shore and protection while she tries to lead the canoes away from her brood with a broken wing act that will go on until she thinks all danger is past. Her antics can provide entertainment for a mile or more of otherwise calm water.

Geese

Although many geese summer in the very far north, there are still many to be found in northern canoe country, usually in small family nesting groups. When molting, geese fly only short distances at best. Frightened by approaching canoes, the molting birds seek shelter along shore in grass and low bush. But a goose out on the water thinks he is hidden if he puts his head in the water—like the classic ostrich—and the canoe can get quite close. When approaching a goose hiding on shore or one cornered by the canoe, be ready; the goose is likely to take flight, heading directly toward the paddlers, and the mature bird looks like a formidable missile. He is not attacking; he just wants out.

Like the duck, he is a valuable source of food. But he is out of season in canoeing weather, and, besides, he and the duck have a summer fish diet. The hunter should wait for a grain-fed legal bird.

Gulls

The snow-white northern gull takes over rocky islands for nesting, and glides and soars on the wind currents when returning to home base—not to be used for campgrounds; the chance of bombing attacks by screeching gulls is great. Watching their swoops and dives as they search for food offers entertainment while paddling along.

Whiskey Jacks

Whiskey jacks are known as Canadian jays to the Audubon Society, and are not water fowls but deserve special mention. They are saucy scavengers who frequent campsites, begging crumbs and picking up leavings—with about the same familiarity as the red squirrel. Completely lacking shyness and fear, the whiskey jack can often be enticed into feeding close at hand, unlike the average songbird.

SNAKES

The farther north, the less likely are poisonous snakes. Whether poisonous or not, the snake seeks a warm, calm spot for his daytime snooze, but avoids heat. He is met along portages and around the campsite lying on a warm rock, behind a log, or hidden behind brush.

Warned of the approach of man, the snake will disappear, but if suddenly startled, while his natural desire may be escape, he will strike when cornered. Treading carefully, watching foot placement eliminates most chance encounters. Above poisonous snake country, the bite of a garter snake will cause few complications, but leather boots through which the snake cannot bite might be worn south of this border.

On rare occasions snakes have been known to seek warmth in the cool of the evening, and whether poisonous or not, the sudden discovery of a snake that has crawled into the tent and found the warm bedding—either before or after it is occupied—can be unnerving. Ordinary procedures in pitching the tent that make it bug-proof will also make it snake-proof. A floored tent in snake country makes sense; otherwise the walls should be tucked in under the ground cloths; if necessary, rocking or tying down the corners and edges. Securing the bug netting even when the tent is unoccupied will keep out snakes as well as bugs. If concerned about an encounter, inspect the bedding before crawling in for the night.

8

MEAL PLANNING AND OUTFITTING

The days of beans and hardtack are long since past; if they ever existed. Modern packaging, dehydration, and freeze-drying make for little change in eating habits and diet, subject to the lack of refrigeration and the inability to replenish perishable supplies.

On any extended trip an occasional debate always occurs over the foods most craved. Some of the conversation may center on exotic dishes, but older campers will most desire salad greens, fresh fruit, and fresh meat. Youngsters usually crave milk, ice cream, milk shakes, candy, soda pop, and hamburgers.

Weight must influence meal planning, but within reason canoes can carry any provisions the crews are willing to portage, and it is unnecessary to "go light" at the sacrifice of a balanced, attractive diet.

Planning the menu for a first trip is difficult. There are always items overlooked and others overstocked. Err on the side of carrying too much rather than too little. The perfectly outfitted trip leaves the bush with almost empty packs—just a few staples rattling around in the bottom of the wannigan. But it is better to have an extra day's food than to look in the wannigans that last day and find the cupboard bare.

The canoeist can do some "living off the land" with fish and berries. Planning a meal or two of fish makes sense, but the traveling party will go hungry if fish refuse to cooperate. It is wiser to

outfit so fish are a supplement, not a necessity.

The Indian lives on "country provisions"; he has no closed seasons. But the vacationer will find most game out of season for him, and in many areas it is illegal to carry firearms in the summer.

There are many good publications on survival techniques, indicating edible berries and greens that grow abundantly in the forest. Without adequate knowledge, do not rely on such fare except in emergency. The neophyte will recognize some natural products like blueberries and raspberries, but it takes an experienced woodsman to find edible products in sufficient quantity to depend on them. Experimenting blindly can be unpleasant; some forest products can be harmful; some even poisonous.

Some trip leaders block out a meal schedule with a set daily menu. In theory, such planning sounds commendable, but in practice there are problems. Perhaps the menu for an evening requires time for preparation, and maybe the day was long and hard and dinner should be quick. Or maybe it is raining and something more simple would fill the bill better. There are many situations where flexibility is desirable.

More flexible planning is accomplished by counting the meals without requiring that either a certain menu be followed for a particular meal, or even that certain combinations of dishes always go together.

First, decide how much concern should be

given to (1) weight and (2) expense. Second, how much meal preparation is to be done from scratch; that is, combining basic ingredients to make different dishes? How much will consist of opening prepared foods and merely heating them? Third, there are alternatives as to the kinds of food carried: (1) some fresh foods keep without refrigeration, and others last only a couple days; (2) canned foods come in great variety; (3) package mixes; for instance, pancake, cake, biscuit, even pizza mix; (4) dehydrated foods—potatoes, for example, are on every grocer's shelf; but there are several companies that market complete lines of dehydrated foods for campers. Their products vary from packages containing only one item to those containing complete meals; (5) freeze-dried foods, about similar to dehydrated in weight, but normally closer in taste and appearance to fresh produce, and more expensive; (6) dry foods not normally classified as dehydrated—like cereals, rice, spaghetti, macaroni, cocoa, coffee, tea, to list a few.

Along with the advent of freeze-dried foods and tremendous increase in interest in backpacking, packages containing complete meals—from soup to nuts—have evolved. And there is no reason why the canoe party cannot outfit with such packaged meals; in which case most of the suggestions that follow are superfluous. Just make sure that expense is a secondary consideration. The use of such meals will also make for a different attitude around the kitchen. There is not much variety in preparation; the meal is readied by adding water, and that is it.

Anyway, as food planning gets under way, locate a source of supply for the desired products. The local grocery has fresh foods, canned ones, various standard household mixes, dry goods, and some dehydrated products. But many dehydrated and freeze-dried foods must be procured elsewhere. Maybe stores or outfitters on the fringe of canoe country have such products in stock, but placing reliance on local suppliers without advance knowledge is chancy. Dehydrated and freeze-dried foods are more surely obtained from a local camping store, the mail-order camping outfit, or directly from the manufacturer. In any event, planning and assembling supplies takes time.

Some sacrifice should be made for the sake of bulk and/or weight. There is little point in carrying a can of soup weighing a pound when a package of dehydrated soup weighs ounces and could substitute easily. A can of spaghetti is quick, but infinitely heavier than the raw ingredients. A couple of pounds of fresh potatoes carried for a week only to be mashed is senseless when a little package can provide almost the same meal. This does not mean all foods should be dehydrated or freeze-dried. First, they are expensive; but more important, such a diet becomes terribly monotonous. In spite of the claims of producers, much lightweight food has a blandness, and the finished product has the unappetizing appearance of dog food, and while probably quite nutritious, it is often hard to distinguish a meal of baked beans from one of corned beef.

Suppose the intended trip is for two weeks and three meals a day are required. Each is quite different, or at least should be for variety. Most people have a preconceived notion of what is meant by *breakfast*, and there is no reason to abandon such an impression, but it is an important meal. The heavy work should be done before noon, and breakfast supplies the necessary energy. Lunch should be relatively quick if there is distance to cover. And the fewer pots and pans to wallop, the quicker the canoes are back on the water. Dinner normally occurs at a more relaxed time when it is possible to concoct more complicated dishes. Besides, if that stuffed feeling exists after dinner, there is no need to portage or paddle on a full stomach. It is possible to sit back, relax, and let the meal digest.

The trip schedule should include occasional "rest days" or "half days"—maybe to fish, or just relax; and in two weeks there is almost certain to be a day or two when weather dictates staying put on a campsite—wind, cold, or rain. Here is the opportunity to bake bread, simmer a pot of soup, bake beans, have pancakes for breakfast. The menu can allow for a few meals that take extra preparation.

The two-week trip will need fourteen breakfasts, fourteen lunches, and the same number of dinners. For the first couple of days, appetites may lag, but as the trip progresses the group will likely become more ravenous. The suggested servings that follow are of course only approximate, but, if anything, lean on the plentiful side. In estimating quantities of dehydrated or freeze-dried products and packaged meals, some reliance must be placed on the producer's advice as to the number of servings per package; but often the quantity involved is overestimated. Without previous experience with a certain product, assume a package labeled as sufficient for four will be about right for three active trippers; and if the party includes teen-agers, their appetites are likely to surpass either adults or younger campers.

BREAKFASTS

Fruit

Fresh fruit—oranges, grapefruit, and the like—can be carried for a couple days. After that, reliance should be placed on dried fruits. Easily available are prunes, peaches, apricots, and apples. They swell when cooked. About two ounces of dried fruit makes a serving for one person; slightly less in the case of apples. There are also available prepared packages of dried fruit ready to cook. Applesauce is one of the most common. The package usually contains sugar in addition to the fruit. Straight dried fruits are better if cooked with sugar; for which, preparation should be allowed in the outfitting.

Fruit Juices

Canned juices are terribly heavy and should be omitted. There are many packaged juices in powder and crystal form. Most of which are somewhat close to the original. Usually they improve if less water is added than recommended. However, the group will travel better on fruit; the juices just provide something tasty to drink in place of water.

Cereal

Either cold or hot cereal, maybe some of each, should be brought along. Cold cereals are available in individual packages for easy serving and carrying. They are light, but extremely bulky.

Hot cereal sticks to the ribs better and provides the basic ingredient for most breakfasts. Starting with the old northern standby of oatmeal, there are many others. Their boxes all specify the ratio of cereal to water, but in general one ounce of cereal will make a serving for one. Some manufacturers even offer an "instant" hot cereal.

Everyone will want sugar and milk for cereal. Try using brown sugar instead of white. Skim-milk powder is satisfactory. There are also a few brands of powdered whole milk that are more expensive, but maybe more tasty. Or canned evaporated milk can be used. Straight from the can, it makes a substitute for cream and is quite rich. It is intended that it be mixed fifty-fifty with water. (Condensed milk is not the same; it is sweetened and looks like a thick syrup and is used in cooking.)

Bacon

A couple of strips of bacon go a long way toward making the meal. Bacon fat should never be discarded. It can be used for frying fish (or anything else), makes a good substitute for shortening (and often a pleasant change), and has countless other cooking uses. Bacon will keep for weeks, though is should be kept out of the direct sun and must be covered from flies. Side bacon, unsliced, keeps better than presliced, and real smoked bacon, if it can be found, keeps better than sugar-cured. Canned sliced bacon is available if preferred. Allow about three or four ounces of bacon per person per meal.

Eggs

Fresh eggs can be carried for at least three or four days. They need careful packing to prevent breakage; with care, sectional cardboard egg cartons will work. It is better to pack the eggs in a box filled with sawdust—an egg wannigan; or pack them in a container otherwise filled with something like flour or cereal.

After the fresh eggs run out, powdered eggs or a prepared egg mix can be substituted. And there are freeze-dried scrambled eggs available. Powdered eggs have a shelf life of six months to a year. Then there are dehydrated egg or omelet mixes that perhaps make a passable egg substitute. A diet of powdered eggs or egg mixes gets tiring, and it would be unusual to include them every breakfast, but a couple of meals might be in order.

Pancakes

Cooking pancakes for more than a couple people is time-consuming, and they are better reserved for a rest day. Still, a camping trip seems to demand a couple of pancake breakfasts.

A choice has to be made whether to use prepared mixes or make the batter from basic ingredients. The latter course leaves more flexibility and is not very difficult.

Pancakes need syrup. The real stuff is extremely heavy and bulky, and unless it is *real* maple syrup, there are packages of syrup mix that do just as well with the addition of a little hot water; or just as good syrup can be made from water, brown sugar, and maple flavoring.

Baked Goods

With a reflector, almost anything that can be baked in the home oven can be prepared in the bush. Normal breakfast additions might include corn bread, biscuits, and muffins (if the reflector has a muffin tin). But since baking takes more time than the traveling party usually spends preparing breakfast, the actual cooking is better done the previous night.

Beverage

No breakfast is complete without a pot of coffee! Or maybe tea. Anyway, a hot beverage. Coffee can be instant or the real stuff. Tea, the same—either tea bags or bulk tea. Youngsters may scorn both, and cocoa might be better.

If there is complete lack of agreement on the morning beverage, supply a pot of hot water and let each person make his own coffee, tea, or cocoa. Space on the fire will not allow for a pot of each, even if there were enough pots.

Fish

For the traveling party, the most available fishing time is after dinner, and so fish often make a breakfast supplement. After the bacon is fried, the pan is ready for the fillets. A meal consisting of fruit, cereal, bacon, and coffee is really all that needs to be provided, and the added fish will fill any void.

LUNCHES

Lunch involves more variation, such as: (1) the cold meal, for which sandwiches or concentrated quick-energy foods come to mind first; (2) the more or less one-pot meal, or that in which there is only one dish as the main course—like baked beans, stew, spaghetti, macaroni, or Spanish rice; (3) the meal made up of a meat, a vegetable, and a starch—like the normal dinner.

The lunch should be packed the night before in one wannigan so that at the lunchsite, only that wannigan and the jewelry are opened. The rest of the outfit remains secured.

The first lunch or two might be sandwiches manufactured the day before, or made on the spot from fresh supplies—meat, cheese, lettuce, tomatoes, etc. Later, cold lunches could be made with canned luncheon meats, precooked ham, cheese, and canned fruit, or something similar that does not require heating. The backpacker maybe prefers concentrated, high-energy foods.

Even so, the time saved by not making a fire is

of questionable value—the party just tires that much more quickly in the afternoon.

Variety in one-pot dishes is not great, but the canoeist might seriously consider the hot meal.

Beans

Baked beans offer a standard, quick, one-pot meal. Dehydrated beans are available, but normally taste less acceptably than canned ones, which come in all sizes, shapes, and descriptions, with or without additives. Figure on a ten- to fifteen-ounce can per person if that is all that is served. The meal is enhanced by adding a can of diced luncheon meat if straight beans are used, or maybe a couple of slices of fried luncheon meat per person.

Better than canned or dehydrated beans by a long shot are those baked on the trail. But this is about an eight-hour project, either overnight in hot sand, or all day at the campfire.

Stew

Canned beef or chicken stews make a good meal, but are terrifically heavy. There are many brands; some with more meat and less potatoes than others. All have a high gravy content, which accounts for the weight. It takes close to a pound of stew per person per meal.

Every producer of dehydrated supplies has a list of stews. In spite of the various names they all taste and look much the same. The packages are light, easy to prepare—usually requiring nothing but boiling for awhile—and make acceptable one-pot lunches. But avoid relying on them completely without having first experimented. They are a boon to the backpacker, but the canoeist need not be so weight-conscious.

Spaghetti or Macaroni

About four to five ounces of dry spaghetti or macaroni will produce a generous serving. Both probably require a sauce. Whether added to the pot before serving or poured over later is immaterial. Adding to the pot reduces the jewelry that must be walloped.

There are innumerable canned spaghetti sauces. Figure on at least one fifteen-ounce can per pound of spaghetti. Some are meat-based, some with mushrooms, etc. There are also much less bulky and lighter packages of spaghetti sauce mixes, weighing only a few ounces. They all require an additional tomato-based supplement—either tomato paste, which weighs only a couple ounces, or a package of tomato soup mix, which weighs a little less. Anyway, figure on at least two packages of sauce and a can of tomato paste or two packages of tomato soup for each pound of spaghetti. Add some cheese; about 1/6 to 1/4 pound does wonders for a pound of spaghetti. The connoisseurs say Parmesan, but fairly mild cheddar is good when diced and mixed with the cooked spaghetti until it melts.

Macaroni, somehow, does not need as complicated a sauce. But ¼ to ⅓ pound of cheddar cheese and a can of tomato paste per pound will make it more enthusiastically received.

There are prepackaged spaghetti and macaroni dinners. They are satisfactory, though less flexible than if building on the basic raw materials—and perhaps heavier, bulkier, and more expensive. Every manufacturer of dehydrated camping foods has spaghetti and macaroni packages, which are also less flexible and more expensive than using basics.

Rice

Spanish rice takes various forms. It takes ⅓ to ½ cup of dry rice for a serving of Spanish rice—about two to three ounces per person. Tomatoes should be added—tomato paste, tomato soup (canned or packaged), or canned tomatoes. About one can per four or five servings. Diced bacon and/or onion helps immeasurably. Cheese can also be added. Such a dish takes longer than the other one-pot meals and maybe should be held for the rest day.

Lunch Beverages

Soup makes a good start to any meal, particularly in cool weather. Dehydrated soups are light, easy to carry, and should not be overlooked.

Tea is the standard bush-man's lunch drink, but a simple pot of hot water would let the tea drinkers make their own with individual tea bags, satisfy the coffee advocates with the instant, and even let the cocoa devotees make their own from individual packages.

Cold beverages are harder to anticipate. There will be days when the midday sun makes everyone wish for a nice cool drink. Water fits the bill for most, but if flavoring is desired, there are innumerable that are merely stirred into cold water. Most are artificial flavorings with a liberal dose of sugar and, as such, produce flavored, sugared water; but some are better than others and only experimentation will find those most acceptable.

Breads

Store-bought bread will hold out for a couple of days. After that, bannock or the equivalent can be provided at lunch. If so, something in the way of spreads will be needed—jams, peanut butter, margarine, honey, butter. Dry baked products will not sell unless used as a base over which to pour a stew—which has plenty of gravy. Crackers will last indefinitely if kept sealed but are terribly bulky, though light, and do not really substitute for bread.

Desserts

As for breakfast, some fresh fruit could be taken for a few days. There are packaged puddings and such products that make excellent desserts; but normally they require longer to prepare than is available at a lunch stop.

The standard dessert is canned fruit or candy bars. Fruit is terrifically heavy, however. About seven ounces per person is needed in order to offer more than a taste. Fruits are packed in a heavy sugar syrup, which if nothing else provides energy. Maybe such desserts should be reserved as treats for particularly long or hard days.

For a few days, sweets from the bakery can be carried—cakes and cookies—but they are hard to pack, perishable, and fragile; likewise, the candy bar. Every camping outlet advertises a compressed, sweet, energy bar. They do not melt in warm weather like the standard candy bar, and travel better; some are advertised as a complete meal. But if the meal is reasonably substantial, they might better be reserved to munch on during the afternoon when the going gets tough. Cookies and cakes can be baked for lunch—candy can even be made—but the problems of packing for travel make such desserts difficult if not impractical. Better to reserve such treats for the campsite on the rest day or for the evening meal.

The third lunch choice is just a quickly prepared dinner.

DINNERS

Dinner, as so defined, demands a meat-vegetable-starch combination.

Meats

One or two meals of fresh meat can be packed for immediate use. Ground beef, steaks, or chops are possibilities. But after the second day out, fresh meat becomes dubious. So future meats must be: (1) freeze-dried; (2) smoked; (3) dried; or (4) canned.

Freeze-dried meats will last for ages until soaked in water. They come close to the real thing, but are expensive, and perhaps lean on the bulky side when the question of packing comes up.

The Indian smokes his fish, fowl, and game during the summer, but, unless he prepares his own, the canoeist is unlikely to employ smoking as a method of preservation for meats other than ham and bacon.

Dried meats are somewhat a thing of the past. Pemmican used to be the staple of the voyageur, and it can be made at home if desired. Beef jerky, which is the base for pemmican, can be home-made or bought from a camping-supply house, but it is more likely desired by the backpacker. Then there are meats like chipped beef, but most should be sealed or refrigerated.

Although less selection is available each year in the canned-meat line as homemakers rely more on freezers, there are various stews, hamburgers, meatballs, ham, luncheon meats, corned beef, corned beef hash, sausages, and others to be found.

If a canned meat is used for a meal in which a vegetable and a starch are included, figure about a six- to eight-ounce serving per person. A corresponding serving in freeze-dried meat weighs about two ounces, but the bulk will be similar.

Try to offer variety in the menu. There probably must be some duplication, but avoid overloading the outfit in favor of one kind of meat. List the possible meats and then outfit with a few meals of each. As a caution, beware of the infinite number of luncheon meats—some are pork-based, others beef, but they all taste much the same.

Figure how the meat meals are to be divided and calculate the number of cans or packages of each that constitute a meal. They can then be combined in any order with vegetables and starches so that no two meals turn up with exactly the same combinations, keeping the party guessing and avoiding a routine in the meal planning and preparation.

Vegetables

The same procedure is followed with vegetables. Some fresh vegetables keep better than others—particularly cabbage, carrots, and turnips, all three of which will last at least a week.

Dried vegetables—usually peas and beans—require a great deal of cooking and are difficult to use on a traveling day. They make a better soup base.

In the canned line, it normally takes five ounces or so per serving. Some of the more common canned vegetables would include peas, carrots, peas and carrots, kernel corn, creamed corn, wax beans, green beans, French-style beans, lima beans, beets, tomatoes, sauerkraut, plus others perhaps less common. The vegetable line offers more variety than any other canned product, and taste is not too far from fresh produce.

Realize that canned vegetables contain a certain amount of liquid and, except for possibly kernel corn, are cooked in their own juices. The water content of a can of tomatoes surpasses all others by a considerable margin—about fifty percent water.

Consider the dehydrated possibilities. Many taste reasonably close to their fresh counterparts —peas, cabbage, carrots, and onions seem to be particularly suitable—but it is advisable to experiment before going overboard. Some taste much like toothpaste!

The selection in freeze-dried vegetables is restrictive compared to canned—perhaps peas, corn, and green beans—but they approach the quality of frozen vegetables and will cut the weight of the outfit by sixty percent to seventy percent— although bulk remains about the same as when cans are used.

Starches

Starches are less varied, and so the same product must be offered more frequently. They divide into fresh potatoes, dehydrated potatoes, rice, noodles, spaghetti, and macaroni. If spaghetti and macaroni are used as meals of their own, their double use should be avoided, with the possible exception of baked macaroni, which narrows the selection.

Fresh potatoes will travel, but weight and bulk are real deterrents. It takes about a half-pound per person, and about an ounce of dehydrated potatoes will make the equivalent in mashed potatoes. A couple of meals of the real thing are appreciated, but perhaps should be prepared in a manner impossible with the dehydrated ones— fried, baked, boiled; almost any method that can be used at home can be used in the bush.

Dehydrated mashed potatoes are a real boon. They are light, compact, and easy to prepare. The servings advertised on most packages are skimpy;

one that advertises as adequate for four persons probably goes for three; sometimes only two. Some brands are flakes, others a powder; try a variety until the best is found. Most brands insist on mixing with milk; the few that advocate water are probably richer.

There are other dehydrated potatoes that are easy to use. The best are potato slices that can either be scalloped or German pan fried. Again they are much lighter than the real ones, although more bulky than mashed.

Canned potatoes are a possibility, but in terms of weight, fresh ones might as well be carried.

Rice comes in a variety of styles, all equally good with regard to weight and bulk. All will require a couple of ounces per serving if used as the starch part of a meal. Time was when there were only "regular" and "instant" rices. Though slightly more difficult to cook, the taste of regular rice is usually preferred in spite of claims that there is no difference. Now there are also rices prepared by frying. Take advantage of the diversity, but do not confuse with wild rice which is different. It is usually used as a side dish or stuffing with fowl and is prohibitively expensive for the ordinary camper. Occasionally a patch of it is found while paddling along; it grows in shallow water and is gathered in the fall by Indians by gliding their canoes through the field and beating the rice stalks with sticks so the rice falls into the canoes.

Noodles offer another possibility—again in various sizes and shapes. Normally they are best served in a meal where there is gravy to pour over them; maybe with chicken or beef stew.

Anyway, split the meals among the various possibilities. Go heavy on dehydrated mashed potatoes. Most other starches demand boiling for a time; the mashed potatoes are made as soon as the water boils and are ready minutes later.

Beverages

The same selection exists here as for the other meals. The evening meal is the best time to brew a whole pot of cocoa. That which is made from raw ingredients can be richer than the "instant" variety made by adding hot water. But if "pure" cocoa is used, sugar and milk must be added. Here is where condensed milk is most desirable.

Soup is, of course, a good way to start the meal. The packaged soups available are legion, and on the cool, rainy evening, soup hits the spot, par-ticularly as an appetizer to be sipped as the main meal cooks.

Coffee and tea are still viable possibilities.

Breads

Bannock is just a glorified biscuit batter, or maybe a cake without eggs. Mixing the batter takes five or ten minutes, and the baking takes another twenty-five to thirty-five minutes, so nor-mally the bannock is done by the time dinner is ready, even after a hard day's travel.

Baked goods can become as fancy as desired, depending on the time devoted to this kind of cooking. Pies, cakes, and cookies are possibilities made with baking powder. Then there is the whole field of yeast—or even sour dough—breads.

Anyway, some baked product as part of the eve-ning meal is desirable. There are prepared mixes for almost everything—biscuits, cakes, pies, and so on—but baking is more flexible if the raw ingredi-ents are carried to whip up the various batters.

Without a reflector, bannock can be baked in a fry pan as does the native woodsman who has never heard of a reflector. Some breads, like doughnuts, and what is called trapper's bread (or squaw cakes), are deep fried. If a gasoline stove is used, there is an oven that can be added that makes baking practical. Some baking can be done in a Dutch oven, or iron pot with a suitable lid, which is particularly adaptable to baking in hot sand.

After the dinner baking is done, bake for break-fast or lunch while the rest of the cookery is being walloped. The finished product is then cooled and replaced in the baking pan for transport. The other meals are too rushed to allow adequate baking time on a traveling day. If yeast bread is baked, make enough so there will be bread for the next couple of meals. Working with yeast is time-consuming, and it takes only a little longer to make a double batch than it does a single setting.

Desserts

Unfortunately by the time dessert is suggested, there are probably no pots left in the jewelry. Maybe on a rest day a dessert can be made earlier to be stored until dinner, thus releasing the pot for dinner uses.

Normally, baked goods count as dessert. A pie or cake will seem more like it than bannock or corn bread. But with a liberal topping of jam, even a bannock satisfies the craving for sweets that grows in the bush.

Packaged puddings are light and easy to carry. Some require milk; some require cooking. Look at the package, but in general those that require cooking work more frequently than the instant varieties. There are canned puddings ready to eat, and a trip to the supermarket will reveal other ideas. Then there are freeze-dried desserts, up to and including ice cream. There are also some desserts to make from raw ingredients at hand—rice pudding being the easiest. But in the long run probably only a few desserts will be asked for; and the party will be well fed on the main meal.

DINNER MENU

Plans have been made as to what meats, vegetables, and starches are to be included. They can now be put together in combination depending on the whims of the party. Once on the campsite, someone wants canned hamburgers, another wants rice, a third suggests peas, someone volunteers to bake a coffee cake—and the menu for the night is planned. The only concern is the need to avoid repeating the same meal a couple of times in a row early in the trip; it will snowball into a similar repetition of some other meal later on. If there are two meals of ham, use one the first week, the other during the second, and so on.

Perishables must be used early; fruit and eggs will not keep indefinitely. Next, look toward weight. Do not save fresh potatoes to be carried over all the portages. But on the other hand, do not use all the canned goods first, making the last stages of the trip on dehydrated and freeze-dried foods alone. Use some discretion so the trip ends with everyone eating as well as at the start. The Indian going into his winter trap grounds outfits with a ton or so of supplies and, on the way in, eats it up as quickly as he can so he will not have to carry it over the portages—which makes for feast and famine—but he can live off the country, which the canoe party cannot. The Indian's meals at the start are exotic, but when he gets down to beans and bannock, they become bland and monotonous; and if down to fish and bannock the last couple days, there is a monotony that makes the trip work and not pleasure.

STAPLES

There is one great area of supplies yet to con-

sider—what might be called staples. Here quantities are difficult to estimate without knowing specific dishes planned, the amount of baking to be done, and the likes and dislikes of the party. In a large group, someone will want an extra bit of something; another will not want as much; and it balances out. With a two-man party there will not be that balance. If neither person likes coffee, it will still be in the wannigan at the end, having been carried for no purpose.

In estimating staples, where each is to be used in cooking must be considered and plans made from there.

Sugar

Use white sugar in beverages and brown on cereals and in baking. Take more brown than white. The craving for sweets soars in the bush. Any extra can always be used to make fudge! Perhaps include some icing sugar to frost a cake. The exact sugar requirement depends on how much is used in baking, but, as a starter, estimate ¼ pound of sugar per person per day—an all-adult party will use less. The white sugar can be cut back to almost nothing by using an artificial sweetener for coffee and tea.

Flour

If prepared mixes are used, just count the expected number of bakings. If batters are made from raw ingredients, the amount of flour depends on how much baking is done, the number of pancake breakfasts, and whether yeast breads are to be made—which use more flour than bannocks. Baking for two meals a day, a reasonable starter is ¼ to ⅓ pound of flour per person per day.

Shortening

The amount of shortening depends on the baking, deep frying, and fish cooking. Half again as much shortening will be needed if the bacon fat is thrown away. Take some liquid corn oil, but not all. A reflector pan cannot be greased with corn oil, though it works well in frying and baking. Start with about ½ ounce per person per day, but not less than five pounds for a two-week trip.

Baking Powder

This is dependent on baking, but some is needed for pancakes at least. Do not run short; it is light, easy to carry, but will not work if it gets wet! It comes in half-pound and pound containers.

With a small party, carry the smaller size rather than keeping it all in one place. Carry a minimum of one pound per week with the small party; a couple of pounds a week with a large one.

Yeast

If bread baking is contemplated, take a couple of packages of dry yeast. One package will do a baking. Having some extras will not hurt or weigh anything.

Salt

Do not be caught short; salt is needed in most dishes. Carry in one-pound containers. Figure a pound a week for the small group, a pound and a half with three or more canoes. Overestimate rather than under.

Spreads for Bannock

Possibilities include jam, marmalade, peanut butter, honey, jellies, butter, and margarine, to name a few. Consumption goes up tremendously if baking twice a day. Go heavy on jam and butter or a substitute; less heavy on the others. As a beginning, two pounds of the various spreads per person per week would be conservative—perhaps less with an adult party; more with youngsters. If butter or margarine is also used in cooking, raise the estimate. If baking is limited, adjust downward, but sweets must be supplied elsewhere.

Butter will not keep in hot weather if purchased right out of the grocer's dairy display (unless someone knows how to wash it). Canned butter keeps, if not opened, for considerable periods without refrigeration, though it should be protected from the hot sun. However, it is not often available. Margarine keeps better, but if carried in cardboard and paper wrapped packages will be squashed easily and once opened makes a messy serving problem, particularly in warm weather. It is better to repack it in a metal can with a suitable lid.

Cornmeal

Cornmeal has a variety of uses in baking, makes a suitable cereal, and can be used as a covering for fried fish. Carry a pound or more depending on anticipated uses.

Other Flours

A few pounds of other than normal white flour makes it possible to vary pancakes in particular—buckwheat is the most normal.

Milk

Five categories: evaporated, powdered cream substitute, condensed, instant skim milk, powdered whole milk.

Evaporated milk substitutes for cream. It comes in "baby" cans—about six ounces—and "tall" cans —about one pound. With a small party, carry all baby cans. With the larger, some tall cans. If used just as a substitute for cream, considerably less than a full can will be needed at any single meal. When opening, punch two *small* holes in the top opposite each other so they can be plugged with slivers of wood. They can also be sealed by moistening a small bit of paper, perhaps a bit of the label, with milk and placing pieces over the holes; they should take like glue as the milk dries. But somehow the opened can defies successful portaging!

Instead of evaporated milk for cream in coffee or tea, a powdered cream substitute can be carried. It has few other uses, but it is easier to pack and does not sour.

Condensed milk is used almost exclusively in cooking—something that needs both milk and sugar, particularly cocoa, frostings, and candies. It is terribly sweet, and a little goes a long way. There may be no use for it at all.

Powdered skim milk is the common variety most easily available. Some people may use it as a drink in addition to using it for cereal and cooking. About ⅓ cup—less than one ounce—makes a cup of milk. In addition to cereal, there will be some cooking needs—baking perhaps, puddings, mashed potatoes, and several other dishes. If used as a drink, quantities needed will soar.

Powdered whole milk is a richer milk drink, but the price rises appreciably. It has the same uses as skim milk for cereals and cooking, and it has about the same ratio of weight to amount of milk produced. Its omission will not be noticed unless a beverage is desired.

Raisins

Raisins make excellent snacks in the middle of the long afternoon. They are also useful in bannocks and bread, and can be used as a pie filling. Raisins can also be added to some hot cereals to good advantage. Take at least a pound.

Dates

Almost the same addition to the outfit as raisins, dates, however, are not as versatile.

Pie Fillings

Dehydrated apples make a good pie. Raisins make a very rich one. Canned fruit could be used; maybe other dehydrated fruits. In season, blueberries or raspberries may be gathered. There are also canned pie fillings. The number of cans per pie depends on the reflector size, but do not carry canned fillings where a similar pie can be made from lighter ingredients.

Baking Soda

Baking soda is used in some baking in addition to baking powder. It can also be used for cleaning, makes an excellent substitute for tooth powder, though the taste is not much, and has first aid uses. It may never be opened, but include a small box; it weighs only a half-pound.

Corn Starch

Used as a thickening agent particularly in puddings and gravies, corn starch, however, may not be necessary.

Pepper

Pepper is a must in every outfit, even if only a little is used. Err on the side of carrying more than necessary. Try to find a brand packed in a container that is also a shaker.

Seasonings and Spices

Standard spices are cinnamon and ginger. Then there are all kinds of other seasonings and spices. Pick what might be helpful—maybe a good number; maybe only a couple. Seasoned salts fall into this category.

Liquid Flavorings

Vanilla is called for in many recipes. A maple flavoring can be used to make pancake syrup, but can also be used in baking. Take a concentrated variety rather than a diluted one if possible; considerably more of the latter product is needed for any result. They are best used in flavoring bannocks to provide variety. At least a teaspoonful will be needed for any project. Most acceptable and adaptable are lemon, orange, butterscotch, imitation rum, and almond.

Soups

Take a variety of the packaged soups without planning specific meals at which they will be used. Some can be used in preparing other dishes—particularly tomato and chicken and rice.

Onions

A little diced onion adds a great deal to many dishes. If weight and bulk are obstacles, dehydrated onions and onion flakes are good as far as taste is concerned. Freeze-dried onions are even better.

Catsup and Mustard

There are some who cannot get along without one or both, but go much heavier on catsup than mustard. Cooking with tomato paste or dehydrated tomato soup cuts back the catsup demand. Dry mustard mixed with a little water makes a potent mustard. There are also relishes and pickle products, but maybe they can be omitted in the interests of weight and space.

Tomato-based Cooking Agents

There are four basic agents from which to choose. Tomato paste is the most versatile. The small can weighs only about six ounces, and a single can goes a long way in providing flavoring—as well as color—to the dish. The next most useful is dehydrated tomato soup, a package of which weighs only ounces. It takes two packages, however, to equal one can of tomato paste, and is not quite as good. Condensed tomato soup can also be used, but, considering weight and bulk, paste is better. Canned tomatoes provide the actual tomatoes that the others lack; however, as previously mentioned, the water content is terribly high. There are dishes, however, where the tomatoes make a definite contribution.

Count the number of meals requiring tomato flavoring; it will be surprising how many call for tomato additives.

Cheese

A medium or mild cheddar is versatile enough to combine with many things. Maybe some Parmesan can be taken. Take a little more cheddar than anticipated—it makes good nibbling. Carry in blocks or wedges, not sliced—that can be done on the spot.

Beverages

Coffee—about the same amount will be used as at home. Take a regular grind unless some special method of preparation is to be used. Carry some instant or freeze-dried; there will be times when just one person wants a cup.

Tea—again the same rules as at home. Bulk tea or a half-gallon bag is good for brewing a pot; otherwise, carry individual tea bags. A few thrown in a pot will substitute for either bulk or larger bags. Instant tea could be considered.

Cocoa—comes in three kinds of packaging: there are individual packages each making one cup; bulk mixes to which water or milk is added; and finally pure cocoa. In order to make a drink, milk and sugar must be added to pure cocoa, and it is best used to make a large pot; it is a bother to dig out the other ingredients for just one cup. But pure cocoa has other uses that the presweetened kinds do not have. So a little of the pure makes sense. How much depends—youngsters who have not acquired a taste for tea or coffee will prefer cocoa.

Fruit juices—packaged rather than canned for weight and packing ease as already noted.

Cold beverages—seem to go best at lunch. Most are presweetened, but make sure; if large quantities of sugar are needed, the supply in that department may need upward adjustment.

Corn Syrup

Corn syrup has cooking uses that may indicate its inclusion.

Molasses

Molasses is used in some baking, and, in particular, baked beans. There may also be someone who uses molasses on his bannock.

Salt Pork

Salt pork keeps for ages without refrigeration and is needed for baked beans; it can also be used in many soups where otherwise a hambone would be thrown in at home.

It can be fried in place of bacon, but should first be boiled to remove the salt. The taste is an acquired one that many people are not accustomed to. The amount per pot of beans depends on the size pot; maybe one to two pounds per pot.

Powdered Eggs

Powdered eggs depend on breakfast desires.

But, in addition, many baking recipes call for eggs, and after the fresh ones are expended, powdered eggs will take up the slack. Whether the recipe calls for them or not, the addition of a couple eggs in almost any baking is welcome. So supplies will depend even more on baking needs.

Egg Substitute

This substitute is not a whole egg product at all. It is a good percent corn starch, and as such will not make an egg dish, but will do the same—almost—for baked goods as powdered eggs. It has the advantage over them in that it is nonperishable. However, there are few suppliers who market it, and it may be impossible to locate it except through special order. Two heaping tablespoons are usually equivalent to one egg.

As a substitute for egg substitute, which sounds redundant, look for a package of French toast mix. As a substitute for substitute, it does an adequate job.

Syrup

Closely tied to the frequency of pancakes, see previous comments advocating the use of brown sugar and maple flavoring.

Chocolate

Baking chocolate has a few limited uses but might be considered if an icing is planned. Pure cocoa can substitute for chocolate in most cases.

Lemon

One or two lemons might prove useful. The juice can be used for tea or cooking, and, if nothing else, a piece of rind added to the prunes is sometimes enjoyable—or maybe just some lemon juice.

BULK AND WEIGHT

By now the list is imposing, and maybe the weight and/or bulk are too great. If so, go back and pare down the list, leaving out luxury items. Perhaps lighter substitutes can be introduced, but do not sacrifice on the basics. Cut on the fringes, but leave intact items like cereal, fruit, bacon, meats, vegetables, starches, flour, shortening, sugar, salt, baking powder, coffee, and tea that make the bulk of each meal. If still too heavy or bulky, go back and substitute dehydrated or freeze-dried products for canned goods. Substituting a fifteen-ounce can for a sixteen-ounce can will not help, but there will be a difference if a small package can replace a large can.

MISCELLANEOUS

Then there are nonedible items that are expendable and not permanent parts of the outfit and must be replaced with each trip. Most have already been mentioned for inclusion in the jewelry, first aid kit, or to be included in an individual's pack—but relisting them briefly may ensure that they are not omitted as the supplies are gathered: For the Jewelry—Matches, soap, scouring pads, pot cleaners, dish towels, a sponge or swab for dishwashing, cooking mittens, and scouring agent for the reflector. Amounts depend on the length of the trip and the size of the group.
For the Individual Pack—Toilet paper (one roll of bumwad per camper, with at least a spare carried in the community supplies), a bug bomb per tent, candles, emergency match supply.
For the Canoe Repair Kit[1]—Repair materials should be checked. Maybe carried in the same container are such things as ax files and a hank of cord that could be listed as items of a supply nature.
For the First Aid Kit—An obvious special item to check. Be sure there is enough waterproof adhesive tape for uses other than medical.

It might also be considered that the community outfit carry a roll of aluminum foil; and while it has been suggested that each individual carry candles, it may be preferable to store them as a unit and have the various tents draw on that supply.

SAMPLE OUTFITTING LIST

Numerous camping manuals contain suggested menus and outfits for a party of an arbitrarily selected size for an equally arbitrary number of days. None are ever supposed to be copied exactly, and they are intended merely as guides.

Since the suggested method of outfitting here avoids a specific menu, to draw one up would be highly arbitrary and of little value. Anyway, given a menu, an outfitting list should still be formed

and items checked off as they are procured and checked again as they are packed.

Here follows a model outfitting list. It provides a series of steps for calculating the amount of each item needed; but the outfitter would probably use this method for some items and not for others—the staples in particular. Obviously the listings of various canned, dehydrated, and freeze-dried products is a guideline. Those listed are available and most have been mentioned earlier, but there are many more possibilities that might be even more appealing to a particular group, and blanks included in the list invite additions under that category.

To use the suggested list effectively, begin by listing the number of breakfasts needed, decide how many of these are to use a certain product, and figure the amount needed for a serving. Then, knowing the size of a package to be purchased, figure how many packages will be needed for a meal—or fraction of a package. Finally, indicate how many of these packages are to be secured to provide for the number of meals it is to be used.

Continue the same procedure with lunches and dinners. As selections are made for parts of various meals, certain dishes need some staple items in their preparation. For example, suppose the party plans to make a one-pot lunch using a pound of spaghetti. If the suggestions made previously are followed, in the staple section the outfitter will also have to check off one can of tomato paste, two packages of dehydrated spaghetti sauce mix, and one-fourth pound cheddar cheese. To be sure this is accomplished, the final column has space for noting items needed to go with that dish, so the additional items from the staple section will not be forgotten.

The staple section should be completed last, perhaps starting with the insertion of those additional items needed to prepare a dish in the breakfast-lunch-dinner section. Regarding other staples, some suggestions have been made earlier, but these are certainly rough approximations, and decisions have to be made before tackling this section regarding some basic cooking philosophies; for instance, baking is the greatest issue—to bake or not to bake—and if baking, how many times a day?

After the list is complete, collecting the outfit starts, and when each item is on hand it is checked off in that column, and shortages, if any, should be noted here.

Then the "Packed" column gets checked last as a final check, as each item is actually packed;

1. For contents of a canoe repair kit, see *Canoeing Wilderness Waters,* pp. 170–96.

SUGGESTED OUTFITTING FORM

Duration of Trip: __________ days   Number of Persons: __________

Packed	On Hand		Number Meals Used	Portion One Serving	Serving per Unit	Number Units per Meal	Total Units	Notes on Preparation

BREAKFASTS

Number Needed: __________

Fruits:
- Fresh:
  - Apples
  - Grapefruit
  - Lemons
  - Oranges
  - __________
- Dried:
  - Apples
  - Apricots
  - Peaches
  - Prunes
  - __________

Bacon:

Cereals:
- Cream of Wheat
- Oatmeal
- __________

Eggs:
- Fresh
- Powdered
- Freeze-dried
- Dehydrated Egg Mix

Pancakes:
- Prepared Mix

ONE-POT LUNCHES

Number Needed: __________

Spaghetti:

Macaroni:

Spanish Rice:

Beans:
- Canned:
  - Baked Beans
  - Beans with Meat
  - Chili con Carne
  - __________
- Dry Beans

Stews:
- Canned:
  - Beef
  - Chicken
  - __________

(continued)

Packed	On Hand		Number Meals Used	Portion One Serving	Servings per Unit	Number Units per Meal	Total Units	Notes on Preparation

Stews: (Continued)
  Freeze-Dried Meals:
    Beef Campers Stew
    Beef Chow Mein
    Beef Ministrone Dinner
    Beef Vegetable Stew

  —————

Cold Lunches:
  Sandwiches:
    Prepared before Trip
    To be Made on Trip

  —————

MEAT-VEGETABLE-STARCH DINNERS   Number Needed: _____

Meats:
  Fresh:

  —————

  Canned:
    Beef Chunks
    Corned Beef
    Corned Beef Hash
    Ham
    Hamburgers
    Luncheon Meats
    Meatballs
    Roast Beef
    Sausages

  —————

  Freeze-Dried:
    Beef Steak
    Chicken
    Diced Beef
    Hamburgers
    Sausages

  —————

Vegetables:
  Fresh:
    Cabbage
    Carrots
    Turnips

  —————

  Canned:
    Beets
    Carrots
    French Style Beans
    Green Beans
    Lima Beans
    Kidney Beans

  (continued)

Packed	On Hand		Number Meals Used	Portion One Serving	Servings per Unit	Number Units per Meal	Total Units	Notes on Preparation
		Vegetables: (Continued)						
		Canned: (Continued)						
		Wax Beans						
		Creamed Corn						
		Kernel Corn						
		Peas						
		Peas and Carrots						
		Sauerkraut						
		Tomatoes						
		———						
		Dehydrated:						
		Carrots						
		Onions						
		Peas						
		———						
		Freeze-Dried:						
		Corn						
		Green Beans						
		Peas						
		———						
		Starches:						
		Potatoes:						
		Fresh						
		Dehydrated						
		Mashed						
		Sliced						
		———						
		Rice:						
		Instant						
		Regular						
		Fried						
		———						
		Noodles:						
		STAPLES						
		Beverages:						
		Coffee:						
		Instant						
		Regular						
		Tea:						
		Instant						
		Bulk						
		Individual Bags						
		½ Gallon Bags						
		Cocoa:						
		Individual Packages						
		Presweetened Bulk						
		Pure Cocoa						

(continued)

131

Packed	On Hand		Number Meals Used	Portion One Serving	Servings per Unit	Number Units per Meal	Total Units	Notes on Preparation

Beverages: (Continued)
Soups:
  Canned

  ——————

  Dehydrated
    Chicken and Rice
    Tomato

  ——————

Baking Needs:
Flour:
  Wheat
  Buckwheat
  Cornmeal

  ——————

Prepared Mixes:
  Biscuit
  Cake

  ——————

Baking Powder

Baking Soda

Yeast

Egg Substitute

Baking Chocolate

Flavorings:
  Almond
  Butterscotch
  Imitation Rum
  Lemon
  Maple
  Orange
  Vanilla

  ——————

Milk:
Powdered:
  Skim
  Whole

Canned:
  Evaporated
    Baby Cans
    Tall Cans

  Condensed

Coffee Cream Substitute

(continued)

Packed	On Hand		Number Meals Used	Portion One Serving	Servings per Unit	Number Units per Meal	Total Units	Notes on Preparation

Baking Needs: (Continued)
  Shortening:
    Shortening
    Corn Oil
    ————

  Sugar:
    Brown
    White
    Artificial Sweetener
    Corn Syrup
    Molasses
    Icing Sugar

Spreads:
  Butter:
    Canned
    Fresh
  Honey
  Jams
  Jellies
  Margarine
  Marmalade
  Peanut Butter
  ————

Desserts:
  Fruit:
    Canned:
      Cherries
      Peaches
      Pears
      Plums
      ————

    Dehydrated:
      Applesauce
      ————

  Puddings:
    Cooked
    Instant
    ————

  Pie Fillings

  Corn Starch

  Freeze-Dried Deserts:
    Ice Cream
    ————

Miscellaneous Foods:
  Dates

  Cheese

    (continued)

Packed	On Hand		Number Meals Used	Portion One Servings	Servings per Unit	Number Units per Meal	Total Units	Notes on Preparation

Miscellaneous Foods: (Continued)
Raisins

Tomato Bases:
  Canned:
    Soup
     Tomato Paste

Bread:
  Fresh
  Crackers
  Pastry
  ————————

Catsup

Mustard

Pancake Syrup:
  Bottled
  Dehydrated Mixes

Seasonings and Spices:
  Cinnamon
  Ginger
  Pepper
  Salt
  ————————

Onions:
  Fresh
  Freeze-Dried
  Dehydrated

Spaghetti Sauce:
  Canned
  Dehydrated

Salt Pork

Miscellaneous Nonedibles:
  Aluminum Foil
  Ax File
  Candles
  Cord
  Dish Swab
  Dish Towels
  Matches
  Mittens
  Pot Cleaners
  Scouring Agent for Reflector
  Soap:
    Bar
    Liquid
  Soap Pads
  Sponge
  Toilet Paper

for instance, maybe the wannigans are packed a day before the trip, but the bacon is left in the refrigerator to be added just before departure—bacon does not get checked off here until actually safe and sound in the wannigans.

OUTFITTING AND PACKING

Now, with everything assembled, comes the monumental task of sorting and packing equipment into various units in which it will be carried. Remember, there should be as few items as possible to handle every time the canoe is loaded or unloaded, but the weight of each container must be kept within limits that can be handled safely. The loads must also be distributed so each canoe and each person carries a share.

The outfit must be organized so that items can be located without turning everything upside down. Start by laying out the various packs and wannigans into which everything is expected to fit. Then start separating the supplies so that all items of one kind are together for the moment. Then stand back and survey it all!

Before packing, organize similar items together.

The first chore to tackle is repackaging some of the food that comes off the grocer's shelves. Cans cannot be improved on, but the items that are sealed in cardboard boxes and paper or plastic containers demand some reworking for a variety of reasons.

As with any kind of camping where traveling is involved, bulk and weight dictate some of the repacking. But canoe travel has the added ever-present possibility of an accident in which non-

protected supplies get wet. The backpacker is naturally concerned about moisture from above; the canoeist is also (and is less able to find immediate shelter). But the canoeist's supplies could get soaked from below, and a wet bag of freeze-dried peas containing three meals leads to eating peas rapidly. Then there is the chance of losing an entire wannigan; if that container had all the canned meat, considerable adjustment would have to be made to the diet.

Have available an unlimited supply of provision bags in assorted sizes. Each must have a method by which it can be tied off; a tie string sewed to the bag is best. A separate tie string always seems to be misplaced, and rubber bands are fine until they break or are lost.

Provision bags can be obtained from a camping-supply retailer in different materials. Cotton cloth bags are the least expensive and most desirable for a majority of purposes. They can be laundered easily and stored until next season. Lightweight transparent plastic bags will not stand the gaff alone, but can be used to line cotton bags to help waterproofing and keep the contents from soiling the cloth. Heavy-duty transparent plastic can stand on its own more successfully, but expense dictates they not be disposed of after one use. They can be cleaned by sponging each one out individually. They need twist ties that are not attached, as do the lighter bags, and perhaps still are better as liners—particularly for items that might be harmed by dampness. Rubberized stuff bags are more waterproof than cotton and have a tie string attached. They are available in only a small range of sizes, have to be sponged clean as heavy plastic, and after a couple seasons develop small pinholes and cracks, destroying their otherwise waterproof properties. Nylon stuff bags are excellent, except for the fact that their stitching lets in water; they are also expensive and difficult to launder. But they are available in many sizes and are equipped with draw strings. But a cotton bag of the same size costs pennies; the nylon equivalent may be three times as much. A few might be used for items of a special nature, but to amass the supply that should be used would be prohibitively expensive.

As packing commences, maybe the first decisions to make concern freeze-dried and dehydrated foods, which come in various kinds of packages. Either product reconstitutes immediately on contact with water and must be used soon. Should an appreciable amount of such supplies get wet, it will be impractical to use all soon enough, and serious food losses could result. Ini-

135

tially, many freeze-dried and dehydrated products were available in cans, but the backpacker objected, and the ecologist insisted that cans be packed out of the wilderness by whoever brought them in. Many producers still waterproof their products and seal the packages well, but unfortunately there are some that use nothing more waterproof than heavy paper. When such packages are stowed, they should be better protected —either with waterproof stuff bags or by inserting plastic liners into cloth bags—and then tied off securely. However, now the bag should be protected against having the contents crushed. A bag of peas otherwise becomes a powder; the hamburger patties will just be diced beef. So each bag now needs to be placed in something rigid. If the bags are waterproofed, a cardboard box will do if the external carrying container is crushproof —like a wannigan.

Then, begin work on the rest of the supplies. Bag anything that comes in a cardboard box where an entire box would not be used at one time. Throw away the cardboard. The boxes cannot be closed off securely once opened; and a half-used box of cereal is sure to spill.

Into this category fall such items as cereal, powdered milk, cornmeal, and rice. As each is tied off, label each bag plainly by writing on the bag with a magic marker or ball-point pen.

Then take items that are packaged in paper or plastic bags where the bag is not strong enough to withstand the beating it might take. Leave these products in their containers; they weigh little and offer some protection. Slip them into bags to be tied off and labeled. It works better to use a separate bag for each package of the fairly large items. More cotton bags will be used, but it is easier on the campsite to handle the smaller bags.

Stowing foodstuffs in cloth bags takes time, but makes tripping much more efficient.

136

Into this category fall such foods as flour, sugar, and coffee (if purchased in bags, which are easier to pack than cans).

Then take those items that are packaged in small individual envelopes and fill cloth bags of reasonable size with these, leaving individual envelopes unopened. In the process, there will be some products that are sold boxed in cardboard and then have either one large or several small envelopes inside. Throw away the cardboard, but do not break open the smaller envelopes. In this category fall dehydrated potatoes, soup packages, and individual cocoa and tea bags.

Also bag dried fruit and various dehydrated mixes, which usually come wrapped in small plastic bags designed for a couple of people—put all of one kind of item in a single cloth bag; sprinkling a package of pancake syrup here and there in the wannigans not only invites breakage of the envelope but also makes finding anything difficult.

Then bag anything that might "leak" through the outfit when the weather gets warm. It is best to wrap securely in aluminum foil over the packaging used by the store. Cheese is an example.

Then there are some products that come packed in boxes where the box should be retained, although the contents would not be used in a single meal. Some should also be bagged to prevent spilling. In this group fall salt, baking soda, corn starch, and baking chocolate.

This leaves a few items still in cardboard boxes. If the entire box is to be used in a single meal, leave the packaging as is. In this category fall spaghetti, macaroni, and noodles.

Then stand back and take another look, and be sure there is nothing left that should be bagged. Any group of small items where it is desirable that all items of that kind be located together should be bagged. Candles, pot cleaners, and dish towels are examples.

Now look to the liquid, semiliquid, and soft, creamy items. Ones that will take several meals to use must be packaged so they can be closed off after each use—jams for example.

Anything of this nature packaged in a plastic or cardboard container should be repackaged before trouble starts. Best are metal tins, which can be sealed with either a pressure lid or a screw-on top. Second best would be heavy plastic jars or bottles obtained from a camping-supply house intended for this purpose. But the prudent experienced tripper will make a collection of reusable tins in which household goods came packaged during the winter, and have these on hand

for the summer trip (or maybe they were saved from previous trips). Look particularly to jam, honey, and molasses. Then there are some items where it is easier to work from a can than it is from the container as it came from the store. Margarine and butter that is not canned are examples; not all of either need be canned or placed in a better container. The original packaging is likely satisfactory until that particular pound is opened, so maybe put a pound in a can and leave the rest alone; although canned butter would have been preferable in the first place. Do the same with margarine; it does not come canned anyway. The plastic "tubs" used for "soft" margarine will crack under pressure.

Then there are a couple of items of a dry nature where working from a metal container is easier. A sugar bowl, for example, is better than a bag for storing something that is likely used at every meal by the coffee and tea drinkers. In baking, the egg-substitute can offers more convenient storage than a cloth bag.

Have a container ready in which to store bacon grease.

Then there is a pile of glass jars that will create problems should they break—not because the contents are lost, or even that it spreads over everything else, but because of the danger from small bits of glass. Each jar should be wrapped in a small paper bag. Breakage is not impossible, but less likely, and the glass will not spread through the pack even if the catsup does! Then when the brown paper is no longer needed around a jar, it gets stuffed in the baking wannigan to be used in bits and pieces as swabs with which to grease the reflector pan, keeping the cook's hands out of the shortening pail. Items in this group are obvious and include catsup, mustard, vanilla, and the various bannock flavorings.

Lastly, the fresh bacon remains, and maybe a fresh ham. (The ham should be boned and then treated as with bacon.) Either will have to be tossed out if flies get in to lay their eggs in the meat. But neither should be sealed in plastic; they both need to breathe. Side bacon keeps longer than sliced. Maybe fold a large side in half by making a slice in the middle down to, but not through, the rind. Place the side in a cloth bag or wrap securely in a piece of cotton cloth. Then slip the package into a second bag and tie it off securely. Double-bagged, side bacon will keep for three weeks if not allowed to sit under the blazing sun (a little mold may appear, but this can be scraped off).

Then take another pause to survey the pile! Now the real packing begins. First, consider how the first day will be spent. Will there be a meal needed before arriving at the campsite for the night? If a lunch is to be eaten on the way, start now using one pack or wannigan as a lunch wannigan. Set aside everything needed for that meal. Even if the menu is a sandwich one, there will be things like beverages, sugar, cream, butter, and jam needed—plus a roll of community bumwad. Pack the lunch on top of whatever else also goes into that wannigan. Use the same lunch wannigan throughout the trip. Do not alternate among the various loads.

Another wannigan should be organized so that it contains all the materials needed to bake a bannock. On making camp late in the day, it is desirable to start baking quickly, and having to paw through all the packs to find the ingredients is time-consuming. Basic needs are flour, shortening, salt, baking powder, egg substitute, cornmeal, and maybe powdered milk. This wannigan should also carry icing sugar, chocolate, cocoa, vanilla, and the liquid flavorings. Set this material aside to go on top of whatever else is carried in that pack.

Add to the jewelry anything that would be needed for washing dishes and walloping pots—not all the cleaning material, just that which would be used for a meal or two. The supply of soap and other needs can be replenished from the other packs as needed.

Decide where the first aid kit and the canoe repair materials will be packed—on top of whatever container houses them.

Now the special loads have been sorted. Next, decide where canned goods will be packed and where the larger, more pliable goods are to go. If using wannigans or containers where it makes no difference whether there are cans against the portager's back or not, put cans in such containers. If using some duffels or babies that are to be carried by throwing them on top of other loads, put the softer, bagged goods there. If using only packs, each load must be planned so the side against the carrier's back will be soft, which may create difficulties unless the outfit is light on canned goods.

Now start packing. The adage "Don't put all your eggs in one basket" holds true. Do not place all the meats in one container. It is better to lose a little of a lot of items than all of one in the event of accident. Check off each item on the outfitting list as it gets packed.

Start by distributing the heavier items—shortening, tins of jam, peanut butter. Distribute the weight equally. Then start on a major item, such as meat. If it takes two cans of something to make a meal, put two cans of that item in a given pack. Do the same with the rest of the canned goods of that nature—vegetables in particular.

Keep working on cans until all are distributed. Then work on the bagged goods. Distribute evenly. If some packs are to contain only bagged items, look first toward flour and sugar, then to cereals and bagged dried fruits. They all take better to rough treatment than other items.

Keep track not only of how full each pack gets, but its weight, and adjust accordingly so that everyone gets a load he can handle. Top off each load with the lighter materials still packaged as they came from the store—spaghetti, macaroni and such items that were not bagged; or lighter items that will not withstand being knocked around—like boxes of freeze-dried or dehydrated foods. Use the small containers as fillers between larger cans and packages—spices, flavorings, tomato paste. Several times during the packing of an individual container the goods should be rearranged, working toward optimum use of space.

By now it should all be done up, except for the items that each individual is to roll in his own pack—bumwad and bug bombs, for instance. There may still be a few perishables that should be refrigerated until the last moment, but otherwise the outfit is ready to roll.

If the packing is reasonably well done, it should be possible to locate a meal without trouble. Every pack should have at least one meal of meat and a meal of vegetable, and enough other items so that if only that pack were available a meal could be started. The baking wannigan would be needed to bake a bannock, and the jewelry would be necessary. Some trippers make a list of the contents of each pack as they go about packing. The theory sounds fine, but, in practice, about the third day out, when adjustments should be made to keep the weights in the packs equal, the lists go for naught!

Take a final check of the outfitting list; everything should be checked as packed. Keep the original list; it probably will not be needed, but there is the off chance of forgetting how many packages of what were supposed to be used per meal. And if the outfitting were done exactly, the original planning better be followed unless some emergency arises.

9

COOKING SUGGESTIONS

There is no such thing as a cookbook for "outdoorsmen." Cooking in the open is the same as cooking anywhere else. Maybe exact temperatures cannot be achieved, refrigeration is lacking, the number and sizes of pots are limited, restraints are dictated by the supplies available, and, frequently, time does not allow for preparation of complicated dishes.

Otherwise, any household cookbook contains recipes and information that any canoeist can use. An "Outdoor Cookbook" just condenses the material and eliminates impractical recipes.

Anyone who can strike a match, build a fire, open a can, and boil water can turn out an acceptable meal in the bush. The better cook, however, adds a little imagination—the extra touch here and there that changes a bland meal into an experience. Above all, everything should be ready to serve at its proper temperature when the cook calls "chow" or "breadline," or whatever the cry for "come and get it" sounds like. Then as each person takes his plate away from the serving line, he should be able to look on the meal with anticipation—appearance is often just as important as taste. Watery cereal may taste as it should, but it will not look nor lift up on the spoon as expected. The black on the bottom of the corn bread can be scraped off, and the pine needle or two in the soup can be fished out, but the diners will enjoy the meal more if it looks right.

While some are more skilled around the fire than others, meal preparation should be a community affair with everyone playing a role—and not always the same role. One person may be a more accomplished baker than the others and willing to handle the bulk of that preparation, but the others should relieve him—maybe to improve their own skills, but mostly to spell him even though he may enjoy his work. There are other entertainments, and no cook should be tied to the fire for such a portion of the trip that he cannot enjoy the other aspects of the bush.

Meal planning and preparation should retain some simplicity. The household cookbook contains numerous recipes that demand hours of preparation—the pot that is put over low heat to simmer for the afternoon—but at home all that time need not be spent looking at the range. The cook can do other things, returning to the kitchen occasionally to check progress; but the open fire needs constant attention, and the cook cannot stray far from base. So the canoesman should leave most of those recipes out of his repertoire on a traveling day. There are some projects of a challenging nature that require time that might be tackled on a rest day, or maybe one when the weather prohibits other activities, and working around the fire becomes an interesting diversion.

In general it should be possible to serve any meal no more than an hour after the fire is laid. At breakfast the group wants to get on the water; at lunch, a little rest is enjoyed; and at dinner there are usually evening entertainments available that make the long, drawn-out meal undesirable.

But cooking does not have to consist of just opening cans or packages and heating the contents—that becomes monotonous.

Everyone should share in preparation—not just the walloping after the meal. If there is a character along who in fair weather never approaches the fire until the meal is served, he has no business forcing his way to the front of the fire in cold and rainy weather, offering to stir the soup or something equally helpful that will keep him next to the warmth.

MEASUREMENTS

With everyone getting into the act, there will be some operating around the kitchen who have little experience on the home range, and trying to read and digest cookbooks and recipes to gain outdoor basics in a short time may seem too confusing.

The recipe in the book gives exact measurements for a particular dish. But few cooks, either in the bush or at home, use absolutely accurate measurements, and few if any recipes require the exactness the recipe would seem to indicate. The practiced cook uses a pinch of this, a shake of that, and a handful of something else.

But without some experience in interpreting how many shakes make a spoonful, the beginner needs some idea of equivalents as he interprets the cookbook measures into those few that happen to be available around the fire. Some standards include:

1 tablespoon (tbsp.) equals 3 teaspoons (tsp.)
1 cup equals 16 tablespoons or ½ pint
1 pannikin (pann.) equals 2 cups or 1 pint

Meals that require merely opening cans and heating the contents pose few problems in estimating how many cans are needed for a meal, and the prepared mixes that indicate the number of servings can be interpreted easily so that the outfitter can judge how far a particular box of a certain food will take him. Bulk ingredients pose more problems—how many bannocks can be made from a seven-pound bag of flour? So, for them, here are some common volume-weight equivalents:

1 cup butter (or margarine) weighs ½ pound
1 cup flour weighs 5½ ounces
1 cup brown sugar weighs 5¼ ounces
1 cup white sugar weighs 7½ ounces
1 cup cornmeal weighs 6 ounces
1 cup powdered milk weighs 3¾ ounces

1 cup regular rice weighs 6½ ounces and will produce 3½ cups cooked rice
1 cup oatmeal weighs 4 ounces
1 cup Cream of Wheat (or similar closely packed cereal) weighs about 6 ounces

With a little knowledge, it can be reasonably estimated how far, for instance, two pounds of rice will go in feeding the group.

SUBSTITUTES

When searching for recipes, some cookbook ideas have to be rejected because the wannigans do not contain some of the supplies called for, but often substitutes can be made so that almost the same dish is produced—perhaps at some sacrifice in richness and body, but still a pleasant diversion from the meal drawn from a standard package. For instance, the following are logical substitutions:

To a large degree, butter, margarine, shortening, corn oil, and bacon fat are interchangeable. Taste may be slightly different, but quite pleasant.

Deep frying can be done in shortening, corn oil, or bacon fat. Butter burns easily. Lard is less versatile than shortening. Margarine can be used, but is perhaps better reserved as a spread.

Greasing a reflector pan before baking should be done with solid shortening. Butter, margarine, and bacon fat can be used with less satisfaction, and corn oil would be a last resort.

Eggs can be replaced with powdered eggs or egg substitute in baking, unless the recipe insists on separating the egg. The egg substitute will not produce scrambled eggs, however, which powdered eggs will do.

Brown and white sugar are almost interchangeable. Brown sugar dissolves and breaks down more quickly than white and, so, makes better syrup and blends more easily in baking.

Except for salt, most spices listed in a recipe can either be omitted or replaced with substitutes.

Milk for cooking can be replaced with either powdered or evaporated milk, diluted fifty–fifty with water. Evaporated milk or powdered whole milk make for a richer drink than powdered skim milk. Condensed milk has few uses outside cooking. Evaporated milk or one of the powdered cream substitutes make the best replacements for coffee cream.

Pure cocoa will replace chocolate in most recipes.

Dehydrated, freeze-dried, or canned products

will replace fresh ones in most recipes. Vegetables are easily substituted for. Dehydrated potatoes easily replace fresh mashed potatoes, and dehydrated slices make good pan fried or scalloped potatoes. Canned and freeze-dried meats will substitute for fresh, particularly in recipes calling for diced meats.

The list goes on, and just because one item mentioned in the recipe cannot be carried or has been used up is often not a cause for rejecting the recipe. The missing ingredient can often be omitted or replaced, making at most a minor alteration in taste—and sometimes a pleasant one.

COMMON PROBLEMS

There are a few common problems that the outdoor's cook will encounter as a result of using methods different from those at home or from using canned, dehydrated, or freeze-dried products instead of fresh or frozen produce. There is another group of difficulties that a practiced cook at home knows from experience; but the outdoor's chef may rarely set foot in the home kitchen, and may need help in producing hot cereal without lumps and fluffy rice over the open fire—just like mother does at home.

Coffee

Normally, coffee in the bush is boiled, so no complicated percolator or drip pot is needed. Use a regular grind of coffee, and use about the same amount as in any other method of preparation. Pour the loose coffee on the water before it starts to boil. Allow it to boil for several minutes; time is to be determined by the strength desired. Remove the pot from direct heat and keep it warm at the edge of the fire. The grounds will settle as soon as boiling ceases. Some suggest dropping an egg shell in to settle the grounds, but this is unnecessary. Some advocate a pinch of salt in the pot; but be sure it is only a pinch!

Tea

Using bulk tea, toss it into hot water just below the boiling point and allow it to steep. The Canadian guide will boil his tea, but the purists deplore this practice. Sometimes after tea color is reached, the leaves refuse to settle. Take the tea off the fire and toss in a cup of cold water; almost all the leaves will go down.

Dried Fruits

Dried fruits may be foreign to many home kitchens. Most can be consumed without cooking, but they swell and soften when soaked in water. Apples, in particular, swell an unbelievable amount. In preparing fruit for breakfast, some soak the fruit in a covered pot overnight. Others wait until morning and boil the fruit for a few minutes instead. Some sugar added to the boiling fruit makes a good syrup—perhaps ¾ cup of brown sugar to ½ pound of dried fruit. A little lemon peel can be added to prunes, and cinnamon goes well in stewed apples.

Cereals

Hot cereals are perhaps less used at home these days, so their preparation may not be familiar to some trippers. A smooth, thick cereal is preferred to a lumpy, watery concoction. Cereal should be added *slowly* to *salted, boiling* water while *stirring* constantly, thereby preventing lumps from forming. After the cereal is so mixed, the pot only needs to be stirred occasionally to check consistency.

Spaghetti, Macaroni, Noodles

The instructions on the package are always explicit in directing that these starches be added to *salted, boiling* water, but in haste there is a temptation to start cooking before the water boils. The strands will stick together in nonboiling water, forming a thick, pasty mess—quite chewy, but not usually considered tasty.

Rice

Regular rice comes both long- and short-grained. Long-grained is generally considered to be more tasty. Those who know usually prefer regular rice to other kinds, provided it is prepared correctly. Just like spaghetti, it should be cooked in boiling water until tender—probably about twenty minutes. The pot should be stirred occasionally to prevent rice from sticking to the bottom, and the water level must be watched. A cup of rice makes about 3½ to 4 cups of cooked rice, so a great deal of water is absorbed. If served directly from the pot, the grains glue together in a sticky mess as the starch that boiled out of the rice cools. At home, fluffy rice is produced by rinsing with cold water using a colander, until the starch is washed out. In the bush, drain the rice, add enough cold water to cover, stir, and drain again. Repeat until the water runs clear; it will be milk white with starch on the first couple of drainings. Unless cooked correctly, rice is disappointing.

Instant, or Minute, rice is easier to cook, and takes less time—about five minutes. It does not need to be drained, but there is a difference in taste.

Vermicelli and rice are mixed in many processed brands. Vermicelli is a product like spaghetti, and preparation usually calls for browning in a skillet, followed by boiling for a short time—five to ten minutes—as the rice cooks. A good number of these products also contain an envelope of flavoring similar to bouillon cubes or dehydrated soup bases. Although cooking starts by frying, the product is not the same as real Chinese fried rice.

CANNED MEATS AND VEGETABLES

With the possible exception of kernel corn, canned vegetables come packed in their own juices and can simply be heated to serving temperature. But a little imagination can be employed as might be done in any kitchen—maybe nothing more complicated than a little salt, pepper, and margarine or butter added when served. Or maybe make the dish look different by creaming the vegetables. A smooth mixture of one or two tablespoons of flour stirred into a half-cup of milk could be added as the vegetables simmer. Or a cream sauce could be made separately by melting a half-cup of butter or margarine over low heat, adding 1½ tablespoons of flour and mixing thoroughly, and then slowly stirring in two cups of milk. Continue stirring over low heat for several minutes, add salt and pepper, and pour over cooked vegetables. Or the sauce can become a cheese sauce by such an addition. If the group likes onions, adding diced onions, or dehydrated or freeze-dried onions, to the vegetables as they cook could be tried. Or maybe carry some spices to use.

Canned meats can also be prepared with a little imagination. Onions make a likely additive. Try chili powder or Tabasco Sauce. The canned-meat area offers more chance for inventiveness than the vegetable area, and only a few ideas follow.

Dumplings for Stews

Most stews are packed with a very high gravy content and may just be heated in the gravy—maybe with some additives. Or maybe top the pot with dumplings.

Make a firm batter from:

¼ cup butter
1 egg
1 cup flour
⅛ teaspoon salt
6 tablespoons milk (more or less)

Drop the batter by spoonful on top of the stew already heated. Do not crowd the pot, and room must be left to cover. Dumplings cook through steaming; try not to uncover until dumplings are done. After the pot is covered, move to such heat that the liquid will simmer. Allow about ten minutes before testing, which is done by pricking with a thin sliver of clean wood. If dough sticks, recover immediately and continue steaming.

Gravy in Canned Meats

Meats like hamburgers and meatballs are packed in a more concentrated gravy. Heating these directly from the can results in heating the gravy quickly to serving temperature, but the meat is tepid at best. If heated more, there is a strong possibility of burning. Adding about ¼ cup of water per can to the pot will produce a thinner gravy, but will allow simmering the meat for a sufficient time to warm it thoroughly.

Meat Loaf

Use canned meat to make a meat loaf. Canned hamburgers, meatballs, or luncheon meat are all suitable bases.

2 cans meat lightly ground with a fork
2 eggs slightly beaten
⅓ cup chopped onion
1 cup bread crumbs, cracker crumbs, or oatmeal
1½ teaspoon catsup, tomato paste, or chili sauce
¼ cup milk
salt, pepper to taste, and perhaps add mustard or chili powder

The actual ingredients can be quite varied. Mold into a loaf and bake for approximately an hour.

Luncheon Meats

These can be served cold, of course, or sliced and fried. They can be used as a base for a meat loaf. Otherwise, they could be diced and combined with various other foods like baked beans, macaroni, or spaghetti.

Corned Beef

Canned corned beef can be served cold, but if heated just as it comes from the can, it burns easily and sticks to the pan. Catsup or a tomato sauce is a natural, so heating by simmering in two cups of water and a package of dehydrated tomato soup or a can of tomato paste makes an attractive serving method. One package of soup makes a good tomato sauce for a couple of cans of meat.

Corned beef could also be used to make a hash, using either diced boiled fresh potatoes or maybe dehydrated mashed potatoes.

Corned Beef Hash

The canned variety of corned beef hash can be sliced and fried or prepared as with corned beef by simmering in a pot by adding water and a tomato base.

It also makes an attractive shepherd's pie by covering the bottom of the reflector pan with hash and topping with cooked dehydrated mashed potatoes—maybe sprinkled with cheese. Brush melted butter or margarine on top to brown the potatoes nicely. Evaporated milk straight from the can sprinkled on top also has the same effect. Bake until the meat is serving temperature and the potatoes have browned.

Chicken

Sliced chicken is packaged without liquid. A good base is provided by simmering in a couple cups of water and a package of one of the chicken-based dehydrated soups—chicken and rice being perhaps better than the others. Canned whole chickens are on the market, but are normally packed in so much broth that it makes carrying them almost prohibitive.

FREEZE-DRIED OR DEHYDRATED FOODS

The suggestions made regarding canned vegetables and meats are equally applicable to the freeze-dried foods—maybe even more necessary. The only real difference is the necessity of reconstituting the food either before or during cooking. Naturally, water thus added then becomes the base for whatever gravy or sauce is to go with the dish.

Freeze-Dried Vegetables

Most instructions indicate soaking in salted water before cooking. Cooking time is perhaps a little longer than for frozen vegetables, but varies greatly with the vegetable. There will not be much difference if the preliminary soaking is skipped and the vegetables are covered with salted water and placed on the fire immediately, cutting preparation time slightly. Be sure to use enough water—the excess can always be drained off; otherwise, as the water is absorbed, there is the risk of burning out the dry pot.

Dehydrated Vegetables

Preparation is similar to freeze-dried, but cooking takes longer. Beware of the dried vegetables off the grocer's shelf. They must be soaked and cooked for hours before being edible, and are used for soup bases when considerable preparation time is available. Split peas (which take less cooking time than whole peas), for instance, make an excellent soup base.

Freeze-Dried Meats

First, those freeze-dried meats like hamburgers, beef steaks, and pork sausage patties usually demand presoaking in warm water until the meat is tender. Cold water takes much longer, and hot water cooks the meat. Soaking time varies, but something like fifteen minutes is standard. Be sure the entire piece of meat is immersed; it is not unusual to require weight placed on top to keep the meat from floating. When tender, remove and drain off excess water, perhaps helping the process by pressing the water out with the back of the spatula. The normal cooking method would be frying, and, as the instructions will say, avoid overcooking, which will dry out the meat excessively.

Second, there are those that are perhaps cooked in the water in which they are reconstituted—maybe diced beef or chicken. Like freeze-dried vegetables, they do not have to be presoaked and cooking can begin as soon as the water is added. They make good bases for stews or maybe something like a spaghetti sauce. If served just as a meat dish, the finished product is infinitely improved by some of the additives suggested for canned stews or meats with gravy. But the gravy base is lacking and the water in which it is cooked is relatively tasteless. Beef or chicken bouillon labeled in the grocery store as a gravy base gives a good start. Then try a tomato base for beef or a chicken soup base for chicken.

There are a few dishes that traditionally seem connected with either camping or canoeing, and perhaps the tripper wants to experiment. Most would not be used in the home kitchen, and may not be included in a standard cookbook. Some are baked products like bannock and trapper's bread and are included in chapter 11. Then there is the traditional leavening agent in sour dough that might be worth some experimentation, which is also reserved for the discussion of baking.

Jerky

The old woodsman's concentrated, compact food was jerky. It was his means for preserving meat in a warm climate, and the ease with which it could be transported made it a logical tripping food. There are some commercial brands available, although prices look high in terms of volume and weight.

It requires about five pounds of lean, red meat to make a pound of jerky. Trim off all fat; cut into strips about one-half inch wide. Dip each strip into heavily salted boiling water until the meat loses its red color. Then hang in a warm, dry place where air can circulate freely around the strips. Finished jerky is almost black and shriveled. It has the texture of shoe leather, but the energy content is high. It can be chewed (with difficulty) just so, or added to stews, although water does not soften it appreciably nor make chewing much easier.

If the drying is accomplished outdoors—which is preferable—hang it in the sun, covering at night, and keeping it protected from rain. A small fire nearby built from nonresinous, sweet wood will help keep off flies and insects. But the meat should not be allowed to cook. It will take a few days to dry completely, depending on weather.

Pemmican

Jerky has no fat content; the fat would turn rancid during the curing. But without fat it makes an incomplete diet, so the standard fur trader's diet was pemmican, which is jerky to which rendered animal fat is added. (The Hudson's Bay Company marketed some in 1970 to celebrate their three hundredth anniversary.)

To make at home, pound strips of jerky into tiny pieces. Melt down raw suet or other animal fat—without boiling. Put jerky into a waterproof bag (plastic is best). The voyageur used a hide

A

C

D

B

E

F

Baking beans in the sand: A) fire is built in hole on sand beach; B) after beans are boiled, pot is lined with salt pork, beans are added, and also an onion —if desired; C) pot is covered with aluminum foil; D) lid is wired down tightly; E) fire and coals are scraped from the hole; F) pot is covered with warm sand, leaving bail protruding.

145

with the hair turned out, and, sewed his pemmican into ninety-pound bales. Several times around the Red River district of Canada the inland trade came to a standstill when politics cut off the pemmican from the buffalo country. Pour enough rendered fat into the bag to cover the jerky, allow to congeal, and seal off the bag.

The fur brigades traveled on a ration of a couple pounds of pemmican per man per day. About all that was lacking in a pemmican diet was fresh fruit. A steady fare of pemmican would be monotonous, but healthy. The old-timers sometimes added wild berries—blueberries particularly—to their pemmican.

Baked Beans

Baked beans now usually come from a can, and few homemakers cook their own. The possibility of using hot sand for an oven makes it possible to bake beans overnight on the trail, or during a rest day, without spending a great deal of time and without tying up the cookery during mealtime.

The oven is created by digging a hole in a sand beach, maybe eighteen inches or so deep, and then building a fire in the hole. There is normally enough trash wood lying around so that fuel need not be carefully drawn and split as for the cooking fire. Stir the sand occasionally while the fire burns, so that more than just the surface sand is heated. An emergency shovel ought to be blocked crudely from a stick of wood; never use a canoe paddle that the hot sand will burn. It will take a couple of hours to heat the sand with a reasonably good driftwood fire. The sand is right when a drop of water sprinkled on it evaporates immediately with a sizzling sound.

For a baking container, a Dutch oven of heavy aluminum or iron is best. A normal, thin aluminum pot transmits heat too quickly from the sand and burns the beans. The pot must have a lid that can be secured firmly to keep out the sand.

The oven, of course, can be constructed using the regular fireplace if it were built on sand, but it is normally more convenient to build a separate bean hole so that a meal can be cooked on the regular fire without the additional chore of trying to heat the sand to oven temperature.

While the sand heats, soak enough dry beans to fill the Dutch oven. If in doubt as to which of several kinds available on the grocery shelf to use, try pea beans first. They will expand during soaking, slightly more than doubling in bulk.

When space over the normal cooking fire allows, place the pot in which the beans are soaking on to boil. Add about ½ teaspoon of baking soda as the liquid starts to boil; it reduces the acidity of the beans. Nine times out of ten the baking soda will cause the pot to boil over. Continue boiling until the beans are tender; a half hour or better. Test by taking a couple on a spoon and blowing on them. When done, the thin outer shell of the bean will peel back. Using a taste test, the bean should be soft. Avoid boiling too long; mushy beans bake poorly and result in a less-attractive dish.

Meanwhile, slice enough salt pork to line the bottom and sides of the Dutch oven. Bacon can be substituted. Then dice about half as much pork or bacon as was used to line the pot.

Spoon the drained beans into the Dutch oven. When the pot is about one-third full, add a couple of chunks of pork, a generous amount of pepper, the same of salt if bacon is used, a little bacon fat or cooking oil, and some molasses and/or brown sugar. The amount of oil, molasses, and sugar depends on the size pot, but each couple of cups of dry beans will demand about ½ cup of each. Molasses and brown sugar can be used in a 1:1 ratio, or the ratio can lean more heavily on one than the other, depending on taste. As each third of the pot is filled, a layer of pork, condiments, and liquid is added. If preferred, the oil, molasses, and sugar can be added all at once from the top. A peeled onion placed in the center of the beans makes a good dividend.

The pot top must fit securely, so avoid overloading. For a more secure seal, place a layer of aluminum foil over the beans, and then seat the top securely using copper wire from the canoe repair kit, copper fishing line, or maybe a piece of the radio antenna, making sure that the bail is positioned upward.

When the pot is secured, scrape the fire and charred wood from the hole. Place the pot in the hot sand, bail up. Then push hot sand around the sides and over the top letting the bail protrude above the sand. Use sand for the covering, not the remains of the fire; too much heat will burn rather than bake.

The beans will bake in about six hours, or by morning if baked overnight. The sand will still be uncomfortably warm, so keep hands and feet out of the area. Pull the oven out carefully by the bail, and brush off all sand before opening. Remove the top and gasket material carefully, and wipe the lip of the pot with a clean cloth to remove all sand. Baking temperatures are erratic, so what the pot contains the first couple of times that the baking is attempted will be something of a surprise. With experience it becomes easier to estimate temperatures. If baked in the home oven, the temperature should have been 250° for the full time. Beans should be browned evenly, of course, but results vary. If underdone, they can be cooked more on the regular cooking fire, being careful not to use so much heat that the beans boil instead of baking. If they are overdone, well— the center should be edible even if the outer rim is a little burned.

Beans are best served warm as they come from the sand, but if baked overnight and carried over until lunch, they can be warmed over a normal fire before serving.

It is possible to bake over or beside the cooking fire if a sand oven cannot be made, but the pot must be watched closely. Since heat comes only from a limited direction, the pot must be turned about every fifteen minutes during the six hours or more that the baking takes. The temperature should be such that the beans bake and do not boil instead, making their preparation without sand tedious and time-consuming.

10

FISH

Fish represent the only country food to be encountered. Game and fowl are invariably out of season, even if the Indian is allowed a snack of moose meat, a duck here and there, or the odd Canadian goose. If game is to be taken, perhaps squirrels and rabbits, a cookbook should be consulted for preparation and cooking.

While the practiced angler needs no reminders on how to treat his catch, maybe the novice does. The first-time fisherman who is satisfied with little or no action is rare, and canoeing areas offer greater chance for success than perhaps more crowded waters easily reached by automobile. Carry at least one fishing outfit, even if very little experience is present. The bug will catch someone!

Naturally, adhere to state or province licensing regulations. Licenses are normally available local to the point of departure; sometimes from the appropriate governmental agency, often also from local outfitters. Resident and nonresident differences are universal, and while a standard license is valid for a year, often there are also shorter-term licenses at a lower cost. Youngsters may also qualify for a less-expensive permit provided there is an adult license in the group. Occasionally the authorities insist on a license for each person in the canoe carrying fishing gear, and some local rules may insist that everyone canoeing the area must have a license.

At canoeing time all game fish are in season, but there may be local restrictions peculiar to certain waters, and sometimes the trip could travel through restricted country; Quebec, for instance, has some sections where the fishing rights have been leased. The fishing laws usually place size qualifications on fish to be kept—which vary with the species—as well as daily and possession limits. Unless the trip is primarily a fishing excursion, it would be very rare for the canoe party to come close to exceeding these limits.

Use barbless hooks if fishing for sport and not the pot. But if release is to be made from a barbed hook, be gentle. If possible, do not remove the fish from the water at all. A pair of long needle-nose pliers will help recover the lure from a gluttonous pike who swallows the bait.

Fish should be cleaned and cooked as soon as possible. However, they are often taken in the evening to be held until breakfast, or caught in midafternoon to be cooked in the evening

The best means for keeping the catch fresh until cooking time is live storage. A light metal or plastic stringer with safety-pin-like hooks passed through the fish's lower jaw allow him to live. Some species are more delicate than others and may not survive even if released from a barbed hook immediately, but often fish can be kept on a stringer for twelve hours and still live if released; and there are times when the fishermen's eyes are

Metal stringer makes live storage easy.

bigger than their stomachs and excess fish should be released. If no stringer is available, a cord strung through the lower jaw will sometimes perform the same function. Do not pass a stringer or a cord through the gills. Chances of survival are nil. Of course, hooking through the lower jaw works only on those species with bony jaws; do not try it with a whitefish, for instance.

Storage at the campsite on a stringer works best; such storage while in the canoe is less satisfactory, unless still fishing. A fish dragged behind a moving canoe obviously acts like a sea anchor, but he will also drown, for he cannot work his gills properly against the water pressure. Fish are better tossed in the canoe while trolling or traveling. The sternsman will object to the odor that permeates the bottom of the canoe once he starts to portage. So, wash the canoe out before storing for the night. The sternsman would probably

rather carry a few more ounces the next day than a canoe that smells of fish.

If the fish cannot be kept alive, the meat will be more firm if the catch is cleaned as soon as practical. Maybe not just as the fish comes from the water, but within a reasonable time. Once cleaned, the fish should be stored under cover in a cool place, avoiding exposure to both flies and heat. If the fish are to be transported before cooking, store in a plastic bag, packed to avoid the heat of the sun, or use a container lined with damp moss or ferns.

If cleaning is to be delayed, storage is satisfactory using the stringer and keeping the whole fish underwater. The meat will stay firm and fresh —at least overnight.

In canoe country, fish are normally cleaned either by filleting or by gutting and cooking whole, with or without the head having been removed.

149

Trout and those to be baked should be gutted. Ones to be planked or roasted need special preparation. The time and energy expended scaling fish is just not worth it. Except for pan-sized trout, release a fish too small to fillet. In a couple years someone may have something on his line worth bragging about. On the other hand, do not scorn the medium-sized fish. Many consider the two- to three-pound walleye better eating than the one in the six- to eight-pound class.

There are two methods of filleting: one demands six cuts with the knife; the second, called a boneless fillet, requires eight, and takes maybe twice as long to accomplish and produces maybe only two-thirds as much meat—but no bones to speak of. A straight fillet is normally used on smaller fish, while the boneless fillet is used for those more than, say, four pounds, and on those with a large number of bones—pike of any size.

If the opportunity presents itself, watch a skilled guide clean a catch. A normal fillet takes him a minute; a boneless, half again as long. Of course he has cleaned a goodly number to gain his skill; so do not expect the job to be so perfect on the first try.

Work on a flat, level, stable surface. A flat rock near the lake is fine. If nothing else is handy, use the blade of a paddle. Under no circumstances use a wannigan top or anything that must either be carried or kept close to other food—the fish odor will linger for days. And do not use the picnic table put on the campsite by park authorities either; it cannot be cleaned easily afterwards.

Use a long, sharp knife with a thin, pliable blade. There should be one in the jewelry. If perhaps a little dull, a couple of strokes with the ax file will get it back in shape before starting. A sharpening stone would be better.

Lay the fish flat, grasping the head so that the tail points toward the knife hand. Make the first cut perpendicular to the fish, just behind the gills and pectoral fin, cutting almost to the backbone and angled downward a little more on the belly side, but not deep enough to reach the stomach.

Then turn the blade parallel to the backbone and cut toward the tail, parallel to the backbone, taking off a slab of meat as thick as possible without penetrating the stomach.

Cut almost to the tail and then turn the fillet over past the tail, leaving it still attached. Place the knife under the fillet, over the skin at the tail, and angle the knife almost parallel to the cutting board. Hold the fish just above the tail, and pull with that hand while working the knife forward, separating the fillet from the skin.

A

B

C

Walleye fillet: A) first cut made behind pectoral fin; B) knife then parallels backbone; C) cutting toward tail, stay close to backbone, avoiding stomach cavity; D) without severing skin, fillet is flipped over tail, and knife is inserted between fillet and skin; E) pulling back on tail and cutting forward, fillet starts to separate from the skin; F) similar start is made on opposite side; G) fillet is separated in same manner on second side; H) after rinsing, two slabs of meat remain.

D

E

F

G

H

Repeat on the opposite side, and there should be two slabs of meat. Wash, and they are ready for the pan.

A boneless fillet separates the fillet from the rib bones that are included in the first method. Some meat is lost, making each fillet smaller, and there will still be a few tiny bones, although the major ones will be removed. Make the same first cut perpendicular to the backbone and behind the pectoral fin. Then, with the fish resting on its belly, slit the skin just to one side of the backbone, and penetrate until the ribs are reached, slitting the length of the backbone in the process, but again leaving a small section of skin attached at the tail. Then continue cutting along the outline of the ribs all the way to the belly skin.

Then flip the fillet over the tail and skin as before. Repeat on the opposite side and there should be two fillets of almost boneless meat.

If the fish is to be cooked whole, or the skin is to be left on—speckled trout and scaleless fish in particular—simply rest the fish on its belly on the board, cut downward behind the gills perpendic-

151

Boneless fillet on a pike: A) make first cut behind pectoral fin; B) knife cut starts just to one side of backbone; C) cut is made parallel to backbone; D) meat is carefully separated along ribs; E) skin is removed as with regular fillet; F) second side starts like the first; G) meat is separated from the ribs; H) skin is removed in like manner.

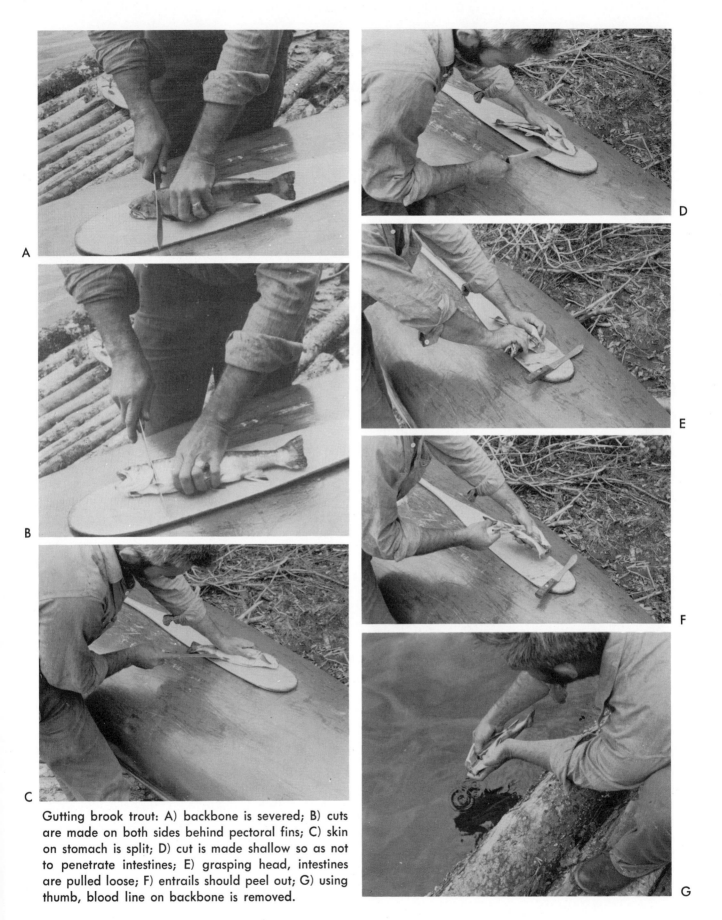

Gutting brook trout: A) backbone is severed; B) cuts
are made on both sides behind pectoral fins; C) skin
on stomach is split; D) cut is made shallow so as not
to penetrate intestines; E) grasping head, intestines
are pulled loose; F) entrails should peel out; G) using
thumb, blood line on backbone is removed.

153

ular to the backbone, severing the backbone, but stopping before reaching the entrails. Then slit the skin on either side of the pectoral fin. Lay the fish on its side and slit the belly without penetrating the stomach, passing the knife to the side of the vent. Grasp the head and pull slightly downward, and the head and entrails all come loose. Wash and remove the blood line on the underside of the backbone with the thumbnail. If the head is to be left on, the same procedure is followed—just removing the entrails without severing the head on the first cut.

Fish remains should never be thrown in the bush; the odor of rotten fish will permeate the area and attract the garbage-dump bear. There should be no leftover fish after the meal either; only those that can be used should be kept for the pot. Anyway, what remains from the cleaning should be burned, buried in the latrine, or tossed far out in the water. The predators will make short work of what is left.

If a particular fish really should make the taxidermist, there is probably little chance of getting him out of the wilderness unless the guide knows how to skin the fish and preserve it in salt. Take all the necessary pictures, and then, regretfully, add him to the pot.

If refrigeration is only twenty-four hours away, it may be worth a try. Take pictures, record the fish's measurement—girth particularly—gut the fish, leaving the head intact, making only a slit in the belly to remove the entrails. Pack the fish in damp moss, a damp cloth, or a plastic bag, and store out of the sun in a cool place. If the fish can be kept cool enough so there will be no spoilage before reaching a freezer, pack the fish carefully without cleaning.

If there is cooked fish left after a meal, it can be carried and reheated. It will not be quite as tasty as when first out of the pan, but there are some who prefer cold fish.

Smoking will preserve fish, but takes longer than is normally available. At home with a properly enclosed smoking rig, the job can be done in less than twenty-four hours. In the bush the Indian usually takes a couple of days to smoke his fish. He makes a three- or four-legged tepee of spruce poles over his smoking fire. Rails are lashed to the frame about three feet off the ground, and small poles are often laid across the rails to form a grate. He then builds a small smoke fire underneath, using the wood that happens to be available. Birch or a sweet wood would give better flavor than the gummy pines. To increase

Indian smokes fish on rails above a smoldering fire.

the efficiency and direct his smoke, he often wraps an old piece of canvas around the frame, leaving a smoke hole at the top and room at the bottom for the fire to breathe. The fire is kept low, burning all day for several days, and the fish are turned periodically when the fire is tended. His finished product is a dark brown color—sometimes mixed with a little black—and may not appear attractive to the vacationer, though it may taste fine. The Indian does the same with any game or fowl taken in warm weather.

Some natives residing in a permanent summer home have an unoccupied tepee or pudding tent nearby, reserved as a summer smoke tent, and so get greater efficiency. Instead of laying fish on a rack, the Indian usually skewers the fish through the tail. The cleaning process is altered so the skin is left on each fillet, and often the belly skin is left intact. The head is first removed, and then, with the fish lying on its belly, two cuts are made on either side of the backbone, as with a boneless fillet, meeting at the belly skin; then backbone, ribs, and entrails are removed as one, leaving two fillets still joined at tail and belly—which are sometimes then separated.

154

A more efficient smoking operation requires a tepee enclosure. Fish are most likely skewered on a wooden rod above the fire.

Fried Fish

Probably the most universal method of preparation, and certainly the easiest and quickest, is to fry fish.

Heat cooking oil in the skillet until warm enough, so that a small piece of fish dropped in it will rise to the surface and bubble. If the pan starts to smoke, it is too warm. Use any cooking oil—shortening, lard, or corn oil. For reasons of economy, however, bacon fat is best, and at breakfast, as soon as the bacon is done, the pan is ready for fish. The purist may object to the bacon flavor; others swear by it. But then the expert may have his own recipe requiring margarine or, more likely, butter for his oil. The novice should avoid both, as they burn when heated to frying temperature.

Oil should be about one-half-inch deep in the pan, depending on the thickness of the fish.

Cut fillets or whole fish into pan-sized pieces. If using whole fish, like trout, cut into pan-sized pieces, making cuts perpendicular to the backbone. Include the tail section; it is delicious. With large, thick pieces, make additional cuts on either side perpendicular to the backbone, but not through, so that the oil can work into the meat during cooking.

Allow fish to dry, and then either cook immediately with no further preparation, or salt and pepper to taste before frying, or roll in a batter or dry flour-based mixture.

The easiest coating is either straight flour or a mixture of flour and cornmeal. The fish is rolled in the dry mixture, lightly coating both sides of the fillets or the inside and outside of the whole fish. Place flour in a plate for rolling, or shake the fish in a plastic or cloth bag containing the mix-

155

Large brook trout should be scored with cuts perpendicular to backbone before frying.

ture. Excess flour must be bushed; it cannot be
retained for other usage; do not replace in the
flour bag!

More complicated batters can be made from
flour so that the batter will just run from the
spoon—not in a straight stream—but only for a
couple of inches, and then the stream breaks and
the batter drops in a "splat." The batter will improve if allowed to stand for a while before using.
Proportions might run: 1⅛ cup flour, 1 teaspoon
salt, ¼ teaspoon pepper, 1 tablespoon oil, ¾ cup
milk, 2 beaten eggs.

Then slip the fish into hot pan, being careful
not to splatter hot oil over the cook. Any water
dropped into hot oil will cause the oil to spit and
jump at the unwary cook, and burns from hot oil
are painful and dangerous, and one of the most
common first aid problems.

Fry until the underside is browned; turn and
repeat on the other side. The fish is done when
browned on both sides if oil has been allowed to
work into flesh. If the fish is so thick or large that
the two sides are browned while the middle is
uncooked, either the oil was not deep enough in
the pan, or it was not allowed to work around the
fish well enough. Tipping the pan slightly during
the cooking helps to ensure that heat also reaches
the center.

Remove the fish from the pan with a spatula
or long-handled fork, allowing the oil to drip off
by holding it a few moments over the pan, and
then let the fish drain completely on paper towels
(which are probably not available), a piece of
clean birch bark, or in a pan slightly tipped so the
drippings will collect away from the fish.

Broiled Fish

Place fillets on a grate, either carried for that

156

purpose or manufactured by weaving green hardwood branches about ¼- to ½-inch thick. Position the grill over the fire so the flame does not quite reach the grill—and burn the wooden one. Cook one side first and then the other. Baste fillets with hot cooking oil or a strip of bacon. Fish alone is quite dry. Add salt and pepper while broiling.

Broiling can also be done by skewering fish on a spit of hardwood. This is done much better with whole fish or fillets with the skin still attached, as the Indian does for smoking. Cooked fish flakes and will likely drop into the fire.

Planked Fish

This is a little harder, but a surer way to broil. Make a flat plank from a piece of sweet wood; do not use gummy pines. Clean fish as the Indian does for smoking, or just make two fillets without removing the skin.

Warm the board by the fire and peg the fish to it, using hardwood pegs—not pines again—or maybe small nails. Prop the board, with the fish attached, beside the fire, where it will get good heat without being touched by the flames. Baste with a strip of bacon skewered on the end of a twig, or peg a couple of thin strips along the top of the fish. Turn the plank several times to get even heat over the entire fish. The fish is done when meat flakes when touched with a fork.

Fish Baked in Coals

Clean whole fish by removing the head and entrails—this works best with lake trout or speck-

Planked fish tacked to hardwood board with pegs; strips of bacon for basting

led trout. Stuff belly cavity with some boiled diced onion, add salt and pepper to taste, and a little butter or other oil, or, better still, a few strips of bacon. Seal tightly in aluminum foil. Large green leaves can be substituted for foil in an emergency, but several wrappings are needed, and large green leaves are hard to find in canoe country! Place the package in the coals—not in a roaring fire— maybe about five minutes on a side; but cooking time will depend on the size of fish and the heat of coals, so it may be necessary to experiment a little.

Fish Baked in Reflector

Use a fish that when cleaned will fill the reflector pan reasonably well; perhaps cut it in half if the pan is small and the fish is large. Lay the halves side by side. Lake trout and large speckled trout again bake best.

Soak the cleaned whole fish in saltwater for fifteen minutes; then drain. Stuff with crumbled leftover bread, finely chopped onion moistened with bacon drippings or melted butter, and salt and pepper. Brush the outside of the fish lightly with bacon drippings or oil, and lay a couple of strips of bacon in the pan under the fish. If the fish is large, make slits in the sides at about one-inch intervals to let heat penetrate better.

Line the pan with aluminum foil or a clean birch bark slab for ease in cleaning afterwards. Place fish on bacon strips, put a couple of strips on top of the fish, and bake in front of a hot fire for ten minutes or so; then move the reflector back slightly to give medium heat, and bake until fish

Larger fish are cut into sections and fried in oil, maybe one-half inch deep. Oil must reach interior of each piece.

Large speckled trout (as shown) or lake trout can be baked in a reflector.

flakes at the touch of a fork—figuring about eight or ten minutes per pound of fish.

Fish Chowder

Fold the cleaned fish in a fresh dish towel or cloth and hang in a pot of boiling water for about ten minutes, or until skin and bones will lift away easily or flesh will come away, using the tines of a fork to pull it away from the bones. Save water in which fish was steamed.

Fry a good quantity of diced salt pork (boil salt pork first to remove some of the salt) or bacon, and add diced onions. When the onions become translucent, pour off into as much of the fish water as will be needed—discarding extra water (amounts depend on how much fish is used, and how thick a chowder is desired).

Add a meal of diced fresh potatoes or dehydrated potato slices, and when potatoes start to soften, add the clear fish meat.

Add milk until chowder color and consistency is reached. Whole milk is much preferred over skimmed for chowder—if using dehydrated milk. Evaporated milk is even better.

Simmer over a slow fire until the potatoes are tender—but not so long that they become mushy —adding salt and pepper to taste. Do not allow to boil after milk is added.

Chowder preparation takes a couple hours, so it is likely a rest-day or half-day project.

More Chowder Suggestions

Bones can be removed from the fish without being cased in the cloth, simply by boiling fish until flesh falls away. Bones must then be picked out carefully so none remain in the chowder water.

Chowders can include almost any ingredients that happen to be available. Kernel corn makes a good addition. Diced ham or luncheon meat can be added instead of (or in addition to) bacon or salt pork. A little butter or margarine also helps. Tomatoes will make more of a Manhattan chowder.

11

BAKING

One of the most intriguing and satisfying exercises around the outdoor kitchen is reflector baking. In a couple of days, fresh baked goods run out or go stale, and carrying bread for an extended period would make the packs so bulky that they would be unwieldy.

There are innumerable mixes for making biscuits, cakes, pies, and almost every conceivable baked product. All are adaptable to the wilderness by substituting the reflector for the home oven. Temperatures cannot be exact, but the reflector, used properly, can be adjusted to do anything done by the home oven.

Using prepared mixes limits the versatility, and a more varied menu can be offered by starting with flour and other raw ingredients and mixing them in different proportions.

All baked breadstuffs require some leavening agent, of which there are four of interest to the tripper. The most universal is baking powder, which makes baked goods of the biscuit-cake variety. For camp baking, a double-action baking powder is used, and the camper can get by quite well going no farther than baking-powder products. The second agent is yeast, which is employed in bread and rolls. For tripping, dry yeast is used instead of cakes, which need refrigeration and have a shorter shelf life. Some recipes call for baking soda, which does not have great leavening power, but is used to combat the acid content of other ingredients in the recipe. It is normally called for in conjunction with baking powder and is used alone only in some cookie recipes. The fourth possibility is sour dough. It is a home-brewed leavening agent, now mainly used by trappers and prospectors who spend long periods in a semipermanent camp. For novelty the tripper may want to make his own. Normally, baking powder and yeast provide enough versatility for anyone.

BAKING POWDER BREADS

The woodsman's baking powder bread is bannock. It is a simple dough made from flour, salt, shortening, baking powder, and water. Adding other ingredients and changing the proportions create different tastes and products, and there is only a fine line of distinction between the bannock and a cake, depending on egg, sugar, and butter content. But baking-powder products include biscuits, muffins, bannocks, cakes, pies, cookies, and then pancakes and doughnuts.

There are probably as many bannock recipes as there are woodsmen. No two veterans mix bannock the same, and most cannot write down their exact proportions. As with most experienced cooks, measurements are only approximate.

Bannocks can be turned out without a store-bought reflector. Some Indians bake with a skillet. He pours his batter into the fry pan, puts it over

Indian method of baking bannock: A) dough is set by heating over fire; B) skillet is then propped up in front of fire.

the fire until the dough sets—like a pancake—and then props the skillet in front of the fire at an angle so his cake will not slip out, and lets it bake.

A reflector can also be created from something shiny like aluminum foil, inventing a rig such that the reflecting surfaces throw heat into both top and bottom of a baking dish. Baking can also be done in a Dutch oven either in hot sand (see *Baked Beans* in chapter 9) or by placing the oven near the fire and turning occasionally. But if baking is to be more than a novelty, a reflector does a better job with less effort. A basic bannock dough, using only the absolutely essential ingredients, is formed by using the following approximate formula: 1½ heaping tablespoons of baking powder; 2 heaping tablespoons of shortening; ⅓ teaspoon salt to every 2 cups flour; and enough water to make a heavy batter. From there the cook is on his own to invent his own mixtures.

160

The keys to successful baking are blending the ingredients and handling the reflector, not what goes into the batter. The first mixing problem is blending the shortening with dry ingredients. If sugar is used, start there. Add the shortening and cream together; then add the other dry ingredients. Some cooks melt their shortening or use corn oil to make blending easier. Some mix the dry ingredients first and then work the shortening in with their hands. Some use a table knife to cut in the solid shortening when tossed on top of the dry ingredients. Whatever method is used, be sure the shortening blends well.

Do not add liquids until everything is set—pan prepared, oven ready, fire suitable. Once liquids get to baking powder it starts reacting, often prematurely dissipating its leavening power.

For bannocks and cakes, the reflector pan should be well coated with shortening, being sure that corners and edges are particularly well treated. Any solid equivalent of shortening will work—butter, margarine, or cold bacon fat. Liquid cooking oil will not be appropriate, except in an emergency.

For pies, biscuits, and cookies, the reflector pan should be dusted with flour rather than greased. For a few special projects like upside-down cakes, dusting over a coating of shortening works best.

With the dry ingredients well blended and the pan and fire ready, start adding the liquids—the dry ingredients can be blended well ahead of baking if desired. Use cool liquids, not hot, nor even warm. Baking powder reacts immediately with heat, and mixing with warm water results in loss of effectiveness before the bannock gets near the fire. Add liquids a little at at time—measurements are only approximate, and a thin batter requires that moisture be steamed out during baking, making the whole process longer than necessary. The batter should be thick and smooth and of such a consistency that it will just pour from the mixing bowl to the baking pan, where it must be leveled with a spoon to fill the corners of the pan.

The mixing from the dry stage to the batter ready to be poured should take only a few minutes, and the last minute or so should involve a folding motion with the mixing spoon to fluff up the batter and allow air to be trapped in it. The batter should then be panned immediately and baking started.

Then the employment of the reflector and the actual baking must be watched. The reflector could be warmed in front of the fire before slipping in the pan, but be sure that the reflector sits level after the pan is added. Obviously, temperatures must be approximated. Cakes call for 325° to 350°, while biscuits demand a hotter oven at home. With the reflector, the temperature is gauged by holding a hand in front of the pan when all is in position. If the hand can be held in place for about three to four seconds before becoming uncomfortably warm, the temperature is about right for bannocks or cakes. Then adjust for a hotter or cooler oven.

Review the previous injunctions about fire building and placement with respect to the wind (see chapter 4), and about various woods and their baking qualities (see chapter 5).

Baking is only one facet of meal preparation, but the top will brown better if there are no pots directly in front of the reflector, at least during the initial baking stages—but often meal preparation makes it impossible to leave such an important area open.

Heat at the front of the oven will be greater than at the rear, so the pan should be turned about two-thirds of the way through the baking. Test the front to be sure it is set before turning. Every woodsman has his own test, from slivers of wood to the proverbial broom straw. A simple expedient, after some experience is gained using the reflector, is tapping the front of the bannock lightly with the knuckles. If the front is firm, it is time to turn. If still soft, wait awhile. Test across the pan; there may not have been even heat at both ends.

Turning prematurely may take the bannock away from the fire at a crucial time, letting it cool and fall, never to regain its full potential. When turning, the pan should be repositioned in front of the fire as quickly as possible. With most reflectors, speed in turning is achieved by taking the whole reflector away from the fire, turning the pan, and then replacing the rig. Turning the pan while the reflector remains in position is trickier and slower; plus getting the cook's hands too close to the fire. The well-equipped jewelry contains a pair of asbestos-palmed cooking mittens for handling the reflector and its pan.

A good reflector with a reasonable fire should bake a bannock in twenty-five to thirty minutes, depending on the thickness of the cake. A moist batter demands more time, and so does a batter that includes fruit, which adds some moisture that must be steamed out. If baking takes more than thirty-five minutes, the fire was poor, the reflector poorly placed, the batter too thin, or,

A

B

C

Reflector bannock: A) batter should just spill from bowl to pan; B) heat is tested by holding hand in front of reflector; C) pan is turned after bannock sets; D) bannock is turned out on wannigan top to cool.

D

most likely, the reflecting surfaces were not polished sufficiently after the previous use.

When done, turn out the bannock on a clean surface; the underside of a wannigan top is particularly adaptable. Bannock cuts and serves better when cool; it is moist and crumbly if cut immediately. Bannock to be transported for a later meal should be stored in the reflector pan after it is cleaned and the bannock has cooled. Allow one side to cool for fifteen minutes or so, and then turn it over to permit the other side to cool, otherwise it will stick to the surface on which it was laid. Be sure to cool a traveling bannock; do not just leave it in the pan; the bottom becomes soggy.

Occasionally, too much heat gets to a spot on the bottom, sticking the bannock to the pan. Usually, tapping the pan with a spoon or dull side of a table knife will free the small area where sticking occurred. A more careful greasing job next time will probably solve the problem, as will more careful attention during the baking. If serious sticking occurred, run a table knife around the bannock's sides before attacking it with a spatula to free the bottom.

The reflector will turn out an upside-down cake, but it should bake from the top down, and a couple of sticks of wood should be stuffed into the lower part of the reflector, or a spare skillet, or anything that will reduce the reflecting quality of the lower surface. Baking time will almost double as a result.

Bannock

Bannock made using only the essential ingredients previously listed is rather bland. A much improved product is produced by using the following recipe:

3 cups flour
½ teaspoon salt
2 heaping tablespoons baking powder
½ cup shortening
2 tablespoons egg substitute or 1 egg
¼–¾ cup sugar
1½ tablespoons powdered milk
1½–2 cups water (more or less to make a stiff batter)

Mix and bake as instructed above. Measurements are only approximate, but proportions are reasonable. Total amount of batter should be adjusted so that the baking pan will be no more than two-thirds full.

Eggs—Spell one of the differences between bannock and cake. In general, the more eggs, the richer the bannock. Fresh eggs are best, powdered eggs next in order, and egg substitute better than nothing—but they can be left out if unavailable.

Sugar—Another distinction between a cake and bannock, but its addition will be noticeable. Bake with brown sugar instead of white. Few who make the experiment will return to white; brown blends more easily.

Shortening—Using butter instead of shortening also turns the bannock into a cake. However, shortening is easier to carry and can be used in other areas where butter makes a poor substitute.

Milk—Powdered skim milk will not be missed. Powdered whole milk will add richness, as will evaporated milk, but weight and bulk make using milk quite optional.

Baking exactly the same bannock recipe twice a day becomes boring both for the cook and the diners. So vary the flavor, texture, and composition of the bannocks with the following:

Corn bread—The purist will demand a slightly different recipe, but an acceptable corn bread can be turned out by replacing a third to a half of the flour with cornmeal. Corn bread will not rise quite as much as bannock. Use a 2:1 flour to cornmeal ratio in a corn bread to be transported. A 1:1 ratio makes a loose corn bread that crumbles easily. The Southern cook will deplore the use of sugar, but most others like it.

Biscuits—Use a basic bannock batter with no additives, and increase the baking powder slightly. Roll out thick dough and cut into biscuit shape—a small food can with both ends removed makes an excellent cutter. Or make drop biscuits with a slightly more watery dough. If a more exact recipe is desired, the labels on many baking-powder cans provide a ready cookbook.

Cinnamon—Add 1 teaspoon of cinnamon to the dry ingredients. Or mix half with the batter and the rest with a couple of teaspoons of sugar that can be sprinkled over the top before baking.

Raisin—Add ½ cup of raisins to the batter, reducing flour slightly. Takes a little longer to bake because of moisture brought in by fruit.

Blueberry—Add a ¾ cup of wild blueberries. Baking takes longer. Raspberries are also likely targets for the berry pickers. Use as fresh fruit, however. The bannock is fine if eaten with eyes closed; the color is a shocking pink!

Vanilla—A welcome additive. Add a teaspoon or so to the batter.

Molasses—Substitute ½ cup of molasses for half of

Reflector is also adaptable to biscuits.

the normal amount of sugar. Use brown sugar for the remainder. A touch of baking soda helps in any baking that uses molasses.

Peanut Butter—Add ½ cup of peanut butter to batter.

Oatmeal—Substitute 1 cup of oatmeal for ¾ cup of flour.

Chocolate—Substitute ½ cup of cocoa for ½ cup of flour, and increase sugar by ½ cup. Baking chocolate is difficult to use since it must be melted first and then maybe mixed with the sugar so that it will blend evenly through the batter.

Liquid Flavorings—A teaspoon of one of many possible liquids will, at small effort and little space and weight, make possible many different flavors. Amount used depends on whether an extract or a concentrated flavoring is available. Some experimenting may be necessary. The most normally acceptable are orange, lemon, maple, almond,

butterscotch, banana, imitation rum, and brandy. Less enthusiasm is likely for those like peppermint, strawberry, and raspberry.

Add the liquid flavoring to the first cup of water mixed with the dry ingredients, so that it will blend throughout the batter. Adding the flavoring directly to the dry ingredients results in isolated spots of concentrated flavor.

Now invent others, but it is possible to bake for a two-week trip without repeating exactly the same bannock twice!

CAKES

When a bannock becomes a cake is a matter of semantics. Three ingredients that spell the change: butter replaces shortening; sugar is added in larger measure; and more eggs are used.

Any standard cookbook contains numerous cake

recipes, many of which are suitable. Avoid ones that call for an inordinate number of eggs, those that require separating the whites and yolks, and those using either the whites or the yolks, but not both. The kind of cake produced in the reflector is limited by the supplies, not the oven.

The easiest way to make "bannock" into "cake" is the use of a frosting. Some require cooking, some just warming, but the easiest are made from icing sugar and are quite rich.

COOKIES

Also consult a cookbook for cookie recipes. Baking time for a pan of cookies is considerably less than for a cake or bannock, but several pans must be done to provide any quantity, and the time expended in baking will therefore increase. So, except for the rainy-day project, most trippers will bake something that takes less effort.

PIES

Piecrust

1½ cups flour
½ teaspoon salt
⅓ cup shortening cut into flour and salt to make a coarse meal
Add water or milk sparingly to make a very stiff, dry dough.

Experts differ, but some add a ½ teaspoon of baking powder to the above ingredients. Using cooking oil instead of shortening will give the crust a mealy taste rather than a flaky one.

For best results, handle the crust as little as possible. Roll out half on a floured, flat surface—the underside of a wannigan top is best. A true rolling pin is a luxury; but one can be whittled from the heart wood of a cedar if someone wants a campground project. Otherwise, any round food container will work—a catsup bottle, corn-oil can. (Remove the paper labels first.)

Dust the reflector pan with flour and mold in bottom crust, making sure edges extend over lips of the pan. If the crust needs patching, use small, thin pieces of dough. Moisten edges to be joined with small amounts of water spread with the fingers, and press the patch into place. Be sure the bottom crust covers entire pan so that filling cannot spill through.

After introducing filling, lay the top crust over the pie, making sure it extends over the lip of the pan. Patch the top crust as necessary. Join the two crusts by pressing down around the lips of the pan with the tines of a fork, and trim off excess. Prick top with the fork in various places to allow steam to escape.

Sprinkle top with a little evaporated milk, or paint with melted butter to brown well. Bake in a moderate oven until crust is firm and flaky. Allow pie to cool slightly before serving. If served directly from the pan, be careful not to score the pan while cutting—use the back side of the sharp knife or a table knife.

Instead of using the reflector pan, pies can be baked in smaller plates if the jewelry has ones that will double as pie tins. The smaller pies will cook more quickly and also allow several kinds to be made at once.

A lattice pattern for the top crust can be made instead of a solid crust; just slice the rolled top crust into strips ¼ to ⅜ inch wide and lay across the top in desired pattern. Slightly less crust will be needed. Some fillings lend themselves to the use of only a bottom shell, in which case only half the above crust is needed.

Pies can also be baked in a Dutch oven, just lining the pot as would be done with any pie plate, and adding the top crust below the top of the pot so that the cover can be placed in position. Baking can be done in a hot-sand oven (see *Baked Beans,* chapter 9), although sand should be of only moderate heat and baking will take only a short while compared with beans; but there is a lot of guess work involved in baking in sand. The pie can also be baked by setting the pot near the fire and revolving the pot at intervals until all of the sides are evenly done.

Fillings

Canned fillings are available for any conventional pie, but more versatility can be obtained by relying on wild fruits, dried fruits, and pudding mixes.

Wild Fruits—Blueberries in particular. Should be carefully cleaned and washed. They can be stewed with sugar to make the filling, or added directly to the crust, with a generous sprinkling of sugar. A cookbook can be consulted for more complicated procedures.

Dried Fruits—Must be presoaked or precooked. Sugar can be cooked with the fruit or added later, but more will be needed than when cooking for breakfast. Most dried fruits—apples in particular—should be slightly diced to make for bite-sized pieces in the pie. Raisins make a very rich pie, which probably would be best if much more shallow than the reflector pan.

Dates can be used to make an excellent date cake, using a stewed sugar-date mixture. Make the crust by combining 1 cup of oatmeal; ½ cup of flour; ½ teaspoon of salt; ½ cup of sugar; and ¼ to ½ cup of margarine or butter. Line the reflector pan with the mixture with hands, using only a bottom crust, or reserve half for a top. Meanwhile, stew ½ pound of dates, 1 cup of sugar (maybe half and half, white and brown), ½ to 1 cup of water, until thick and syrupy. Pour date syrup over crust, add top crust if desired, and bake like a bannock. Cake is done when crust starts to pull away from the sides. Cool, and serve directly from the pan. The date squares are quite rich!

YEAST BREADS

Yeast is the base for bread and rolls, while baking powder is used for biscuits and cakes. Yeast is tricky when worked in the open. Success depends not so much on what ingredients go into the dough, but how it is handled and at what temperature.

Temperature control is vital. At fifty degrees or below, yeast will not rise at all. Best working temperature is about eighty degrees. At 120 degrees the yeast stops working, and at about 140 degrees the yeast is killed. To achieve the required eighty-degree temperature, a warm, sunny day is best. Otherwise the temperature must be created artificially using the campfire.

Yeast bread needs a minimum of about five hours, and often longer. Rising times can be shortened by doubling the amount of yeast, but flavor will be slightly altered.

Basic Bread

Take about one cup of lukewarm water. Add one package of yeast, one tablespoon of salt, and two heaping tablespoons of white sugar. Stir to ensure dissolution, and let stand in a warm spot for about fifteen minutes.

Meanwhile, measure about five cups of flour into a large pot or bowl. Warm the flour in the sun or by the fire. After warming, add yeast mixture, one cup of melted shortening, and about 1½ to 2 cups of lukewarm water. Mix well, working dough with hands. Gradually add as much more warm flour as the dough will take—about three to four cups. When dough will take no more, ex-

Yeast bread: A) yeast mixture is added to warm flour; B) additional warm flour is worked in; C) after being allowed to rise twice, bread is panned; D) panned bread is allowed to rise once more; E) pan will be turned after first side is done; F) finished loaves are lightly covered with butter.

166

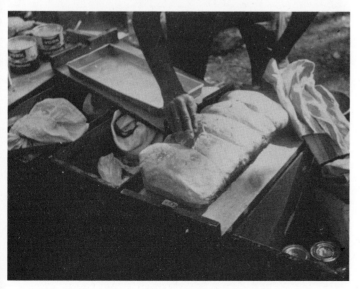

tra flour will gather in the bottom of the pot. Form into a ball, cover pot, and allow to stand in eighty-degree temperature until dough doubles in bulk—about two hours.

Punch dough down by pressing the center of the ball with the fingers. Punch several times, reform the ball, and turn the dough over. Avoid handling too much. Recover the pot.

The second rise should take about an hour, when again dough should double in bulk. Remove from pot, pat dough flat, cut off amounts intended to be about one-third as large as a finished loaf. Form each piece into a loaf shape (probably no bread tins are available).

Dust reflector pan with flour, and lay in as many loaves as it will accommodate, remembering that loaves will triple in bulk. There will be two or three times the number of loaves that can be fitted into most reflector pans using the indicated quantities. But it is normally more convenient to bake several times, giving bread for several meals, than it is to make a small setting good for only one meal. Actual baking time is not much longer than for bannock, but rising time makes the job time-consuming.

Extra loaves that will not fit in the pan immediately should be laid on a flat floured surface —like a wannigan top. Panned bread should then be covered with a cloth—a clean dish towel—and allowed to rise again in eighty-degree conditions

After rising about an hour, the bread is ready to bake. Loaves should have doubled in bulk. Start baking in a warm oven for about ten minutes, and then move the reflector back and continue baking for about half an hour in a moderate oven. To brown the top, brush with evaporated milk or melted butter. To test to see if the bread is done, loaves should easily come free from the pan, and a hollow sound is heard when the bottom of the loaf is tapped. If the loaves were placed touching the sides of the pan to start with, finished loaves should have drawn back slightly from edges. If in doubt, bake a little longer, though baking too long will make a thick, heavy crust.

Then bake the second batch, leaving the first to cool where air can circulate before packing, if it is to be transported for a future meal.

Do not be discouraged if the first attempt with yeast turns out slightly heavy. The major problem is heat—too much or too little—and experience will lead to improvements. It takes at least an afternoon to set bread. It is sometimes possible to set bread at lunch, carry the pot along in the canoe on a warm day, punching down at required times, and finally panning the bread at the campsite. By the time camp is established, the bread will be ready to bake.

As outlined here, the dough was kneaded only during the mixing stages; other recipes will indicate much more handling of the dough.

Raisin Bread

Follow the preceding recipe, tossing warm raisins in with the warm flour before adding yeast. About ¾ pound of raisins will be about right for this amount of dough.

Rolls

When bread dough reaches the panning stage, flatten into ovals about ¼- to ⅜-inch thick. Fold each oval over on its short axis to form Parker House rolls. Pan and cover and let rise for about thirty to forty minutes. Baking time runs about twenty to thirty minutes in a hot oven.

DEEP FRYING

Doughnuts, fritters, and what is called "trapper's bread" are made from basic baking doughs, which are then deep fried. Some use baking-powder doughs; others, yeast doughs.

Enough cooking oil or shortening is heated in a skillet so that the frying will float—maybe about half an inch. The best frying temperature is about 375°, but in the bush the test is made by dropping a small sliver of dough into the fat—just as for fish—and the oil is hot enough when bubbles appear around the dough. Too low heat allows the bread to soak up oil; too hot, it will burn on the outside before the inside cooks. If oil is smoking, it is too hot.

Trapper's Bread

Trapper's bread is made from either a thick bannock dough, made with less liquid to give about the same consistency as for biscuits, or, better still, from a yeast dough. Using bannock dough, fry about ten minutes after cutting, letting the dough dry a little, but before baking powder reacts too much with the liquids. With yeast dough, roll out and fry after the second punching; it is not necessary to pan dough and let it rise again.

Press either dough flat with hands, and cut into rectangles about two inches by four inches and ¼- to ½-inch thick. Cut an oval hole in the center to allow the oil to bubble up through the hole, thereby cooking the center equally with the outside edges.

Fry about four to six minutes on a side, or until golden brown on both sides. Serve after draining

A

Trapper's bread from yeast dough

B

C

Eastmain Cree trapper's bread

and partial cooling, with butter and jam—just like biscuits.

Trapper's bread from the yeast dough solves the problem of any leftover dough, over and above that needed for a couple of bread bakings. It also offers a quick bread for the meal at hand, while the longer baking can be accomplished and the bread is stored for future meals.

Baking Powder Doughnuts

> 3⅓ cups flour
> 1 tablespoon baking powder
> ½ teaspoon salt
> 1⅓ cup sugar
> ⅜ teaspoon nutmeg
> 1 egg
> 3 tablespoons shortening
> ¾ cup milk—for a thick dough

Eastmain Cree doughnuts

Roll out to biscuit thickness and cut into circles—maybe using a vegetable can with both ends removed as a cutter. Cut a center hole (not for decoration, but to let the oil bubble up). A catsup bottle top makes a good cutter here. Allow to stand about ten minutes before cooking.

Deep fry until brown on both sides, turning when one side is done. Drain and cool, and maybe coat with sugar or a cinnamon-sugar mixture.

Raised Doughnuts

Dissolve one package of yeast in about ¼ cup warm water, to which has been added one tablespoon of sugar.

Scald 1¼ cup milk and pour over a ½ cup of soft butter and a ½ cup of sugar. Add ¾ teaspoon of salt, and allow to cool, and add two well-beaten eggs (cooling enough not to cook eggs).

Pour the two mixtures together and add slowly five cups of flour to make a soft dough. Knead gently on a floured board, working in all possible flour. Roll into a ball, place in a greased bowl, cover, and allow to rise until double in bulk—about two hours. Turn out on board again, knead again slightly, reroll, and replace in bowl, cover, and let rise again until double in bulk again—about an hour.

Roll to about one half-inch thickness on floured board, let stand a couple minutes, and cut into doughnut shapes, and cover and allow to rise about one-half to three-quarters of an hour.

Deep fry until golden brown, turning after first side is done. Cool, and sprinkle with sugar, cinnamon-sugar, or glaze.

SOUR DOUGH

Both baking powder and yeast are more reliable and more easily controlled than the sour dough of pioneer days, but for fun it might be worth experimenting with. It is a home-nurtured yeast that, once started, replenishes itself with each use, and at every baking, the "starter" is increased and some used for the baking, and some set aside to use the next time.

The initial starter can be made from flour and water, but it is more easily made by thoroughly mixing two cups of flour, two cups of lukewarm water, and one package of dry yeast, placing in a covered jar or crock—do not use metal—in a warm place away from drafts overnight. It should now have a pleasant yeasty smell. Using a package of yeast is cheating by pioneer standards, but

assures that the starter will really go. The starter should be stored in a cool place and "fed" at least once a week. It may turn a slightly orange color—but if it takes on a green tint, start over again.

Using the starter, baking is similar to any yeast bread procedure—same rising times and punching instructions.

The night before baking, add to the present starter enough flour and lukewarm water in equal quantities to make enough for the baking and still leave a cup to retain for the future. Take two cups of starter, add four cups of flour, two tablespoons of sugar, one teaspoon of salt, and two tablespoons of melted shortening come morning. Set aside the remaining starter for the future. Mix dough and follow bread instructions.

Sour dough can also be used as the leavening agent for other dishes—flapjacks, muffins, and waffles. Even though the canoe tripper will find commercial products easier to store and more reliable, the experiment can be inviting.

PANCAKES

No trip seems complete without at least one pancake breakfast. Of course they could be prepared every morning, but as the size of the party increases the time for a pancake meal rises, thereby delaying breaking camp until after the winds rise.

2 cups flour
1 teaspoon salt
1 tablespoon baking powder
1 tablespoon white sugar
2 tablespoons powdered milk (optional)
1 egg
1 heaping tablespoon shortening before melting (or use corn oil)
2 cups water—more or less
1 teaspoon vanilla

Mix dry ingredients, melt and add shortening, and then add water (mixing vanilla with first cup of water), and blend until a smooth, thin batter is obtained. Allow to sit a few minutes before cooking, while the pan heats.

The secret of good pancakes lies in the cooking, not the batter. Heat skillet or grill over warm fire with just enough bacon fat or cooking oil to cover surface lightly; too much gives a deep-fried pancake. The pan should be hot enough so that the fat is about to smoke—but not quite. Drop batter onto the pan by the spoonful, without allowing

Some large pancakes get flipped.

the skillet to cool—better to leave the skillet on the fire and bring batter to it, rather than the other way.

Let the pancake cook until bubbles appear through the batter, not only around edges, but some toward center. Turn once with spatula and cook about half as long on reverse side. Serve immediately with butter, syrup, or any other topping.

Then there is the camping school that advocates cooking cakes the same size as the pan being used. Avoid too much batter; the inside never seems to cook! But then the pancakes can be skillfully flipped. Just make sure there is enough batter left to try again if necessary.

Cooking temperature is important. A low, steady fire is better than an erratic, blazing one. If the initial greasing of the pan disappears partway through cooking, add a couple more drops of fat between the cakes or along the sides of the

pan. Best results are achieved using a clean skillet; the one just used for bacon should be scraped clean with the edge of the spatula if not washed before starting the pancakes; otherwise, they stick badly. The one used for fish must definitely be scoured before use.

Cornmeal Pancakes

2 cups flour
1 cup cornmeal
1 tablespoon baking powder
1 teaspoon salt
1 egg
2 tablespoons powdered milk (optional)
1 tablespoon white sugar
½ cup melted shortening (corn oil maybe?)
Water to make a smooth batter

Cook just as any other pancake batter, but watch more closely—cornmeal burns more easily

171

than flour. Cook in small cakes. The pan-sized ones burn before cooking through. Lay off the flipping—cornmeal cakes are more delicate than those of straight flour.

Buckwheat Cakes

> ½ cup flour
> 1 tablespoon baking powder
> ½ teaspoon salt
> 2 teaspoons sugar
> 1½ cups buckwheat flour
> 2 tablespoons melted shortening
> 2 tablespoons powdered milk
> Water to make a smooth batter.

Let stand fifteen minutes before cooking. Cook in small cakes for best results.

Maple Syrup

Pour two cups of brown sugar into a ½ cup of boiling water, and stir until sugar dissolves. Add one teaspoon of maple flavoring and allow syrup to boil for a couple minutes. Adjust water-sugar ratio to make syrup as thick or as thin as wished.

12

WHERE TO FIND IT

The suggestions to follow cannot be complete, and there are constant changes in marketing. Many possible sources of canoeing equipment will be omitted in any listing, but these can be contacted by mail.

CANOES

Canoe manufacturers will supply a catalog, but without knowing the manufacturer and the product, buying from a catalog alone is chancy. It is better to see the craft before ordering, and much better to field test it. The major manufacturers usually have distributors located in areas other than the company's base, and with their catalog normally supply a list of local distributors.

There is an excellent annual, "Canoe/Kayak Buyer's Guide," published by *Canoe Magazine*, 1999 Shepard Road, St. Paul, Minnesota 55116. Or contact the American Canoe Association, 4260 East Evans Avenue, Denver, Colorado 80222.

Aluminum

Alumacraft Boat Company
315 West St. Julien Street
St. Peter, Minnesota 56082

Appleby Manufacturing Company
P.O. Box 591
Lebanon, Missouri 65536

Browning Aerocraft
900 Chessing
St. Charles, Michigan 48655

Great Canadian, Inc.
45 Water Street
Worcester, Massachusetts 01604

Grumman Boats
Marathon, New York 13803

Jayco, Inc.
P.O. Box 460
Middlebury, Indiana 46540

Lowe Industries
Interstate 44
Lebanon, Missouri 65536

Lund American
New York Mills, Minnesota 55410

Michi-Craft Corporation
19995 19 Mile Road
Big Rapids, Michigan 49307

MonArk Boat Company
P.O. Box 210
Monticello, Arkansas 71655

Rich Line
P.O. Box 591
Lebanon, Missouri 65536

Sea Nymph Boats and Canoes
P.O. Box 298
Syracuse, Indiana 46567

Smoker-Craft
Smoker Lumber Company, Inc.
New Paris, Indiana 46553

Starcraft Canoes
2703 College Avenue
Goshen, Indiana 46526

Canvas

Chestnut Canoe Company
Fredericton, New Brunswick

Great Canadian, Inc.
45 Water Street
Worcester, Massachusetts 01604

Old Town Canoe Company
Old Town, Maine 04468

Treadwell Woodwork and Marine
R.R. # 1
Baysville, Ontario

Fiberglass

Some of the following producers manufacture a very limited selection of models, so some searching may have to be done to locate canoes with required length, width, and depth.

Aero-Nautical, Inc.
Skimmar Boat Division
154 Prospect Street
Greenwich, Connecticut 06830

American Fiber-Lite
P.O. Box 67
Marion, Illinois 62959
(Fiber-Lite)

Aqua Sports Canada, Ltd.
525 Champlain
Fabreville
Laval, Quebec H7P 2N8

Bemidji Boat Company, Inc.
Highway 2 West
Bemidji, Minnesota 56601

Black River Canoes
Box 327
Route 301 South
LaGrange, Ohio 44050

Blue Hole Canoe Company
Sunbright, Tennessee 37872

Brownline Canoes and Kayaks
2539 Bitters Road
San Antonio, Texas 78217

Chicagoland Canoe Base, Inc.
4019 North Narragansett Avenue
Chicago, Illinois 60634

Custom Fiberglass Products
P.O. Box 101
Industrial Park
Mount Juliet, Tennessee 37122

Dolphin Canoe Company
Industrial Park
Wabasha, Minnesota 55981
(also Waterproof Canoe-Pac)

Easy Rider Fiberglass Boat Company
10013 51st Avenue S.W.
Seattle, Washington 98146

Fiberglass Engineering
Box 3
Wyoming, Minnesota 55092

Grand Fiberglass Products
5705 36th Avenue
Hamilton, Michigan 49419

Grayling Canoes
1271 South Bannock Street
Denver, Colorado 80223

Great Canadian, Inc.
45 Water Street
Worcester, Massachusetts 01604

Green Mountain Outfitters, Inc.
P.O. Box 66
Forestdale, Vermont 05745

Iliad
55 Washington Street
Norwell, Massachusetts 02061

Indian River Canoe Manufacturing
1525 Kings Court
Titusville, Florida 32780

Jayco, Inc.
P.O. Box 460
Middlebury, Indiana 46540

Lincoln Canoes
Route 32
Waldoboro, Maine 04572

Mad River Canoe
P.O. Box 363
Spring Hill
Waitsfield, Vermont 05673

Midwestern Fiberglass Products
Breezy Acres
P.O. Box 247
Winona, Minnesota 55987

Mohawk Manufacturing Company
963 North Highway 427
Longwood, Florida 32750

Moore Canoes, Inc.
5235 Winthrop Avenue
Indianapolis, Indiana 46205

Northern Fiberglass Industries, Inc.
747 Payne Avenue
St. Paul, Minnesota 55101

Old Town Canoe Company
Old Town, Maine 04468
(also Royalex)

Pack 'N Paddle, Inc.
701 East Park
Libertyville, Illinois 60048

Pinetree Canoes, Ltd.
Box 824
Orillia, Ontario L3V 6K8

Precision Fiberglass Parts, Inc.
P.O. Box 416
Port Campus # 2
Hood River, Oregon 97031

Quapaw Canoe
600 Newman Road
Miami, Oklahoma 74354

Rivers and Gilman Moulded Products, Inc.
Main Street
Hampden, Maine 04444

Sawyer Canoe Company
234 South State Street
Oscoda, Michigan 48750

Seminole Canoe and Boat Company
P.O. Box 43
Sanford, Florida 32771

6-H Products, Ltd.
80 Hickson Avenue
Kingston, Ontario

Trailcraft, Inc.
Concordia, Kansas 66901

Tremblay Canoes, Ltd.
P.O. Box 655
St. Felicien, Quebec

Voyager Canoes
Box 78
Marinette, Wisconsin 54153

Voyageur Canoe Company, Ltd.
King Street
Millbrook, Ontario LOA 1GO

Whitewater West
727 South 33rd Street
Richmond, California 94804

Wood

Burley Falls Canoe
Burley Falls, Ontario KOL 1KO

C and L Canoe and Guideboat Distributors
Malone, New York 12953
(*Fiberglass Covered*)

Native Cedar Canoes
Reckards Canoe Shop
Rockwood, Maine 04478

Stalek Canoes
16 East Chase Street
Baltimore, Maryland 21202

Wilderness Boats
Route 1

Box 101A
Carlton, Oregon 97111

Wonacott Canoes, Inc.
P.O. Box 1902
Wenatchee, Washington 98801

Kits

Grayling Canoes
1271 South Bannock Street
Denver, Colorado 80223
(*Fiberglass*)

Outdoor Sports
Box 1213
Tuscaloosa, Alabama 35401

Riverside Canoes
Box 5595
Riverside, California 92507

Sportscraft
Box 636
Allentown, New Jersey 08501
(*Canvas*)

Trailcraft, Inc.
Concordia, Kansas 66901
(*Canvas and Fiberglass*)

Wonacott Canoes, Inc.
P.O. Box 1902
Wenatchee, Washington 98801
(*Wood*)

PADDLES

Most of the major canoe manufacturers also market or manufacture paddles and such accessories.

Angle Paddles
Route # 3
Elk River, Minnesota 55330

B and M Company
P.O. Box 231
West Point, Mississippi 39773

Cannon Products, Inc.
2345 North West 8th Avenue
Fairbault, Minnesota 55021

Carlisle Ausable Paddle Company
110 State Street
Grayling, Michigan 49738

Caviness Woodworking Company, Inc.
P.O. Box 710
Calhoun City, Mississippi 38916

Country Ways
3500 Highway 101 South
Minnetonka, Minnesota 55343
(*Kits*)

Dafron Industries, Ltd.
Nathan S. Joudrey and Son, Ltd.
Blockhouse, Nova Scotia

Raymond A. Dodge
1625 Broadway
Niles, Michigan 49120

Foster Oar Company
P.O. Box 1185
Conway, Arkansas 72032

The Happy Outdoorsman, Ltd.
433 St. Mary's Road
Winnipeg, Manitoba

Hurka Industries
1 Charles Street
Newburyport, Massachusetts 01950

Moise Cadorette
1710 Principale
St-Jean-Des-Piles, Quebec GOX 2VO

Nona Boats
977 West 19th Street
Costa Mesa, California 92627

Sawyer Woodworking
8891 Rouge River Highway
Rouge River, Oregon 97537

Shaw and Tenney, Inc.
20 Water Street
Orono, Maine 04473

Sports Equipment, Inc.
Mantua, Ohio 44255

Tecumseh Custom Canoe Paddles
R.D. 1, Box 141
Greenville, Ohio 45331

Voyageur Enterprises
P.O. Box 512
Shawnee Mission, Kansas 66201

GENERAL CANOEING SUPPLIERS

Most deal in a broad line of products, producing some canoeing accessories of their own, while also acting as distributors for other manufacturers. Many of the general camping supply houses to be listed later offer similar services, although the camping population to which they cater is broader.

Blackhawk Outfitters
941 North Washington
Janesville, Wisconsin 53545

Canoe Imports
74 South Willard Street
Burlington, Vermont 05401

Cannon Valley Outfitters, Inc.

Cannon Products, Inc.
2345 North West 8th Avenue
Faribault, Minnesota 55021

Colorado Whitewater Specialists, Inc.
1127 West Elizabeth
Fort Collins, Colorado 80521

Hanson's Trail North
960-A Troy-Schenectady Road
Latham, New York 12110

Bart Hauthaway
640 Boston Post Road
Weston, Massachusetts 02193

Northwest River Supplies
542 North Grant
Moscow, Idaho 83843

Rutabaga Whitewater Supply
1002 South Park
Madison, Wisconsin 53715

Seda Products
P.O. Box 997
Chula Vista, California 92010

The Summit Shop
185 Wayland Avenue
Providence, Rhode Island 02906

Whitewater West
727 South 33rd
Richmond, California 94804

SPECIALIZED CANOEING ITEMS

Some specialized items are also available from the firm marketing a wider range of products useful to the canoeist, but here are a few suppliers offering useful equipment:

AC Mackenzie Company
Box 9301 Richmond Heights Station
St. Louis, Missouri 63117
(*Poles*)

Mo Trailer Corporation
1030 South Tenth Street
Goshen, Indiana 46526
(*Canoe Trailers*)

Northern Star Products, Inc.
1972 Grand Avenue
St. Paul, Minnesota 55105
(*Sailing Accessories*)

Omega Marketing
P.O. Box 487
Marblehead, Massachusetts 01945
(*Life Jackets*)

Stearns
St. Cloud, Minnesota 56301
(*Life Jackets*)

Wildwater Designs
Penllyn, Pennsylvania 19422
(*Life Jacket Kits*)

MAPS

Maps produced as part of the United States or Canadian topographical surveys are hard to improve upon. Sometimes the necessary sections can be secured locally, but if tripping far from home, the maps should be secured as the journey is planned. Request an index for the region, indicating the scale desired. Four miles to the inch is adequate for most travel; two miles to the inch would show more detail; while one mile to the inch probably means carrying so much paper that it would become unwieldy, unless traveling virgin territory where the party must grope its way along.

U.S. Geological Survey
520 Illinois Street
Fairbanks, Alaska 99701
(*Alaska*)

Department of Energy, Mines and Resources
Surveys and Mapping Branch
615 Booth Street
Ottawa, Ontario K1A OE9

U.S. Geological Survey
Map Distribution Office
1200 South Eads Avenue
Arlington, Virginia 22202
(*East*)

U.S. Geological Survey
Distribution Section
Federal Center
Denver, Colorado 80225
(*West*)

The major criticism of these maps would be the omission of portage information; and if the region being traveled has restrictions regarding camping and fishing, such information is lacking.

Eastern and western indexes of maps available from various sources can be purchased from U.S./Canadian Map Distribution Bureau, Lt., Midwest Distribution Center, Box 249, Room 640, Neenah, Wisconsin 54956.

Listing all sources of maps of a local nature that might be helpful to the canoeist would be difficult in capsule form. A local office of the U.S. Army Corps of Engineers may have produced useful maps. Many Canadian provinces have provincial maps distributed by their Departments of Conservation, Fish and Game, Natural Resources, or Tourism.

Then there are some maps of an even more local nature, usually produced in conjunction with a description of canoe routes in the area. The book service of the American Canoe Association, 4260 East Evans Avenue, Denver, Colorado 80222 can help with sources. In the east try Appalachian Mountain Club, 5 Joy Street, Boston, Massachusetts 02108. A useful listing of additional sources is contained in Bill Riviere's *Pole, Paddle, and Portage* (Van Nostrand Reinhold, 1969) or *Backcountry Camping* (Doubleday and Company, 1971).

ROUTES

Previous suggestions regarding the securing of local maps would be repeated for suggestions as to the actual route. Many state and provincial departments of conservation and the like—titles vary—offer descriptions of canoe routes. In addition, a camping-supply house located in a canoeing area can often supply information on routes in the area. Usually the mail-order catalog lists the availability of such routing information. In addition to the organizations already listed, and the camping suppliers to be named later, some route information can be obtained from:

Canoe Routes
P.O. Box 53
Litton, Indiana 47441

Wilderness Sports Corporation
P.O. Box 85
Eagle Valley, New York 10974

GENERAL CAMPING SUPPLIERS

Most of the following suppliers operate a salesroom at their base and a mail-order business. Many market products of their own manufacture, directed toward the general camping market, and also act as distributors for the products of other manufacturers. They all supply catalogs on request, although some charge for their catalogs. Sometimes the catalog charge is applied toward the first purchase, but often just results in adding your name to a subsequent mailing list as a result of a purchase.

Some are strongly oriented toward the lightweight camping industry, and the kinds of products of interest to the canoesman will be in the clothing, pack, tent, and cooking areas. Others are more general, or even inclined toward the needs of the canoeist, and many also act as distributors for one or more of the major brands of canoe.

The following list is by no means complete, and of course there are many fine camping outlets of a local nature where the buyer has the advantage of actually seeing his purchase rather than selecting from a catalog.

Alpine Designs
6185 East Arapahoe
Boulder, Colorado 80303

Eddie Bauer
1737 Airport Way South
Seattle, Washington 98134

L. L. Bean, Inc.
Freeport, Maine 04032

Cabela's
Sidney, Nebraska 69162

The Camp and Hike Shop
4674 Knight-Arnold Road
Memphis, Tennessee 38118

Camp and Trail Outfitters
112 Chambers Street
New York, New York 10007

Camp Trails
3920 West Clarendon Avenue
Phoenix, Arizona 85063

Colorado Outdoor Sports Corporation
P.O. Box 5544
Denver, Colorado 80217

Co-Op Wilderness Supply
1432 University Avenue
Berkeley, California 94702

Eastern Mountain Sports, Inc.
1047 Commonwealth Avenue
Boston, Massachusetts 02215

Gander Mountain, Inc.
Box 248
Wilmot, Wisconsin 53192

Don Gerow
Sanborntown, New Hampshire 03269

Don Gleason's Campers Supply
9 Pearl Street
Northampton, Massachusetts 01060

Gokeys
21 West Fifth Street
St. Paul, Minnesota 55102

Great World
West Simsbury, Connecticut 06092

Hancock Village Outfitters, Inc.
Hancock, New Hampshire 03449

J. B. Herren
23341 Mulholland Drive
Woodland Hills, California 91364

Herter's, Inc.
Waseca, Minnesota 56093

Hudson's
105 Third Street
New York, New York 10003

Indiana Camp Supply
Box 344
Pittsboro, Indiana 46167

Kelty
1801 Victory Boulevard
Glendale, California 91201

Doug Kittredge Sports
Mammoth, California 93546

Laacke and Joys
1425 North Water
Milwaukee, Wisconsin 53202

Moar and Mountain
63 Park Street
Andover, Massachusetts 01810

Northern Prairie Outfitters
206 Northwest Highway
Fox River Grove, Illinois 60021

P and S Sales
P.O. Box 45095
Tulsa, Oklahoma 74145

Sierra Designs
4th and Addison Streets
Berkeley, California 94710

The Ski Hut
1615 University Avenue
Berkeley, California 94703

Skimeister Sport Shop
Main Street
North Woodstock, New Hampshire 03262

The Smilie Company
575 Howard Street
San Francisco, California 94105

Waters, Inc.
111 East Sheridan Street
Ely, Minnesota 55731

FREEZE DRIED FOODS

Major camping-supply houses carry one or more lines of freeze-dried and/or dehydrated foods, but here are some of the manufacturers and distributors primarily concerned with lightweight camping foods.

Bernard Food Industries, Inc.
1125 Hartrey Avenue
Evanston, Illinois 60204

Bowes Company, Ltd.
75 Vickers Road
Islington, Ontario M9B 6B6
(*Powdered Drinks*)

Chuck Wagon Foods
Micro Drive
Woburn, Massachusetts 01801

Dri Lite Foods, Inc.
11333 Atlantic Avenue
Lynwood, California 90262

Freeze-Dry Foods, Ltd.
579 Speers Road
Oakville, Ontario

S. Gumpert of Canada, Ltd.
31 Brock Avenue
Toronto 3, Ontario

Marshall Produce Company
Marshall, Minnesota 56258
(*Egg Mix*)

Oregon Freeze Dry Foods, Inc.
P.O. Box 1048
Albany, Oregon 97321

Rich-Moor
P.O. Box 2728
Van Nuys, California 91411

Salada Foods, Ltd.
855 York Mills Road
Don Mills, Ontario

Ad. Seidel and Son, Inc.
2323 Pratt Boulevard
Elk Grove Village, Illinois 60007

Stafford Foods, Ltd.
37 Hanna Avenue
Toronto, Ontario M6K 1X1

Stow-a-Way Industries
166 Cushing Highway (Route 3A)
Cohasset, Massachusetts 02025

KITS

A relatively new source of camping equipment
has started with the introduction of kits for the
home assembly of clothing, sleeping bags, packs,
and tents. Considerable saving can be made by
investigating this field if the purchaser has a
sewing machine and some proficiency in its use.

Altra, Inc.
5441 Western Avenue
Boulder, Colorado 80301

Frostline Kits
452 Burbank
Broomfield, Colorado 80020

Mountain Adventure Kits
P.O. Box 571
Whittier, California 90608

SunDown Kits
Box 1023
Burnsville, Minnesota 55337

SPECIALISTS

Differentiated from the general supply house
would be some manufacturers and distributors
who probably would not be able to supply all the
equipment needed by the canoeist, but could help
greatly in their areas. Some produce only one
item which could help; others are much broader
in their offerings.

Air Lift
2217 Roosevelt Avenue
Berkeley, California 94703
(*Air Mattresses*)

Anzen Products
15314 East Proctor Avenue
City of Industry, California 91745
(*Waterproof Rec-Pac*)

Atlantis
P.O. Box 12342
Waitsfield, Vermont 05673
(*Foul Weather Gear*)

Beckel Canvas Products
P.O. Box 20491
Portland, Oregon 97220
(*Canvas Products*)

Browning
Morgan, Utah 84050
(*Packs, Sleeping Bags, Stoves, Tents*)

Camp 7
802 South Sherman
Longmont, Colorado 80501
(*Sleeping Bags*)

Camp-Ways
12915 South Spring Street
Los Angeles, California 90061
(*Plastic Containers*)

Canoe California
Box 61C
Kentfield, California 94904
(*Gear Bags, Packs*)

Charter Oak Distributors
50 Walnut Street
Middletown, Connecticut 06457
(*Fishing*)

Clear-Creek
14361 Catalina Street
San Leandro, California 94577
(Tent)

Coleman Company
250 North St. Francis
Wichita, Kansas 67201
(Clothing, Lanterns, Stoves, Tents)

Converse
55 Fordham Road
Wilmington, Massachusetts 01887
(Boots, Foul Weather Gear)

Dana Home Products
Port Ewen, New York 12466
(Stoves)

William R. Donovan Company
Newark, New York 14513
(Waterproof Rubber Bags)

Early Winters, Ltd.
300 Queen Anne Avenue North
Seattle, Washington 98109
(Tent)

Eureka Tents, Inc.
625 Conklin Road
Binghamton, New York 13902
(Tents)

Fafner Enterprises
1043 South Harvey Avenue
Oak Park, Illinois 60304
(Waterproof Camera Box)

Feather Weight
P.O. Box 376
Tignall, Georgia 30668
(Sleeping Bags, Down Products)

Hirsch-Weis/White Stag
5203 S. E. Johnson Creek Boulevard
Portland, Oregon 97206
(Tents)

Holubar
Box 7
Boulder, Colorado 80302
(Clothing, Sleeping Bags)

Hy-Score
200 Tillary Street
Brooklyn, New York 11201
(Stoves)

Instant Corporation
Box 1136
Barnard, Vermont 05031
(Tump Line)

JanSport
Paine Field Industrial Park
Everett, Washington 98204
(Frames, Packs)

Johnson Woolen Mills, Inc.
Johnson, Vermont 05656
(Jackets, Shirts)

Lende Foam Products
Bolton, Massachusetts 01740
(Sleeping Pads)

Maran
P.O. Box 931
Kent, Washington 98031
(Frames, Packs)

Netcraft Company
Box 5510
Toledo, Ohio 43613
(Fishing)

The North Face
1234 5th Street
Berkeley, California 94710
(Packs, Sleeping Bags, Tents)

Optimus International
P.O. Box 907
La Miranda, California 90637
(Stoves)

Pacific/Ascende
P.O. Box 2028
Fresno, California 93718
(Sleeping Bags)

Pak Foam Products
390 Pine Street
Pawtucket, Rhode Island 02862
(Foam Pad)

Primus-Sievert
354 Sackett Point Road
North Haven, Connecticut 06473
(Stoves)

Phoenix Products, Inc.
U.S. Route 421
Tyner, Kentucky 40486
(Waterproof Bags)

Recreation Creations, Inc.
Silver Lake Road
Dingman's Ferry, Pennsylvania 18328
(Waterproof Camera Box)

Recreational Equipment, Inc.
P.O. Box 22090
Seattle, Washington 98122
(Clothing)

Sheldon's, Inc.
Antigo, Wisconsin 54409
(Mepps Fishing Lures)

Snow Lion
P.O. Box 9056
Berkeley, California 94701
(Sleeping Bags)

Stag Trail Country
5203 South East Johnson Creek Boulevard
Portland, Oregon 97206
(*Sleeping Bags*)

Stebco Industries
1020 West 40th Street
Chicago, Illinois 60609
(*Air Mattresses, Life Jackets*)

Tent Works Ltd.
Camden, Maine 04843
(*Tents*)

Tough Traveler
1138 State Street
Schenectady, New York 12304
(*Duffels, Packs*)

Tyco Camping Company
8344 Leesburg Pike
Vienna, Virginia 22180
(*Jungle Hammocks*)

Voyageur Enterprises
P.O. Box 512
Shawnee Mission, Kansas 66201
(*Packs, Tents, Waterproof Bags*)

Woods Bag and Canvas Company, Ltd.
401 Logan Avenue
Toronto 8, Ontario
(*Packs, Sleeping Bags, Tents, Tump Lines*)

INDEX

184